Practice in TESOL

To Síofra and Tiernan, who always remind me of the important things in life.

Practice in TESOL

Fiona Farr

EDINBURGH
University Press

© Fiona Farr, 2015
© the chapters their several authors, 2015

Edinburgh University Press Ltd
The Tun – Holyrood Road
12(2f) Jackson's Entry
Edinburgh EH8 8PJ
www.euppublishing.com

Typeset in 10/12 Minion by
Servis Filmsetting Ltd, Stockport, Cheshire,
and printed and bound in Great Britain by
CPI Group (UK) Ltd, Croydon CR0 4YY

A CIP record for this book is available from the British Library

ISBN 978 0 7486 4553 4 (hardback)
ISBN 978 0 7486 4554 1 (webready PDF)
ISBN 978 0 7486 4552 7 (paperback)
ISBN 978 0 7486 9642 0 (epub)

CONTENTS

USEFUL ABBREVIATIONS

AMEP	Adult Migrant English Programme
AR	action research
BAAL	British Association for Applied Linguistics
BANA	Britain, Australia, North America
BNC	British National Corpus
CALL	computer-assisted language learning
CLT	communicative language teaching
CPD	continuous professional development
CUP	Cambridge University Press
DDL	data-driven learning
EAL	English as an additional language
EAP	English for academic purposes
EFL	English as a foreign language
ELO	expected learning outcome
ELT	English language teaching
ERIC	Educational Resources Information Centre
ESL	English as a second language
ESOL	English for speakers of other languages
ESP	English for specific purposes
FCE	First Certificate in English
ICLE	International Corpus of Learner English
IELTS	International English Language Testing System
IRF	initiation response feedback
L1	first language
L2	second language
LAD	language acquisition device
MATSDA	Materials Development Association
MOOC	massive open online course
OUP	Oxford University Press
PBL	problem-based learning
PLN	personal learning network
RP	reflective practice
SETT	self-evaluation of teacher talk
SLA	second language acquisition

STT	student talking time
TBLT	task-based language teaching
TESOL	Teaching English to speakers of other languages
TP	teaching practice
TTT	teacher talking time
VLE	virtual learning environment

SERIES EDITORS' PREFACE

Editors Joan Cutting, University of Edinburgh and Fiona Farr, University of Limerick

This series of textbooks addresses a range of topics taught within **TESOL programmes** around the world. Each volume is designed to match a taught 'core' or 'option' course (identified by a survey of TESOL programmes worldwide) and could be adopted as a prescribed text. Other series and books have been aimed at Applied Linguistics students or language teachers in general, but this aims more specifically at students of ELT (English Language Teaching – the process of enabling the learning of English), with or without teaching experience.

The series is intended primarily for college and university students at third or fourth year undergraduate level, and graduates (pre-service or in-service) studying TESOL on Masters programmes and possibly some TESOL EdDs or Structured PhDs, all of whom need an introduction to the topics for their taught courses. It is also very suitable for new professionals and people starting out on a PhD, who could use the volumes for self-study. The **readership level** is **introductory** and the tone and approach of the volumes will appeal to both undergraduates and postgraduates.

This series answers a need for volumes with a special focus on **intercultural awareness**. It is aimed at programmes in countries where English is not the mother tongue, and in English-speaking countries where the majority of students come from countries where English is not the mother tongue, typical of TESOL programmes in the UK and Ireland, Canada and the US, Australia and New Zealand. This means that it takes into account physical and economic conditions in ELT classrooms round the world and a variety of socio-educational backgrounds. Each volume contains a number of tasks which include examples from classrooms around the world, encourage comparisons across cultures and address issues that apply to each student's home context. Closely related to the intercultural awareness focus is a minor theme that runs throughout the series, and that is language analysis and description, and its applications to ELT. Intercultural awareness is indeed a complex concept and we aim to address it in a number of different ways. Taking examples from different cultural contexts is one way, but the volumes in the series also look at many other educationally relevant cultural dimensions such as sociolinguistic influences, gender issues, various learning traditions (e.g. collectivist vs individualistic) and culturally determined language dimensions (e.g. politeness conventions).

TESOL students need **theory clearly related to practice**. This series is practical and is intended to be used in TESOL lectures and workshops, providing group tasks and independent activities. Students are invited to engage in critical thinking and to consider applications of concepts and issues to their own particular teaching contexts, adapting the tendencies and suggestions in the literature to their own countries' educational requirements. Each volume contains practical tasks to carry out individually, in small groups or in plenary in the classroom, as well as suggestions for practical tasks for the students to use in their own classrooms. All the concepts and issues encountered here will be translatable into the ELT classroom. It is hoped that this series will contribute to your improvement as a teacher.

The series presents ELT concepts and research issues **simply**. The volumes guide students from the basic concepts, through the issues and complexities, to a level that should make them alert to past and recent teaching and research developments in each field. This series makes the topics accessible to those unaccustomed to reading theoretical literature, and yet takes them to an exam and Masters standard, serving as a gateway into the various fields and an introduction to the more theoretical literature. We also acknowledge that **technology** is a major area within TESOL and this series is aware of the need for technology to feature prominently across its volumes. Issues of technological integration and implementation are addressed in some way in each of the volumes. The series is based on state-of-the-art research. The concepts and issues raised are intended to inspire students to undertake their own research and consider pursuing their interests in a PhD.

Editorial Advisory Board

As well as the two editors, the series has an Editorial Advisory Board, whose members are involved in decisions on commissioning and considering book proposals and reviewing book drafts. We would like to acknowledge and thank members of the Board for all of their work and guidance on the Textbooks in TESOL series:

- Prof. David Block, ICREA/University of Lleida
- Dr Averil Coxhead, Victoria University of Wellington, New Zealand
- Prof. Donald Freeman, University of Michigan, USA
- Mr Peter Grundy, Northumbria University, UK
- Dr Annie Hughes, University of York, UK
- Prof. Mike McCarthy, University of Nottingham, UK
- Dr Liam Murray, University of Limerick, Ireland
- Dr Anne O'Keeffe, Mary Immaculate College, University of Limerick, Ireland
- Dr Jonathon Reinhardt, University of Arizona, USA
- Prof. Randi Reppen, North Arizona University, USA
- Assoc. Prof. Ali Shehadeh, UAE University, United Arab Emirates
- Assoc. Prof. Scott Thornbury, the New School, New York, USA
- Prof. Steve Walsh, Newcastle University, UK

Edinburgh Textbooks in TESOL

Books in this series include:

Changing Methodologies in TESOL	Jane Spiro
Mixed Methods Research for TESOL	James Dean Brown
Language in Context in TESOL	Joan Cutting
Materials Development for TESOL	Freda Mishan and Ivor Timmis
Practice in TESOL	Fiona Farr

ACKNOWLEDGEMENTS

Books don't just happen, especially books about classroom practice. There are a great many scholars on whose previous work I have relied in writing this volume and I am grateful to these fellow professionals and researchers. Over the last year, I have had the pleasure of writing with two great colleagues, Angela Farrell and Elaine Riordan, who contributed chapters to this book, and I'm thankful to them for sharing their own empirical research and for being so responsive to my many requests. I also wish to acknowledge the essential part that my past and present undergraduate and postgraduate students have on my thinking and research. I deeply appreciate your patience and generosity in allowing me to collect data, to sample materials and to discuss ideas with you in formal and informal ways. This book comes from you and is for the yous of the future. The previous volumes in this series have helped to shape and clarify my thinking and approach, and, for this, I acknowledge the work of my fellow-authors: Jane Spiro, Paul Wickens, Liam Murray, John Eyles, J. D. Brown, Joan Cutting, Florence Bonacina-Pugh, Kenneth Fordyce, Nicola Galloway, Eleni Mariou, Freda Mishan and Ivor Timmis. My series co-editor for these volumes, Joan Cutting, deserves special mention for her insights, commentary and general good humour as this book progressed. It continues to be a pleasure to work with you on this project.

Most of the work for the final chapters of this volume happened as I undertook a new and demanding role as Dean of Teaching and Learning at the University of Limerick. Making time for my writing was only possible with the quiet but effective support of Prof. Sarah Moore, and with the energy and efficiency of Una Clancy and Vicky Kelly, both of whom made things happen and got things done to assist me in the Centre for Teaching and Learning during this period. Sincere thanks to them and all of the CTL team. My family deserve final pride of place in my acknowledgements. To my dad, for years of investment, and not just financial. For your constant support, Sean – go raibh míle míle maith agat. And most importantly of all, for this, my second book, I have had *two* big little inspirations, who shared me with my laptop when they could have pulled me away. Síofra and Tiernan, this book is for you.

The publishers and author would like to thank the following for permission to reproduce previously published material:

Figure 3.2 from Römer, U. (2011) 'Corpus Research Applications in Second Language Teaching', *Annual Review of Applied Linguistics*, Vol. 31, pp. 205–25, by permission of Cambridge University Press.

Figure 9.1 from Wallace, M. (1998) *Action Research for Language Teachers*, by permission of Cambridge University Press.

Extracts from Crookes, G. (2003) *A Practicum in TESOL: Professional Development through Teaching Practice*, reproduced by permission of Cambridge University Press.

INTRODUCTION:
FROM LEARNER TO TEACHER

1.1 INTRODUCTION

This is a book for beginning and novice teachers and is suitable for use as part of your teacher education programme or as a self-study resource. It builds on previous volumes around this topic while including some new perspectives and approaches. The path that you choose to take to becoming a teacher is entirely at your discretion, and in today's world, you have many options and choices in relation to where and how you get your formal and informal education and information. This book aims to support and direct you along that path in ways that allow the wisdom of the years of practice-based TESOL experience, knowledge and research to inform your choices. I have also drawn on my own experiences as a teacher and teacher educator over a number of years, as well as on my research, to produce a volume which I hope is accessible and useful for you as a newcomer to the world of English language teaching. It does come with a caveat. Although there is a lot we know about teaching and learning, there is also a lot we do not know. There are times when I still find myself puzzled when something unanticipated happens in one of my classes, which I would not have predicted in a million years. And therein lies the joy of teaching – ever changing, ever challenging and ever rewarding.

You may ask: why another book on practice? I asked myself that precise question as I contemplated embarking on the journey that has produced this volume. The first thing to say is that there are excellent practice-oriented volumes on English language teaching, some that I came through my own teacher education with and to which I still return on a regular basis. You will see them referenced throughout the chapters here. There remain what I consider three good reasons for writing this volume:

- *Evidence-based teaching.* Due to the copious amounts of research that have been conducted since the mid-1980s or so, we are better informed than ever in relation to effective teaching and learning practices and approaches. The downside of this is that it can be difficult for a beginner teacher to make sense of it all in a way that might inform their practice. In fact, it would be almost impossible to read even a small amount of it as you balance the other demands of the task of teaching. In this book, which is strongly research-informed, I have tried to access the relevant readings and use my own schematic filters to mediate it in a way that is useful for you as a beginner teacher.

- *Technology*. I do not need to tell you about the impact that information and communication technologies have had on our lives. As a result, we are in an unprecedented stage in the history of English language teaching, which requires a serious (re)consideration of our pedagogic approaches as a result. I attempt to remain true to good pedagogic foundations in this book, while considering how technology impacts on what we do, and how it can be used to enhance language teaching appropriately for more autonomous and digitally literate learners (Gillen 2014).
- *A broader perspective on practice*. For a number of years I have been writing and talking about the impact and importance of teaching practice and feedback, reflective practice, professional development and research, as *core* principles and priorities. I have taken the liberty in this book to include all of these around the more conventional topics such as lesson planning and materials development. The objective from the outset is that you consider teaching more holistically and see that you have a responsibility as a professional to engage with all of these activities from the beginning.

1.2   YOU AS A TEACHER

Learning to become a teacher involves both inward and outward perspectives and considerations. For this reason, you will be asked throughout the chapters of this book to consider your own personality and approach to learning, which will have an inevitably strong influence on your teaching style. As part of this process, you will contemplate how to draw on your strengths and minimise the influence of any traits not conducive to good classroom practice, as you begin to define yourself as a teacher. There may be practical and emotional adjustments associated with making the transition from having previously been a learner to now becoming a teacher. You will be engaged in a range of explorations about your own previous learning and teaching experiences with the aim of awakening how this personal practical knowledge is likely to impact on your teaching practices and beliefs. Ultimately, this will provide a strong foundation for the transition to creating your own teacher identity. This is vital in order not to fall automatically and uncritically into teaching in the ways you were taught as learners, whether good or bad.

There are a number of language teaching methods which have created/developed specific roles for teachers, learners and materials. These are reflective and characteristic of the times at which they emerged and the related social, cultural and political influences. While this is not a book about methodology, it is usefully read in conjunction with such a volume, for a more fully informed approach. *Changing Methodologies in TESOL* by Spiro (2013) is suggested as a useful accompaniment to this volume for this purpose. As a methodological overview, she includes the account of the roles, activities and goals within four methodological approaches illustrated in Table 1.1.

These methods are likely to influence your own emerging teacher identity, which will continue to evolve right through your professional career. In addition, the impact that the use of information and communication technology can have on the role of the teacher is explored explicitly and implicitly in the core chapters that follow. These

Table 1.1 Language teaching methods (adapted from Spiro 2013: 28)

	Audiolingual approach	Grammar-translation	Communicative approach	Humanistic approach
What the teacher does	Models correct language	Explains grammar rules	Facilitates real-life exchanges and situations	Mentors and supports individual learning
What the learner does	Mirrors and imitates examples of correct learning	Becomes a 'linguist' in understanding rules	Simulates and practises language for real-life settings outside the classroom	Negotiates personal learning goals with the teacher
Learning activities	Drilling correct language Chanting	Practising structures	Dialogues and role-play in lifelike contexts	Personalised learning
Learning goals	To use language forms correctly	To understand language rules and use them accurately	To communicate appropriately in social settings	To develop confidence and fluency in real-life settings

accounts engender a critical engagement from the outset as you begin to define your own role, approaches and identity.

1.3 THE STRUCTURE OF THE BOOK

This volume contains eight core content chapters, each dealing with a discrete topic, which you will need to consider as part of your engagement with teaching practice. The topics inevitably overlap and work together to help mould and inform your practice. I have tried to organise the chapters so that they allow you to progress logically through the typical stages of the practice cycle, although you may choose to read and use them out of sequence. The teaching practice (TP) cycle reflected includes a consideration of the learners, the teacher and the materials; engaging in classroom observations to watch and learn from others; planning for teaching; preparing for what happens when you are in the classroom teaching; engaging in a post-teaching discussion with a TP tutor; ongoing reflective practice and professional development; and teacher engagement in research.

Each core chapter (2–9) is structured as follows:

- Introduction
- Input
  This is in three sections, *each one containing*:
  - An explanation of basic concepts and findings from research-based studies

- – Three tasks, to be used in class and outside as self-study, one applying the concept to teaching, one suggesting a research topic and one based on an online activity
- Further reading
  This is in two sections, *each one containing*:
  - – A summary of a research-based article or chapter
  - – Bite-size chunks from the article or chapter
  - – Two tasks, to be used in class or as self-study, one applying the concept to teaching, and one suggesting a research topic, both focusing on applications and ways of adapting input
- Summary
- A list of suggested additional readings

The book also contains a number of appendices. The first four relate to the contents of Chapter 3 on materials development. They illustrate a range of published and online materials, as well as corpus-based materials and concordances. The other appendices (5–9) should be read in conjunction with Chapter 6, which discusses what goes on in the classroom during practice teaching. These include a review and glossary of key terms, and a discussion of teacher behaviours, strategies and options in this context.

THINKING ABOUT YOUR LEARNERS

2.1 INTRODUCTION

Probably the most obvious and banal statement you will read in this book is that teachers exist because of learners and therefore learners should be the first consideration when making decisions about what you plan to do and how you plan to do it. Yet, over years of watching teaching, it sometimes seems to me that the materials, the syllabus, the teacher's priorities and a range of other factors sometimes take primacy in teachers' thinking. It is easy to be lured into going straight to good-quality and visually attractive materials that are convenient to use and attractive to learners. We need to remind ourselves that taking the learner as the starting point is essential but not always easy when teaching a variety of different learners, sometimes in relatively large groups. Learners, as individuals, are complex, but with the benefit of theoretical and empirically based research findings we now know something about how learning happens, though a complete understanding may never be possible because of the huge range of ever-changing influences and contextual variables. You have been a language learner, so it is a useful starting place to ponder what you think influenced your learning experiences and your attainment. You may want to think about variables that were associated personally with you and those which related to the environments in which you studied. Were you more successful, more relaxed, more confident and more engaged during some of your experiences than others? Why was this the case? What was the difference that made the difference? These are the types of questions we will begin to explore in this chapter, but this time you will be considering them from the perspective of a teacher who wants to create the best possible learning setting and experience for your learners.

This chapter explores the many learner variables that can influence the planning and execution of a language lesson. These operate in overlapping and intersecting ways, which may make it difficult for you as a teacher to understand how they work together in practice. The fact is that the relationship between them is complex and all we can do as teachers is to be aware of the influences and try to cater and plan for them in ways that we deem best for our own teaching situations. The sections below examine learner variables, self-directed and autonomous learning, and language proficiency levels in an attempt to begin to facilitate this process of raising your awareness. The sections begin with a discussion of the importance of taking into account learners' social and cultural background, and individual attributes such as age, learning styles and motivation (Dörnyei 2001, Oxford 1996) are considered in some detail. Finally, language proficiency levels are addressed in relation to a number of different frameworks that exist internationally, including commonly used criteria in popular coursebooks and an overview of the Common European Framework of Reference.

2.2   LEARNERS AS INDIVIDUALS

2.2.1   CONCEPTS, FINDINGS AND TEXTS

It is difficult to untangle the myriad of individual learner variables that affect language learning as they operate in fluid, flexible and evolving ways. Yet for the purposes of your awareness, your understanding and ultimately your planning and teaching, such unravelling (for the purposes of illustration) is what I will attempt to do in the following sections, which are organised around a number of relevant themes: the learners' backgrounds, age, aptitude, styles and strategies, and motivation.

The learners' backgrounds
The following scenarios represent just a small range of potential English language teaching contexts in which you may find yourself during your professional careers. Teaching English:

• for academic purposes (EAP) to a group of Masters students in an Irish university
• to managerial staff in a General Motors plant in France
• to a group of South American immigrants in New York
• in a Japanese secondary school
• in a summer camp for children in Spain
• as a private tutor to two children in a family home in India
• to a group of refugees in London.

All of these include learners from different social, economic, political and cultural backgrounds, which will influence their learning and therefore your teaching. Many of the scenarios illustrate EFL contexts in a range of international settings with learners of different ages, with different needs and motivations for learning English, all of which will be discussed in the following sections. They also represent some private and some public educational settings (which will be discussed further in Chapter 5 on lesson planning).

The New York and London examples represent those studying English in a bilingual or ESOL context (Schellekens 2007) who, regardless of their previous socio-economic status, now find themselves with limited access to resources and sometimes even language provision. They do not automatically have a strong voice or other entitlements in their new country of residence. They may have only instrumental motivation to learn English, or no motivation at all. Due to culture shock or other psychological or physical trauma they have come through, they may be extremely vulnerable and in need of pastoral care and other social supports. They may experience discrimination and racism inside and outside of the classroom, and they may come from a very different culture of learning and educational system from the one in which they now find themselves. In the 1980s, the Ontario Institute for Studies in Education (OISE) led a major five-year project entitled the Development of Bilingual Proficiency (DBP) (Harley et al. 1990), which researched variables related to language proficiency, the effects of instruction and the age of the learners. The project examined learners from a number of different source-language backgrounds and in a variety of learning contexts. In this bilingual setting, typically associated with various types of international movement to a new country for economic or political reasons with the intention of living there, the project revealed some interesting findings illustrating the very complex nature of individual influences on degrees of attainment and progression. Some of the findings include suggestions relating to age of arrival, such as 'an advantage for older immigrant children on largely academic types of second language tasks, but no such advantage on vocabulary knowledge or communicative style, the latter being interpreted as reflecting personality rather than linguistic proficiency' (p. 131). In terms of starting age for classroom L2 learning for immersion programmes, the findings 'showed some advantages for the early start, but these advantages were not evident across the board' (p. 132). Predictors of bilingual proficiency were exposure to heritage languages and to a lesser extent attitude (p. 125). This research went a long way towards highlighting the complexities around individual variables and has much to teach us about approaching language learning in such contexts. There are many decisions that need to be made in relation to topics and language content (for example, whether literacy is an issue) for your own group of learners.

Age
Although not a simple concept in itself, there is now ample research to suggest that age is an important variable in language learning. The younger a learner is when they begin to study a language, the higher their relative chance of success will be. Chomsky (1986) referred to this ability of younger learners as the language acquisition device (LAD), which is believed to be most effective up to the age of seven, a period during which children show the psychological and physical flexibility and malleability to reach native-like standards of proficiency. 'By contrast, older children and adults seem to retain "interference" from their mother tongue' (Spiro 2013: 39). Bearing this in mind, along with a strong consideration of maturity levels and learning preferences at different ages, we will now briefly discuss factors that need to be taken into account when teaching children, teenagers and adult learners.

Young learners already represent quite a diverse group, ranging in age all the way to adolescence. There are different developmental characteristics that need to be understood at each age. Piaget (1963, cited in Murray and Christison 2011: 73) proposes a framework with stages of cognitive and affective development: sensory-motor stage (0–2 years, when children do not yet think conceptually); preoperational stage (2–7 years, when language and conceptual development is rapid and children are egocentric); concrete operations (7–11 years, when children can apply logical thought to concrete problems and begin to use language for social purposes). Considering the age and stage of your learners has implications for the language learning activities you develop or select. Murray and Christison (2011: 79) provide the following general guidelines for teaching young learners:

- Activities for young learners should be simple enough so that they can understand what is expected of them. The younger the child, the simpler the activity should be . . .
- Because human development progresses through a series of stages, teachers must consider what young learners are capable of doing. The goal of the activity needs to be achievable, and the activity itself needs to be stimulating . . .
- For very young learners and for beginning English learners, activities should be orally-based, directed towards listening and speaking.
- The ordering of skills for young learners should be listening, speaking, reading, and writing. Children should only be asked to write words they can read . . .
- Written activities should be used sparingly until children have had the chance to master the mechanics of writing . . .
- Activities that help young children develop balance and spatial awareness at the same time they are learning language are ideal activities, such as variations of TPR (Total Physical Response, a teaching methodology based on the coordination of language and physical movement).
- Building literacy skills works best in young learners when they learn to read and write about ideas and concepts they already use in oral communication.
- Activities that help children develop social skills in conjunction with language are also desirable. Children need to become aware of themselves in relation to others, to share and cooperate . . .
- Children also need to learn how to learn. In order to help them achieve this goal, their learning must not be confined exclusively to the classroom, the textbooks and the teacher . . .
- Activities for young learners should give them an opportunity to experiment with different ways of learning and organising their work, so that they can become aware of themselves as learners and can determine their preferred ways of learning.
- Activities should promote a positive affective climate in the classroom so that learners feel comfortable responding.

I would also add more explicitly that children love fun, laughing and silliness, and where these can be promoted through activities, they should be. Creativity is also a wonderful attribute of most children and because they have not yet learned to be self-conscious, they are happy to share their creative endeavours with others and to do so with a sense of pride, both of which should be encouraged. Volumes such as Hughes and Hadfield (2005) have a range of suggestions for suitable activities for use with young English language learners.

Teaching adolescent learners brings with it a different set of characteristics and considerations. Learners will have had a range of diverse learning and living experiences and will have attained different levels of proficiency, both of which can contribute to a lot of heterogeneity in groups of this age. According to Murray and Christison (2011: 91), 'there are five key areas of development related to adolescents – intellectual, physical, social, emotional, and moral. In whatever context teachers of adolescent learners may find themselves, these developmental factors are at work, and they are at work whether teachers are teaching content, language, or integrating language and content.' They suggest a range of supports that teachers can provide in each of these five areas:

- Intellectual development, when they are making a transition from concrete to abstract thinking processes such as reasoning and reflecting. Suggestions include opportunities to work collaboratively, helping them to connect abstract concepts to real lives through reflection time, and to apply their knowledge to real-life contexts; differentiating instruction so that they have choices to suit how they learn and how they express themselves; creating tasks that help them develop complex thinking; giving them choices to pursue tasks that are interesting to them; talking to them in one-to-one meetings to find out what they are doing and thinking; and modelling academic tasks that will also be useful for them outside the classroom.
- Physical development, when they are experiencing rapid and irregular growth. Suggestions include methods that give learners opportunities to move around and collaborate; culturally appropriate discussions related to physical development, puberty and sexuality; and opportunities for scheduled physical fitness activities every day.
- Social development, when adolescents are very egocentric, concerned about what others think of them and about fitting in with their peers. Suggestions include taking time to understand and empathise; establishing clear expectations for social interaction in the classroom; requiring students to apply their knowledge to social issues of interest; and teaching them the language needed to function democratically in groups.
- Emotional and psychological development, when emotions are animated and there can be a rapid shift between different emotions, often without a logical reason. Suggestions include providing students with opportunities to write and reflect; offering sincere positive feedback when appropriate; and helping students to set and achieve their personal goals.
- Moral development, which is often idealistic and based on a specific cultural context. Students can be keen to make changes to the world but become frustrated with how difficult and slow the process can be. Suggestions include engaging students in community activities; teaching students culturally appropriate ways of resolving conflicts, using relevant language forms; and creating complex learning experiences that involve problems from real-life contexts.

Examples of activities to support these developmental needs as well as advice about dealing with the types of discipline problems that you may encounter with teenagers can be found in volumes such as Lindstromberg (2004).

In terms of age, many English language teachers find themselves at some point teaching postsecondary-level adults. This is a large part of the market share for English language schools and universities. Their needs generally tend to be relatively specific and although some will want to study general English, many will want to follow a programme in some sort of English for specific purposes (ESP). Early in my career when I was teaching in an adult education school in France, I ended up teaching business English to a group from General Motors, and a combination of academic and scientific English to a nuclear physicist. Both were daunting experiences and I remember the feeling of never being more than one step ahead of the students in my preparation, understanding and knowledge. ESP is always a challenge if the language domain is not one with which you are very familiar, and there is a balance to be found between general English and specific English. Research and curriculum development in areas such as EAP is at a relatively advanced stage and teachers are spoilt for choice in terms of resources and materials (for example, Hyland 2006). This may not be the case for all ESP and you may have to put a considerable amount of energy into researching, preparing and negotiating content with the groups or individuals concerned.

Aptitude

The concept of aptitude is not unproblematic, and it has been debated in some detail in second language acquisition circles since the 1950s (Spiro 2013: 36–7). In the early discussions, aptitude was considered to have specific components such as memory, auditory ability and grammatical sensitivity, which could be demonstrated in a number of ways. This stance later encountered some opposition based on alternative theoretical propositions and criticisms of the aptitude approach. In the 1980s Krashen and Terrell proposed that because all learners had a 'natural order' for learning, the aptitude debate was inappropriate (Krashen and Terrell 1983). Others challenged the notion of aptitude as being a static or culturally neutral notion, and argued that it was context specific and had the capacity to change. In other words, just because an individual may have been a good language learner at one time and in one place, this may not carry through to other contexts of language learning. Language learning aptitude does not work in that way, and there is plenty of empirical evidence to support this argument. Skehan (2014: ch. 3) provides a detailed historical account of the theoretical and practical development of the aptitude movement before discussing some relevant research in this area. He also developed a framework for considering aptitude in a way that is directly integrated with language processing (Skehan 2002). He suggests four components in this framework: noticing (an awareness of how language works), patterning (an awareness of specific language patterns), controlling (a type of controlled practice to use the patterns that have been noticed) and lexicalising (freer opportunities to use the language in context).

Styles and strategies

Learning style refers to the preferences that individuals display in terms of being predisposed to the ways in which they think about, process and understand, in this case, language. Research suggests that learners perform better and are more comfortable when they learn in ways that fit best with their own style. There are many models that have been proposed from the world of educational psychology to explain and categorise learning styles, including well-known examples such as the sensory style model specifying visual, auditory and kinaesthetic preferences (see, for example, Dunn et al. 1975, 1978). Visual learners tend to like to see things, for example, lists, crosswords, pictures, movies etc. Auditory learners prefer to hear things or speak aloud. In addition, kinaesthetic learners tend to be tactile, for example, touching things, moving and acting. Other students may be holistic (seeing the big picture with activities such as predicting or guessing or planning) or analytic (liking a detailed approach such as analysing language items and rule learning). They may be tolerant of ambiguity (feeling comfortable with inductive approaches where they have to figure things out, such as in problem-based learning) or intolerant of ambiguity (liking to know exactly what they have to do and how to do it) (for an overview, see Reid 1987). There are many models that present learning styles, often in contrast (see, for example, Jensen 1998), and while these are useful to help you appreciate the range of possibilities, they should not be accepted as being absolute. Learners may be anywhere on a cline between styles, they may change styles in different contexts, and, of course, we should encourage them to develop what may not be intuitive stylistic approaches for them. Strategies, on the other hand, are the range of techniques that learners use, either purposefully or subconsciously, to advance their learning; for example, some learners use rote learning to memorise vocabulary lists. Strategies are discussed in more detail in the section below on autonomy, but it is worth noting that research has found links between styles and strategies (Ehrman and Oxford 1990) and has also found 'that students can stretch beyond their learning style to use a variety of valuable L2 strategies that are initially uncomfortable. Strategy training is particularly useful in helping students use new strategies beyond their normal stylistic boundaries' (Richards 2002: 127).

Motivation
The field of psycholinguistics has been concerned for a number of years with what motivates learners and the effects of that motivation on the learning process. Gardner is one of the most prominent early names associated with the study of motivation. He is probably best known to language teachers for the distinction between a social type of motivation which he called 'integrative', based on the wish to integrate with the host culture, society and language, and what he called 'instrumental' motivation, which is typically associated with wanting to learn a language in order to pass an exam or to progress to more senior career positions, for example (Gardner and Lambert 1972). In more recent years, the study of motivation has changed considerably with a move towards a more complex, dynamic and situated approach, looking at variables such as identity, culture and religion (see, for example, Dörnyei and Ushioda 2011). Four phases to the study of motivation have been identified by Ushioda and Dörnyei (2012: 396):

- The social-psychological period (1959–1990), characterised by the work of Robert Gardner and his associates in Canada
- The cognitive-situated period (during the 1990s), characterised by work drawing on cognitive theories in educational psychology

- The process-oriented period (turn of the century), characterised by a focus on motivational change
- The socio-dynamic period (current), characterised by a concern with dynamic systems and contextual interactions.

Whatever the approach, the research shows strong links between high motivation and language learning success, and so it is an important variable to consider and worth exploring with your learners.

TASK 2.1   AGE-RELEVANT TASKS

Think of a topic and discuss how it could be used as the basis for a lesson with children, with adolescents and with adults. Discuss how you would mediate it differently for the different age groups.

TASK 2.2   CULTURES AND LANGUAGE LEARNING

A. Select two cultures with which you are relatively unfamiliar. Research them (online or by talking to teachers or individuals from those backgrounds) and summarise any issues that may arise in a classroom in your home country for students from these backgrounds (for example, related to religious beliefs, social conventions, gender etc.).
B. Take the following topics, research them and assess any impact that socio-cultural background may have on the way that they are used as the basis for a lesson:

food, animals, fashion, transport

TASK 2.3   LEARNING STYLES

Do an online search for three different models of learning styles. Evaluate their usefulness and assess associated potential advantages and disadvantages of using such models to inform teaching and learning.

2.3   AUTONOMY IN LANGUAGE LEARNING

2.3.1   CONCEPTS, FINDINGS AND TEXTS

Benson's book entitled *Teaching and Researching Autonomy in Language Learning* (Benson 2013) is an important text examining all aspects of learners taking control over their own learning, and the benefits of building this capacity. We also now talk about learner responsibility and engagement as related concepts. The term 'autonomy' should not be confused with or considered synonymous with learners working alone or independently, as autonomy can occur successfully in many different dynamic and group contexts. Dickinson (1987, cited in Nunan 2013: 192) makes a useful distinction between self-instruction (when students are working without the direct control of a teacher, but the teacher may or may not be responsible for the key decisions that relate to what will be learned and how), self-direction (where the learner is responsible for all of the key decisions in relation to learning but may not be responsible for how these decisions are implemented) and autonomy (where the learner is responsible for the decisions and the implementation). This may be worth bearing in mind as you read what follows in this section. You may have a specific focus on different versions of these and at different times depending on your teaching context. In addition, Nunan (2013: 193) argues that:

> autonomy is not an absolute concept. There are degrees of autonomy and the extent to which it is feasible or desirable for learners to embrace autonomy will depend on a range of factors to do with personality of the learner, the goals in undertaking the study of another language, the philosophy of the institution (if any) providing the instruction, and the cultural context within which the learning takes place.

Bearing this in mind, this section will focus on how you as a teacher can foster self-direction and autonomy appropriately among your students in ways that are supportive and constructive for their language learning. Six broad headings related to the practices or approaches to the development of autonomy will be used to frame the discussion. According to Benson (Benson 2001: 111) these are: resource-based approaches; technology-based approaches; learner-based approaches; classroom-based approaches; curriculum-based approaches; and teacher-based approaches. These approaches are very often combined and arguably interdependent.

Resource-based approaches

The focus in resource-based approaches is on the interaction between the learning and the resources, including lesson plans (see Chapter 5), the selection of materials (see Chapter 3) and how assessment and evaluation takes place. It has been suggested that learners at the beginning of the learning process do not know what is best for them and so a gradual approach to increasing autonomy is most suitable. Resources can play a central role in this gradual development. Nunan (2013: 194) suggests a five-level gradient, taking account of learning content and process, which is appropriate for this purpose, and gives examples of how materials can be used and modified to match each of the levels:

1. Making learners *aware* of the goals, content and strategies underlying the materials they are using (for example, being explicit about aims and learning outcomes at the beginning and end of an activity, or asking learners to think about their preferred strategies and styles for particular activities).

2. Learners become *actively involved* in their learning by making choices about content and procedures (for example, offering students a choice between two parallel tasks, which they can individually select from depending on their own needs and interests).

3. Encouraging learners to *intervene* in the learning by making modifications to

     goals, contents and tasks (for example, asking learners to modify tasks from a course-book, or create follow-up tasks specific to their own requirements).

4.   Learners *set* their own goals, *create* their own content, and *develop* their own tasks (for example, providing students with a text and asking them to develop a set of questions or tasks around it).

5.   Learners *transcend* the formal learning context into more self-directed and autonomous modes, making links between the classroom and the world beyond it (for example, asking students to record a conversation, to notice how the 'listener' shows they are engaged, to list some strategies and try them out in their next conversation).

Self-access is also a key deliberation in any discussion about resources and developing autonomy. In fact, it has become even more important since the explosion of commercially produced materials and the availability of open educational resources in online environments, which, along with pedagogic contexts, bring their own sets of ideological messages not always as transparent as they might be to the user. Littlejohn (2013: 183) suggests that 'self-access work may be seen as having an important role in defining learners as more active agents in their own education'. Self-access centres, many of which are becoming more virtual than physical, attract or experience student engagement because of a directive or advice from a teacher, to gain extra credit or because students identify a need for themselves. Centres typically come with some sort of language learning advisor and a range of resources and banks of materials (videos, literature, online materials, skills courses etc.). In relation to the underlying ideological position proposed to the learner, Littlejohn (2013: 186) proposes three questions that might usefully be asked:

- What role in the discourse is proposed for the learner: initiate, respond or none?
- What mental operation is to be engaged? (Lower-order to higher-order cognitive demands as per Bloom's revised taxonomy – see Chapter 4 for a fuller discussion.)
- Where does the content in the task come from? From within the task itself, from the teacher or from the students?

While these questions are important in deciding the level of the materials and tasks in class, they are even more important in directing students to self-access materials, where there is very little if any advisor or teacher moderation available to the learner as they negotiate their way through what could potentially be a random selection of activities. And the reverse is also true: learners could be working in a self-access environment with materials that are completely directive and controlled. In other words, self-access does not automatically equate to self-directed or autonomous learning in its own right. There are a number of key issues in determining the effectiveness of self-access. Sturtridge (1997, cited in Benson 2001: 115–16) provides a framework for considering the issues in a number of areas, most of which still hold true even if they need to be considered in the light of the online self-access environments that tend to prevail today:

- Management:
  - Is there adequate consultation between management and teachers in the planning and implementation of the centre?
  - Are activities in the centre integrated into the curriculum?
  - Are learners involved in the planning and management of the centre and are they aware of its role?

- Facilities:
  - Is the centre easily accessible to its potential users?
  - Is it appropriately resourced in an on-going way?
  - Are available resources appropriately and imaginatively used and displayed?
  - Does the access and retrieval system encourage the development of autonomy?

- Staff training and development:
  - Do those working in the centre to encourage growth and change engage with staff development? Does it cover the roles of teachers and learners in self-access?
  - Does the centre have adequate feedback systems for staff comments and proposals?
  - Are the centre's staff connected with and involved in research into its uses?

- Learner training and development:
  - Is regular training available to those who want to use the centre? Does this extend to dealing with aspects of autonomous learning?

- Learner culture:
  - Does the centre accommodate different learning styles and the strengths and weaknesses of the students who use it?

- Materials:
  - Are the materials adapted for self-access use?
  - Do the materials foster autonomous learning skills as well as language development?
  - Does the range and availability of the materials facilitate exploration and choice for the learners?

Technology-based approaches

Information technology and interactive technology in our lives and in language learning environments are here to stay and ever expanding (Farr and Murray 2016). This brings many opportunities for self-directed learning, although it also has limitations (see Chapter 4 for a further discussion of the limitations). There is a range of specific and generic software suitable for the development of language skills. Here I will discuss them in relation to what have traditionally been known as the receptive (listening and reading) and productive (speaking and writing) language skills (other technological tools such as the availability of language analysis tools and associated corpora will also be discussed in Chapter 3). In technological terms, we have reached a phase of interactional potential, which fits very well with the espoused aims and methodologies of the teaching profession. I will briefly discuss one example of this here. It relates to the possibilities offered by telecollaboration as discussed in Helm and Guth (2016), 'which can be defined as online intercultural exchange between classes of foreign language students in geographically distant locations'. As such, it has good potential to assist the development of language and intercultural competence in self-directed and autonomous ways and is situated within interactionist and socio-cultural theoretical frameworks. Early forms of telecollaboration in the 1980s were based on eTandem models where learners worked in partnership with learners who were native speakers of the language being learnt. Learners typically work autonomously and set their own objectives and organisational structure around the exchanges. The Cultura model, where learners complete tasks and collaborate around the results, allows learners to communicate in their first language (or the language of their institution), providing rich language input for the other party. Both of these models are based on the idealised native speaker, a concept that has come into question and has influenced emerging frameworks which are now characterised by much variety in terms of languages, users, technologies and pedagogic design. Whatever approach is taken, its success is largely dependent on the commitment and time investment of the collaborating teachers, who play a vital role on the organisational and pedagogic design side of the projects, without which there is the potential for failure.

Learner-based approaches
The focus in learner-based approaches is on behavioural and psychological changes that will enable learners to take more responsibility for and control of their learning. As such, it has a cognitive and an affective dimension. The first comprehensive account of what learners do when they learn and the effectiveness of the related actions came with the work of Rebecca Oxford (1990, 2001). She proposed a categorisation of six strategy orientations: affective strategies (to increase/promote positive feelings); social strategies (learning through interaction with others); memory strategies (techniques to help memorisation); metacognitive strategies (an awareness of which strategies work and purposeful use of them); cognitive strategies (such as noticing, analysing, applying etc.); and compensatory strategies (ways to deal with not understanding or knowing how to say something). Although there has been some critique of a strategy-based approach (for example, Rees-Miller 1994), Benson (2001: 145) asserts that 'the balance of evidence suggests that strategy training can lead to an improvement in learning performance given the right circumstances'. He cites Charmot and Robin's (1994) five important components of strategy training:

- Discovery and discussion of strategies that learners are already using
- Presentation of new strategies by explicitly naming and describing them
- Modelling of strategies
- Explaining why and when the strategies can be used
- Providing extensive practice with authentic tasks and opportunities for

students to discuss their own applications of the strategies and their effectiveness.

In addition to the vast bodies of literature now available on language learning strategies, there are many models of learner styles, or preferences that learners naturally display in the way in which they like to receive, process and output new linguistic information (see Chapter 5 for a critical account of some of the existing models). In any sort of strategy or style awareness or development for students, you need to be careful of labelling them one type or another, as this could pigeonhole them and prevent diversity and an ability to develop in other ways. This is a substantial risk in the light of the shortcomings around existing models and the lack of empirical evidence suggesting direct impact on learning.

Classroom-based approaches
In the conventional educational context of the classroom, there are ways in which autonomy can be developed through opportunities that are collaborative and supported. Classroom activities can be configured in ways that are deliberately more learner-centred and controlled but fully scaffolded by the teacher. Learners can be involved in planning, and research has shown this to be effective in many different contexts (Benson 2001: 152–4). They can also have a role to play in assessment, specifically in self-assessment, which can be a mechanism to improve learning through awareness raising and noticing (Schmidt 1993). It can also be motivating and empowering for them to be involved in evaluating learning, as this has traditionally been the domain of the teacher, but they need to be supported and inducted to ensure it is a positive and beneficial experience. There may need to be a gradual approach to self-assessment that coincides with the development of a range of other classroom activities that promote independent and critical thinking. Assessment is not confined to progress made in language production. It can also centre on the extent to which learners have attained their goals in specific lessons, and might take the form of them reflecting on what they have learned and identifying future needs, directions and actions, much in the way that the reflective cycle works for you as a student teacher (see Chapter 8). Planning, assessment and to a great extent what happens in the classroom, however, can be determined largely by the educational culture in which you work and may be constrained by school, national or international curricula and exam systems.

Curriculum-based approaches
A process or learner-centred approach to syllabus design is the epitome of learner involvement in negotiating and directing what happens with the curriculum as a whole. This approach is most closely associated with the work of Candlin and Nunan (Nunan 1988) on the Adult Migrant English Programme (AMEP) in Australia in the 1980s. However, in my experience, due to a number of influencing factors, this approach is rarely possible or desirable in its true form. In many cases, some negotiation may be possible and desirable but not to the extent that the product merits the title of a learner-centred syllabus, which it has been suggested has serious

shortcomings for most settings, including lack of explicit progression between levels and a perception that teachers are not doing their jobs properly (Murray and Christison 2011: 6). However, some learner participation in decisions around the syllabus has a number of advantages and is likely to ensure ownership from the very beginning. Models of good practice in negotiated syllabus design will generally include learner support in areas such as reflective practice, self-directed learning, learning strategies, needs analysis, and identifying and articulating individual and collective learning outcomes. This will ensure that the learners are not overwhelmed or ill equipped for the job of negotiated syllabus design and understand the sound pedagogic principles on which such an approach rests. And even with these supports, the role of the teacher will continue to be pivotal to a successful outcome.

Teacher-based approaches
The role of the teacher in self-directed and autonomous learning contexts necessarily changes from having a transmission focus to being what has been variously labelled: facilitator, helper, advisor, co-ordinator etc. There may be resistance to this change by both teachers and learners. Teachers who have come through more traditional educational systems and teacher education programmes will have spent their entire apprenticeships of observation observing teachers as informers and custodians of knowledge, and so this becomes their frame of reference. The one thing that the technological revolution has done is to democratise access to information. There is practically nothing that can't now be googled and found, or at least that is the perception of younger generations. (Recently, when my 9-year-old daughter Síofra mislaid her Hallowe'en party mask I found her sitting on her bed with her iPad searching for 'options to find mask in house'!) This has meant that a partial redefinition of teacher role has already been orchestrated by the impact of technology on society. Teachers can also feel that professionalism means adhering to the traditional roles, as this may be a strong, sometimes implicit, rather than explicit, expectation from the institution, the students and other stakeholders. Some cultural ideologies put the teacher at the centre of the learning process. For instance, in Confucian heritage cultures, the teacher is viewed as an authority to be respected as the source of knowledge. Learners from such backgrounds may resist role rebalances because of their own previous experiences and expectations, or simply because more active engagement and self-direction will require significantly more effort on their part. In addition to the teacher's role relative to the learner, there is the added dimension of teacher as self-directed learner and practitioner. A progression into reconfigured teacher roles will require reflective practice and development activities as outlined in Chapter 8.

TASK 2.4   YOU AS AN INDEPENDENT LEARNER

Consider some of your past educational experiences as a learner.
Can you identify some in which you were more self-directed?
What were the characteristics of these situations?
How do these align with Benson's six approaches discussed in this section?

TASK 2.5   LEARNER PERCEPTIONS

Prepare some questions about various aspects of self-directed and independent learning. Interview some English language learners. Write a short report on your findings and present it within a small group.

TASK 2.6   ONLINE LANGUAGE LEARNING RESOURCES

Find an online English language resource centre. Evaluate a selection of the materials that it contains using Sturtridge's questions on materials (above). Share your findings in small groups.

2.4   LANGUAGE PROFICIENCY LEVELS

2.4.1   CONCEPTS, FINDINGS AND TEXTS

There are many ways of placing a learner on a scale that represents their current language level or level of proficiency. This may be necessary to place them in the correct class or to determine their suitability for a particular job or entrance to an English-speaking university. Large ELT publishing companies such as Cambridge University Press (CUP) and Oxford University Press (OUP) design their materials for different levels. Coursebooks, for example, are usually available for somewhere between six and eight levels, each of which takes approximately 80–100 hours to complete. These will have descriptors along the lines of 'beginner', 'elementary', 'pre-intermediate', 'intermediate', 'upper-intermediate', 'advanced' and 'proficiency'. The materials contained within coursebooks, graded readers, and skills, grammar and vocabulary practice books will be pitched for a typical learner at the relevant level, and the materials will be indicated as being suitable for one of the levels. This is a practical, if somewhat imperfect way to help teachers to select and pitch teaching materials at the proficiency level of their learners. There is also a range of place-ment tests that learners can take to determine their level, for example, the Nelson Quickcheck Placement Test, the Harvard English Language Placement Test or the Oxford Online Placement Test. Many private English language schools use these or their in-house tests during orientation, in combination with an interview to place the learner at the appropriate level.

In addition to the publishers' frameworks, there are also more granulated descrip-tors of levels. One well-known example, which has gained much currency since its introduction, is the Council of Europe's Common European Framework of Reference (CEFR). This framework was the result of over twenty years of research and at the time of writing is available in thirty-nine languages. The following descriptions of the framework, its purpose, and scope come from the CEFR website (http://www.coe.int/t/dg4/linguistic/cadre1_en.asp):

> It was designed to provide a transparent, coherent, and comprehensive basis for the elaboration of language syllabuses and curriculum guidelines, the design of

teaching and learning materials, and the assessment of foreign language
proficiency . . .
  The CEFR describes foreign language proficiency at six levels: A1 and A2, B1
and B2, C1 and C2. It also defines three 'plus' levels (A2+, B1+, B2+). Based on
empirical research and widespread consultation, this scheme makes it possible to
compare tests and examinations across languages and national boundaries . . . It
also provides a basis for recognising language qualifications and thus facilitating
educational and occupational mobility.
  The CEFR's illustrative scales of 'can do' descriptors are available in a bank of
descriptors together with many other related descriptors.

Table 2.1 gives an illustration of the CEFR global scale along with the matching
descriptors.
  All of these frameworks are useful as descriptive accounts of learner language
level. In addition, they facilitate the use of a common understanding and discourse
between teachers in many different international contexts. Of course, we must consider that proficiency level is a concept that is brought into question by some of the
literature, which rejects the exclusive place of the native speaker standard in the light
of English as a lingua franca models and ideologies (for a full discussion, see Cutting
2015: ch. 2).

TASK 2.7   COURSEBOOKS AND LANGUAGE LEVEL

Select a language level typically used in coursebook descriptions (for example, 'upper
intermediate'). Compare and contrast a range of coursebooks from different publishers for that same level, using the descriptions provided in the contents and unit
outlines. What are the similarities and differences? If they differ, why do you think
this is the case?

TASK 2.8   CEFR AND COURSEBOOKS

Using either the same range of coursebooks as in the previous task, or a different
range, examine whether they are mapped in terms of the CEFR. If they are not, use
the detailed CEFR from the framework's website and try to establish where each book
sits on it in terms of level.

TASK 2.9   THE ENGLISH PROFILE PROJECT

A. Read about the English Profile Project online. What can you learn about its aims
    and outcomes?
B. Read one research article from the associated journal, which can also be found
    online. Share a summary of the article in a small group.

Table 2.1   Common European Framework of Reference levels: global scale

Proficient User	C2	Can understand with ease virtually everything heard or read. Can summarise information from different spoken and written sources, reconstructing arguments and accounts in a coherent presentation. Can express him/herself spontaneously, very fluently and precisely, differentiating finer shades of meaning even in more complex situations.
	C1	Can understand a wide range of demanding, longer texts, and recognise implicit meaning. Can express him/herself fluently and spontaneously without much obvious searching for expressions. Can use language flexibly and effectively for social, academic and professional purposes. Can produce clear, well-structured, detailed text on complex subjects, showing controlled use of organisational patterns, connectors and cohesive devices.
Independent User	B2	Can understand the main ideas of complex text on both concrete and abstract topics, including technical discussions in his/her field of specialisation. Can interact with a degree of fluency and spontaneity that makes regular interaction with native speakers quite possible without strain for either party. Can produce clear, detailed text on a wide range of subjects and explain a viewpoint on a topical issue giving the advantages and disadvantages of various options.
	B1	Can understand the main points of clear standard input on familiar matters regularly encountered in work, school, leisure, etc. Can deal with most situations likely to arise whilst travelling in an area where the language is spoken. Can produce simple connected text on topics which are familiar or of personal interest. Can describe experiences and events, dreams, hopes & ambitions and briefly give reasons and explanations for opinions and plans.
Basic User	A2	Can understand sentences and frequently used expressions related to areas of most immediate relevance (e.g. very basic personal and family information, shopping, local geography, employment). Can communicate in simple and routine tasks requiring a simple and direct exchange of information on familiar and routine matters. Can describe in simple terms aspects of his/her background, immediate environment, and matters in areas of immediate need.
	A1	Can understand and use familiar everyday expressions and very basic phrases aimed at the satisfaction of needs of a concrete type. Can introduce him/herself and others and can ask and answer questions about personal details such as where he/she lives, people he/she knows and things he/she has. Can interact in a simple way provided the other person talks slowly and clearly and is prepared to help.

2.5   FURTHER READING ONE

Kadir-Hussein, A. and Che-Haron, S. (2012) 'Autonomy in language learning',
***Journal of Education and Practice*, 3: 8, 103–11.**
This journal article investigates autonomy among learners studying Arabic in
Malaysia. It begins by contextualising notions of autonomy in the context of the
changing roles of teachers in constructivist approaches to education, where learners
are expected to play a major part in actively discovering and processing information
in order to build their own knowledge.

> In response to the above Holec (1981) introduced autonomous learning which
> emphasized learners taking charge of their own learning. These abilities involve
> establishing learning objectives, defining content and learning process, selecting
> methods and techniques to achieve learning objectives, monitoring the
> procedure of learning, and evaluating what has been acquired. Being
> autonomous also means that a learner is capable to make decisions concerning
> the learning with which he is or wishes to be involved. (p. 103)

They highlight the fact that Holec's definition of autonomy emphasises learner
behaviour, while Little's (1995) focuses on the psychological aspects of learning and
Benson (2001) adds a political dimension in the inclusion of freedom of choice in
what and where to learn. For the purposes of their study, the researchers use the
five autonomous learning activities proposed by Holec: (1) determining learning
objectives, (2) defining the contents and learning progress, (3) selecting methods
and techniques to achieve learning goals, (4) monitoring the procedure of language
acquisition, and (5) evaluating what has been acquired. The literature review section
of the article outlines some empirical studies that have been conducted on autonomous language learning which in some cases showed resistance to autonomy and the
redefined roles of teacher and learner because of a lack of confidence (Yaping 2005),
while others seemed motivated and ready to take responsibility (Rukthong 2008). The
authors cite three studies on autonomy from the Malaysian context, showing some
general resistance and a reliance on teachers. One study in particular, ThangSiew
(2009), found a difference between students in public and private universities, with
the latter found to be more responsible and self-directed. The next section of the
article describes the methodology the researchers employed for their own study.

> The present study adopted a survey by Jianping Xu (2009) which was developed
> specifically to measure language learners' abilities to involve [themselves] in
> autonomous learning by looking at the degree to which they are able to conduct
> autonomous language learning in five specific areas. (p. 105)

A questionnaire was designed around Holec's five autonomous activities with
six questions relating to each of them for the Jianping study, and the authors of
this article adopted four of the sections for the purposes of their study. This was
administered to a group of Arabic language learners and results reported in this paper

were from 179 responses. On the basis of these results the respondents were found to be positively predisposed and ready for autonomous language learning in general, especially in relation to productive activities such as those based on communication, writing and translation. The authors conclude that:

> The findings revealed that CELPAD [Center for Languages and Pre-Academic Development] Arabic language learners were ready to learn autonomously and had positive attitudes and inclination towards autonomy, therefore appropriate and proper trainings are needed to expose and foster autonomy among them. (p. 110)

FURTHER READING ONE TASK

1. On the basis of Holec's five dimensions outlined in this article, design a short questionnaire, with three questions for each dimension. Ask a group of six of your peers or students to complete the questionnaire and prepare a short analysis and conclusion of the results.
2. Plan the type of training the authors refer to in their conclusion for this group of Arabic learners in Malaysia, taking appropriate cultural considerations into account.

2.6   FURTHER READING TWO

Zoltan Dornyei has a very informative and useful personal webpage, www.zoltandornyei.co.uk, where you will find most of his published articles and book chapters related to motivation and language learning in a downloadable format.

FURTHER READING TWO TASK

1. Select a reading of your own choice, summarise it and discuss in a small group.
2. What aspects of the chapter, book or article that you have read will you use to inform your own teaching and how?

2.7   SUMMARY

This chapter focuses on the ways in which variables related to individual learners can influence their English language learning. It begins with a discussion of social and cultural background and considers some different teaching scenarios with learners from different backgrounds studying in either ESOL or EFL settings, and how both past and present settings can be significant. Section 2.2 continues with an examination of how age impacts on learning and appropriate approaches for children, adolescents and adults. Following this, aptitude, suitable learning styles and strategies, and motivation are deliberated. Section 2.3 considers notions of self-directed and autonomous learning in some depth and looks at the ways in which these can be promoted in the classroom, in self-access and through technology. The degree to which learners are ready and willing to become more independent can influence the rate and success of their learning in terms of process and product. The final content-based section of this chapter gives a short outline of the ways in which proficiency levels are measured and articulated for different purposes. The two points of focus are on levels related to published language learning materials and the CEFR, its aims, scope and level descriptors. This chapter begins a focused discussion on taking the learner as the starting point for teaching, but other influences and related issues will come up in later chapters when discussing the teacher, materials, observing and planning lessons for English language teaching.

2.8 ADDITIONAL READINGS

Benson, P. and Voller, P. (eds) (2013) *Autonomy and Independence in Language Learning*, Abingdon and New York: Routledge.

Dörnyei, Z. (2001) *Motivation Strategies in the Language Classroom*, Cambridge: Cambridge University Press.

Kramsch, C. (1998) *Language and Culture*, Oxford: Oxford University Press.

Little, D. (1995) 'Learning as dialogue: The dependence of learner autonomy on teacher autonomy', *System*, 23: 2, 175–81.

Spratt, M., Humphreys, G. and Chan, V. (2002) 'Autonomy and motivation: Which comes first?', *Language Teaching Research*, 6: 3, 245–66.

3

THINKING ABOUT YOUR MATERIALS

ELAINE RIORDAN

3.1 INTRODUCTION

Tomlinson (2001: 66) defines materials as 'anything which can be used to facilitate the learning of a language. They can be linguistic, visual, auditory or kinaesthetic, and they can be presented in print, through live performance or display, or on cassette, CD-ROM, DVD or the internet'. Whether operating within a fixed syllabus using prescribed resources, or being free to select and design from scratch, in your role as a teacher, you must inevitably make decisions in relation to the materials to be used in TP. These decisions will be made on the basis of a number of issues; for example, institutional requirements; the level, age, needs and interests of your learners; the skill(s) and language area(s) being practised; and the resources and time available to you. Becoming familiar with the abundance of materials available for TESOL is no easy task, and this chapter hopes to offer you an insight into some of the existing material, and get you thinking about how to use, exploit and adapt materials for your own teaching. From my experience in training TESOL teachers, what they often find the most difficult task is how to use the material that is already prescribed; for example, they can find it difficult to extract the language focus of a given piece of material, or they are unsure how to present it to their learners. Another issue is that some student teachers feel the need to stick rigidly to each activity offered in a coursebook, which can sometimes result in a tedious lesson, and thus neglect the needs of the learners. Moreover, when student teachers are designing their own lessons, difficulties they face include creating a coherent lesson, matching materials to appropriate levels and exploiting the materials for language input. These types of skills are refined through practice and experience, and the tasks in this chapter are designed to help you to reflect on such issues.

This chapter begins by surveying the vast world of commercially and freely available materials for TESOL (for example, coursebook series, specific skills materials, software packages and mobile applications), and goes on to discuss some important issues around their usage. The next section attends to the use and development of authentic materials. In an attempt to provide stimuli for you when drawing on authentic materials for your language lessons, an overview of some of the underlying principles for teacher interpretation, mediation and evaluation is offered. The following section investigates language corpora and their potential for language learning materials. This is approached from a critical perspective so that you are in a position to make informed decisions in relation to the suitability of such resources.

3.2 PUBLISHED MATERIALS

3.2.1 CONCEPTS, FINDINGS AND TEXTS

Materials can have a number of functions, namely informative, instructional, experiential, eliciting and exploratory (Tomlinson 2012), and your responsibility as a teacher revolves around combining such materials with appropriate methodologies and effective TPs. As there are so many published materials on the market, this section offers you a flavour of what is out there, and hopes to get you thinking about dealing with such materials.

Coursebooks
Appendix 1 presents some examples of well-known coursebooks which range in levels, and cover all (or some) of the language skills. As well as popular books for general English, there are materials designed to cater for specific skills, for example reading skills, grammar, vocabulary and so on; coursebooks for exam-based classes such as the Cambridge suite of exams (for example, KET, FCE) and IELTS; and materials designed for ESP, EAP and young learners (see Appendix 1). For more information on the broad range of materials available to you in your professional practice, please consult the publishers' webpages (for example, Cambridge University Press, Macmillan English, Oxford University Press and Pearson Longman), where you can also get further resources in their coursebook companion websites.

Considering the wealth of published resources available, it is worthwhile to refer to relevant research in relation to coursebooks. Some advantages and disadvantages of using a coursebook are summarised in Table 3.1 (see, for example, Mares 2003, Rubdy 2003, Tomlinson 2001, 2012, Ur 1991).

Another issue often cited in the literature concerns the global coursebook, which can be defined as material which has been designed in English-speaking countries, and for use in English language classes around the world. These types of coursebooks have been criticised as they appear as uniform, with bland topics,[1] and a lack of focus on the local needs, interests and cultures of learners (see Gray 2002, Mishan 2005). Indeed, Tomlinson (2012: 158) notes that 'many global coursebooks are not considered to be sufficiently engaging or relevant for their actual users'. He goes on to state that he 'would like to see more localised textbooks and more global textbooks which are designed to be flexible and to offer teachers and students opportunities for localisation, personalisation and choice' (ibid.; see also Tomlinson 2008b for examples of localised materials, and Farr et al. 2010 and Chambers et al. 2011 for using corpus-based materials with localised data). Tomlinson (2012: 165) also discusses the various views in relation to the ideology of coursebooks, which can represent 'a view of teaching and learning, a view of the target language and the culture(s) they represent and the worldview of their producer' which he believes can be dangerous due to the status coursebooks have in classrooms, as users may accept the views portrayed within them. However, he believes that teachers and learners are critical with their use of coursebooks, and he suggests that in order 'to protect the intended consumers it is important that teachers and language courses focus on developing constructive

THINKING ABOUT YOUR MATERIALS

Table 3.1   Advantages and disadvantages of coursebooks

Advantages	Disadvantages
Carefully prepared and structured; therefore provide a solid framework to work from	Typically represent only the American or British English varieties
Attractively presented	Can be culturally inappropriate
The most convenient form of presenting material	Reductionist in the language points covered
Consistent in the delivery of materials and tasks	Can often follow a typical format, which can be demotivating
Provide stimuli for methodological development	Result in a uniform syllabus and approach and therefore may not suit every type of learner
The language is controlled	Impose styles of learning
Help students revise; thus promoting autonomy	May not be suitable to the students' levels
Offer continuation; give students a sense of progression and cohesion	If answers come at the end of the book, students may rely on them too much
Come with guides, teacher's book, procedures and aims outlined	Remove power from teachers
Offer reassurance to teachers	May result in too much dependency from teachers, and in turn, a lack of creativity

criticality as one of their objectives'. Therefore, you, as the teacher, may want to reflect on and reveal the ideological stance within given materials, and indeed adapt materials to reflect local cultural preferences (see also Prodromou and Mishan 2008).

As well as aiming for localised coursebooks, authors call for materials to be 'humanised' (see Moskowitz 1978). This can be achieved by 'adding activities which help to make the language learning process a more affective experience, and finding ways of helping the learners to connect what is in the book to what is in their minds' (Tomlinson 2003a: 163). Considering the above, Tomlinson (2001: 67) advises that 'no coursebook can be ideal for any particular class and an effective teacher needs to be able to evaluate, adapt and produce materials to ensure a match' (see Section 3.3 for more on materials evaluation). On a positive note, it is believed that teachers 'seem to be more constructively critical of their coursebooks and to be more willing, confident and able to localise and personalise their coursebooks for their learners' (Tomlinson 2012: 170).

Taking the above considerations into account, the task of finding a coursebook to suit teaching needs is a challenge (Cunningsworth 1995). However, Rubdy (2003: 45) offers a framework for the selection of materials, which includes assessing materials in the light of the:

1.   learners' needs, goals and pedagogical requirements;
2.   teacher's skills, abilities, theories and beliefs; and
3.   thinking underlying the materials writer's presentation of the content and approach to teaching and learning respectively.

Once a coursebook has been chosen, it can then be used in a number of ways, ranging from following it strictly and using every activity in sequence to not using it at all, or using it but supplementing it with other materials, although not necessarily in a sequenced order (Ur 1991). Unfortunately, Tomlinson (2013a: 45) notes that while coursebooks appear to be used in most classrooms, 'there is surprisingly little treatment in the literature of how coursebooks should be used and of how they are actually used in the classroom'. My advice to any new teacher would be to use (or at least examine) coursebooks to begin with in order to become familiar with the materials, types of tasks and so on for the level you are teaching. On the other hand, do not be afraid to be critical, selective and creative in the choices you make (materials adaptation is discussed further in Section 3.5).

Online material
As well as coursebooks, copious material can be sourced online, where whole lessons, activities and games can be taken freely (or for a small cost). As far back as 1997, Carrier noted the difficulty in trying to produce a list of online sites because existing ones are disappearing or changing and new ones are emerging every day, and in the era of Web 2.0 this is even more pronounced. However, examples of online sites which I have found particularly useful are given in Appendix 2. While some of these resources are excellent, time may be required to evaluate and adapt the materials so they suit your and your students' needs. To this end, materials evaluation (see Tomlinson 2003c), discussed in Section 3.3, is a key factor for you to consider.

In addition to sourcing material on the Internet, online learning is also now widely acknowledged as a route for language learning (see Levy 2009, Wang and Vásquez 2012), whereby SLA factors such as input theory, social and collaborative learning and scaffolding can be facilitated (see Blake 2008, Mishan 2013). To this end, as seen in Appendix 2, there are specifically designed computer-assisted language learning (CALL) packages for English language learners (see Mishan 2013 for a more detailed discussion of CALL courseware). A final area to underline is the field of mobile learning (see Chinnery 2006). There are a number of apps (iOS and Android) now available, examples of which are listed in Appendix 2. Again, the teacher must go through these packages and decide on their usefulness for their learners (see Mukundan and Nimehchisalem 2008). For more examples (and theoretical background) on how to use technologies for language teaching in terms of vocabulary, grammar and the four skills, see Derewianka (2003) and Chapelle and Jamieson (2008). While this section has attempted to offer you an overview of issues and content in published materials, the following tasks encourage you to become more familiar with what is available, before moving on to a discussion of authentic materials.

TASK 3.1   EXPLORING MATERIALS

In groups, familiarise yourselves with some of the materials available for EFL/ESL courses. Take a look at the following publishers' sites, and explore what is on offer, or examine some of the coursebooks listed in Appendix 1. Discuss your findings with your peers. I would also encourage you to share details of available material that you have with one another, or if your institution has a virtual learning environment (VLE), create a shared document with the class whereby everyone can upload a summary of their chosen material.

Example publishers:

- Cambridge University Press   http://www.cambridge.org/
- Macmillan English   http://www.macmillanenglish.com/
- Oxford University Press   http://ukcatalogue.oup.com/
- Pearson Longman   http://www.pearsonelt.com/

TASK 3.2   RESEARCHING ONLINE LEARNING MATERIALS

In 2012, Tomlinson wrote a state-of-the-art paper on materials development, where he predicted that in the future 'materials will increasingly be delivered electronically through computers and smartphones' (2012: 171). In groups, research the expanding area of online learning and online materials. Read at least one research article, and interview one student about what (if any) technology they use for language learning. Report to your group with your findings.

TASK 3.3   LESSON/ACTIVITY ANALYSIS

There a number of websites dedicated to English language teachers. Pick one website from Appendix 2 (or search for other sites), and explore it. Find one activity/lesson plan and analyse it. Think about the following and share your thoughts in groups:

- skill(s) practised
- function(s) practised
- language point(s) practised
- language level
- task type(s)
- topic
- content
- pedagogical approach

3.3   AUTHENTIC MATERIALS

3.3.1   CONCEPTS, FINDINGS AND TEXTS

Authentic materials are those designed originally for native speakers (for example, brochures, newspaper articles, songs, literature), which can be adapted for use in the language classroom (see Mishan 2005 and Shomoossi and Ketabi 2007 for a critical discussion of authenticity). Tomlinson (2012: 162) notes that 'an authentic text is one which is produced in order to communicate rather than to teach, and an authentic task is one which involves the learners in communication in order to achieve an outcome, rather than practice the language'. He also holds that the text does not necessarily need to have been written by a native speaker and that it may have been simplified for reasons of clarity or communication. Nor does the task necessarily have to be a real-life task. It can be a task which practises real-life skills. To this end, Mishan (2005: 75) presents a set of guidelines for consideration when designing authentic tasks:

1. Reflect on the original communicative purpose of the original text.
2. Ensure tasks are text appropriate.
3. Elicit response to/engagement with the text.
4. Ensure tasks approximate real-life tasks.
5. Activate learners' existing knowledge of the target language and culture.
6. Involve purposeful communication between learners.

The benefits of authentic materials have been proposed by many. For example, Edge (1993) believes that they represent the real objective of language learning, with the complexities that published materials often tend to avoid. In addition, Mishan (2004: 219) outlines 'the richness of authentic texts in terms of their cultural and linguistic content, the opportunity to select materials that are relevant, appropriate, and interesting to particular groups of learners, [and] the motivational aspects of learning from authentic rather than didactic material'. Mishan (2005) also puts forward the 3 Cs framework of culture, currency and challenge to explicate the merits of authentic texts, in that authentic texts encapsulate the culture of the target language; are current and up to date in terms of language and topic; and are inherently challenging for learners. Moreover, in a study which examined task behaviour with EFL learners in a South Korean university, Peacock (1997) found that overall class motivation was higher for learners when using authentic materials compared to purpose-written material, although there were no differences with regard to learner self-reported motivations. He also found that time was a factor in that during the early stages of the study, the learners preferred purpose-written materials but later on they preferred authentic materials (from days 9–20). The students in his study noted that they found the authentic material less interesting than purpose-written material, and therefore Peacock suggests that 'learners were more motivated by authentic materials, but not because they were more interesting' (1997: 152).

A summary of the implications (from SLA research) of the use of authentic materials has been proposed by Mishan (2005: 41; see also Tomlinson 2008b, 2013b) as follows:

*   Authentic texts provide the best source of rich and varied comprehensible input for language learners.
*   Elaborative changes to a text enhance comprehensibility better than does simplification.
*   Authentic texts impact affective factors essential to learning, such as motivation, empathy and emotional involvement.
*   Learning style (individual or culturally conditioned) need not be an impediment to the efficacy of the use of authentic texts and tasks for learning.

- Authentic texts are suited to a naturalistic, consciousness-raising approach to learning TL grammar.
- Authentic texts are particularly suited to the deployment of the more holistic mode of language processing, top-down processing.
- Authentic texts (from the audio and audio-visual media in particular) stimulate 'whole brain processing', which can result in learning that is more durable.

Moreover, while authentic materials are predominantly found in English-speaking countries, with advances in technology the Internet now offers a wide-ranging and extensive supply (see Mishan 2005 for various examples of authentic tasks, and also Tomlinson 2012).

Having outlined the implications of authentic materials for language learning, I must also note that there are many ways in which we can utilise such materials. They can be used:

- independently to focus on a specific skill or teaching point
  - holiday brochures to practise modal verbs
  - menus to practise the semantic field of food, and requesting/ordering
- alongside a piece of material from a coursebook
  - using a listening text in a coursebook, with an authentic piece of listening on a similar topic; and either doing a jigsaw listening, or getting students to compare the genres of the texts
  - using authentic materials as extension activities to follow up on issues covered in a coursebook
- to supplement a piece of material from a coursebook
  - if a reading exercise in a coursebook is outdated, then an authentic piece can be found from a newspaper instead.

Alongside the many benefits of using authentic materials, we should be aware of the effort and time required to prepare these materials. We also need to be careful in how we use them (as with any material), because if used incorrectly, they can demotivate learners. For example, Nguyen (2008) outlines how Internet technology can inform syllabus design and offer an abundance of immediate authentic materials, but cautions that 'the teacher is clearly a crucial element in the success or failure of a lesson' (2008: 139). To this end, you as the teacher are responsible for materials development, adaptation, and evaluation, which are discussed briefly below.

Materials development and evaluation

Materials development has been defined as 'both a field of study and a practical under-taking' in that it studies 'the principles and procedures of the design, implementation and evaluation of language teaching materials [and] it involves the production, evaluation and adaptation of language teaching materials, by teachers for their own class-room and by materials writers for sale or distribution' (Tomlinson 2001: 66). As there is not enough room in this volume to discuss the area in detail, to give you an overview

Table 3.2   Trends in materials development (based on Tomlinson 2003b: 7–9)

Positive trends	Negative trends
Increased samples of language use being incorporated into materials, which encourage discovery learning	Grammar being returned to its central place in the curriculum (which goes against research into learners' and teachers' needs and wants)
More materials incorporating corpus-based data emerging	More prominence given to speaking and listening in coursebooks rather than writing and reading
More focus on spoken grammar in materials	Literature neglected in coursebooks
More focus on affective engagement of learners in materials	A lack of controversial issues being dealt with
More personalised materials (in terms of learners' views, lives and so on) being used	Predominant learning style catered for in coursebooks is analytical
More use of the Internet	Follow an assumption that learners can only deal with short texts as they have short attention spans
More interactive packages emerging	Follow an assumption that learners do not want to be engaged in intellectually demanding tasks while language learning
More institutions producing their own locally driven and relevant materials	Learners are underestimated in terms of their intellectual, linguistic and emotional skills

of the present state of this field, Tomlinson (2003b: 7–9) summarises current trends in materials development, examples of which are presented in Table 3.2.

Another area to underscore is materials evaluation; and whether you are using coursebooks or other materials with your learners, you ultimately have the job of evaluating the material so you can make decisions about implementation. This can take the form of predicative evaluation (evaluating before you use material) or retrospective evaluation (evaluating after you have used the material; see Ellis 1997, Tomlinson 2003c). While there is not enough scope to address this in full here, please see Mishan and Timmis (2015) in this series for more on materials evaluation (see also Mishan 2005 and Tomlinson 2012). You can find more information about issues in this field from the well-known Materials Development Association (MATSDA; http://www.matsda.org), as well as an accompanying journal, *Folio* (http://www.matsda.org/folio.html).

TASK 3.4   EXPLOITING AUTHENTIC MATERIAL

A. Figure 3.1 is a piece of authentic material taken from an online source. In groups, decide (1) what language focus (grammar, vocabulary and so on) this type of material lends itself to and (2) how you would use the material.

Fluffy Frozen Strawberry Dessert Recipe

By Derezione

Stephanie shared this on our **Instagram** account the other day:

Chocolate comes from cocoa, which comes out of a tree. That makes it a plant. Therefore chocolate counts as a salad. The End.

Now that we know that chocolate is really a healthy food, this dessert also qualifies as healthy because it's loaded with strawberries and nuts. (Oh, how I wish that were true!) ☺
But really though- life is about being happy. And happiness often comes in the form of dessert. I am a firm believer of moderation in all things- dessert every now and again is good for the soul. And this dessert is extremely good for the soul! It's creamy, frozen, has fresh strawberries, and a nutty crust that tastes like cookies. What more could you want?!

Figure 3.1   Authentic material: recipe

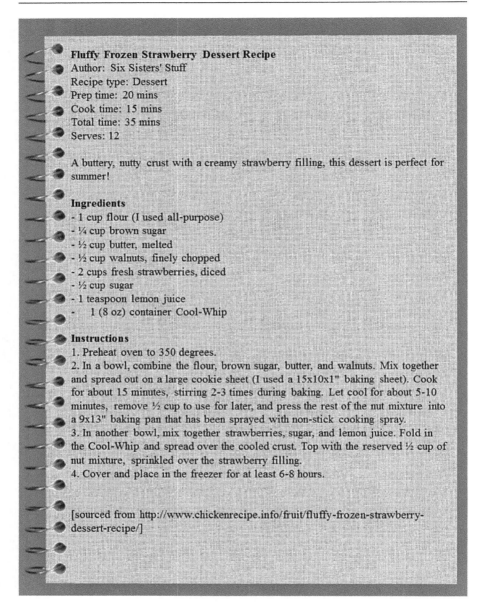

Fluffy Frozen Strawberry Dessert Recipe
Author: Six Sisters' Stuff
Recipe type: Dessert
Prep time: 20 mins
Cook time: 15 mins
Total time: 35 mins
Serves: 12

A buttery, nutty crust with a creamy strawberry filling, this dessert is perfect for summer!

Ingredients
- 1 cup flour (I used all-purpose)
- ¼ cup brown sugar
- ½ cup butter, melted
- ½ cup walnuts, finely chopped
- 2 cups fresh strawberries, diced
- ½ cup sugar
- 1 teaspoon lemon juice
-    1 (8 oz) container Cool-Whip

Instructions
1. Preheat oven to 350 degrees.
2. In a bowl, combine the flour, brown sugar, butter, and walnuts. Mix together and spread out on a large cookie sheet (I used a 15x10x1" baking sheet). Cook for about 15 minutes, stirring 2-3 times during baking. Let cool for about 5-10 minutes, remove ½ cup to use for later, and press the rest of the nut mixture into a 9x13" baking pan that has been sprayed with non-stick cooking spray.
3. In another bowl, mix together strawberries, sugar, and lemon juice. Fold in the Cool-Whip and spread over the cooled crust. Top with the reserved ½ cup of nut mixture, sprinkled over the strawberry filling.
4. Cover and place in the freezer for at least 6-8 hours.

[sourced from http://www.chickenrecipe.info/fruit/fluffy-frozen-strawberry-dessert-recipe/]

Figure 3.1   (continued)

B.   For Figure 3.1, design an activity for learners, and ask your peers to assess the activity in terms of the six guidelines offered by Mishan (2005: 75), given at the beginning of Section 3.3.

TASK 3.5   LEARNER FEEDBACK ON AUTHENTIC MATERIALS

Examine EFL students' perceptions of the activity you have designed in Task 3.4. Show the activity to a few language learners, and get their opinions (via questionnaires, interviews or focus groups) of your activity compared to materials in coursebooks. Share the findings with your peers.

TASK 3.6   ARTICLE ANALYSIS

Go to the MATSDA website, and look at the 'sample articles' section of the *Folio* journal (http://www.matsda.org/folio_article.html). Choose one article, read it and share what you learn with your peers.

3.4   CORPUS-BASED MATERIALS

3.4.1   CONCEPTS, FINDINGS AND TEXTS

A corpus is a collection of texts, spoken or written, stored on a computer, available for research and teaching through concordancing software (see Section 3.6 for types of corpora). It is therefore 'a rich resource of authentic data containing structures, patterns and predictable features' (Leech 1997: 3). Some of the functionalities of corpora and corpus tools include the generation of:

*   The most frequent words
*   Concordances (specific words in context)
*   Key words (words which are unusually and statistically frequent in one corpus compared to a larger corpus)
*   Clusters, also called chunks or lexical bundles (see Biber et al. 1999, McCarthy 2006), which are strings of language or a combination of words in sequence
*   Lexicogrammatical profiles, including collocations, semantic prosody, connotation and syntactic or semantic restrictions (O'Keeffe et al. 2007).

The focus of this section is to explore how corpora can help us to design materials for the language classroom. To highlight this, Römer (2011: 207) makes a distinction between the various applications of corpora to pedagogy, which can be seen in Figure 3.2.

Indirect applications
Indirect applications include the use of corpora by researchers, but also, and of more relevance to this chapter, by materials writers. To this end, a number of materials have been designed based on corpora. Most dictionaries now rely on corpora (since the

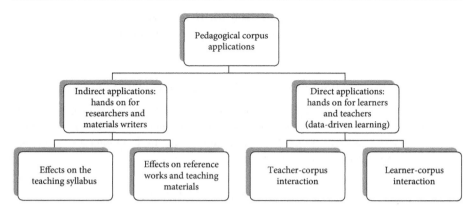

Figure 3.2   The uses of corpora in second language learning and teaching (Römer 2011: 207, courtesy of Cambridge University Press)

COBUILD project; see Hanks 2009, Sinclair 1997), and, as can be seen in Appendix 3, grammar reference books, corpus-informed coursebooks and corpus-informed skills books have been published. Although there is a lack of corpus-informed coursebooks on the market, most coursebooks are based on the results of corpora in some way, in that the Academic Wordlist (Coxhead 2000), West's (1953) General Service List or Cambridge's New General Service List (Brezina and Gablasova 2013) are used (see McCarten 2010 and McCarten and McCarthy 2010 for more on corpus-informed coursebook design). Another indirect application is that corpora have had an impact on teaching syllabuses, for example the Lexical Syllabus (Sinclair and Renouf 1988), and a coursebook which follows this approach is *Innovations* (published by Heinle & Heinle).

Direct applications

This chapter will focus more on the direct applications of corpora where teachers and learners can use the corpus for language awareness-raising tasks (Chambers et al. 2011, Flowerdew 2012, Reppen 2010). Data-driven learning (DDL), a term coined by Johns (1991), is typically associated with corpus linguistics, whereby learners work through corpus data to examine language (see Chambers 2010 for a history of DDL, and Mishan 2004 and Gilquin and Granger 2010 for how to use DDL in language teaching). Before moving on, I suggest you watch Randi Reppen's talk on YouTube, where she discusses the applications of corpora in the language classroom (http://www.youtube.com/watch?v=Qf46lOnMCfs).

Vocabulary, grammar and each of the skills are drawn on next in order to provide you with examples of how corpora can be used for materials design (in Appendix 4 you will find the names and details of a range of spoken and written online corpora and concordancers). Firstly, in the area of vocabulary, corpora can show us how words are organised into patterns such as collocation and colligation (see McCarten 2007), what type of words we need for a 'basic' vocabulary as well as for an

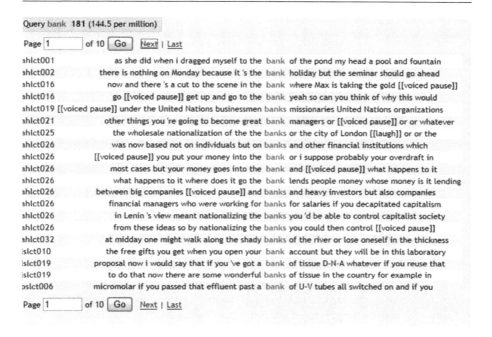

Figure 3.3   Concordance of bank in BASE (via Sketch Engine)

'advanced' vocabulary, and more specialised vocabulary in areas such as business and academic English (O'Keeffe et al. 2007; see also Brezina and Gablasova 2013). Some corpus-informed vocabulary materials already exist; for example, see Nelson's website for ready-made business English materials (http://users.utu.fi/micnel/business_english_lexis_site.htm), and for academic English see *Exploring Academic English: A Workbook for Student Essay Writing* (published by NCELTR) and CUP's *Academic Vocabulary in Use* (see also Coxhead 2010 for more on corpora in EAP).

Examples of activities for vocabulary practice could include investigating the various meanings of a word, the subtle differences in synonyms and antonyms or what prepositions go with certain adjectives. You can also make gap-fill activities for learners, using Lextutor. An example of how words are polysemic can be seen in the concordance lines in Figure 3.3,[2] where you can clearly identify that the word *bank* can have multiple meanings. You could give these example concordances to your learners and encourage them to discover the various meanings of the word.

When dealing with grammar, corpora can allow learners to see repeated patterns, and encourage noticing. Indeed current corpus-informed grammar practice materials include *English Grammar Today* (published by CUP), a workbook which complements the same publisher's reference guide *English Grammar Today: An A–Z of Spoken and Written Grammar*. Examples of corpus-based activities to design include investigating verb patterns; phrasal verbs; functions of auxiliary verbs; use of articles; and form and functions of modals and conditionals. An idea for an activity

Extract for **COULD** With <u>no associate</u> on EITHER side sorted 1 wds **left** of key

```
20 randomly selected lines from 1494 hits      (normalized to 1484 per million for comparison)    Click keyword for Larger Context
026. ▢ quiet week of the " phoney war I had plenty to think about. COULD I really be part of a war machine? I was given a day o
051. ▢ aid he had always worked for the benefit of his country and COULD not be held responsible for how the hard currency he p
061. ▢ ly, considered to be compatible with the common market, and COULD therefore be granted discretionary exemption from the
065. ▢ on our modern commuter stations, but we were jam packed and COULD not be parted from our scant luggage. I found a friend
114. ▢ res, climbed 17p to 248p. Top analysts reckon that the boom COULD continue with investors switching their cash from the
118. ▢ en laughter. The implication was that Gen Noriega's bravado COULD in no legal sense be taken as a declaration of hostili
166. ▢ ay, who feared that Gen Noriega's former links with the CIA COULD prove embarrassing in open court. "Do we really want h
168. ▢ might be. The alternative condition of the exclusion clause COULD, following the German example, require three constitue
182. ▢ 1st Republic, he said. The word " Socialist in this context COULD also become an anachronism very soon. Civic Forum want
221. ▢ foreign exchange markets that rapid political developments COULD weaken the Bundesbank's fight against inflation. The D
226. ▢ s or dryness. The number of votes for wets, damps and dries COULD be accurately counted and a proportionate entitlement
232. ▢ 1 believed that the existing rail network in the South East COULD cope with any extra traffic after 1993 despite the fac
238. ▢ mediately after the advertising campaign and the electorate COULD concentrate on one method of voting, but since that ti
241. ▢ orded how many infants had been christened in it. Elisabeth COULD remember when batterie de cuisine actually looked like
246. ▢ ted wickets to the opposition. Slow bowlers And now England COULD have a fight on their hands in their second innings on
255. ▢ September 1974 the Union Committee had a meeting. Everybody COULD see that safety at the factory was getting worse. The
273. ▢ more sophisticated contextual subject access features,      COULD encourage the searcher to use the catalogue and ultima
278. ▢ al strike -- in which sheer weight of numbers and firepower COULD have been expected to guarantee ultimate success. Very
304. ▢ r "illegal transactions. Buyers of certain subsidised goods COULD be required to show their identity cards in shops. Koh
337. ▢ cerned in it a vulnerability: something he could defend. Be COULD offer her financial security; a home -- on Man;
```

Built by Lextutor on 2014/7/22

Figure 3.4   Concordance of could in the BNC (via Lextutor)

for learners focusing on the functions of modal verbs can be seen in the concordance in Figure 3.4, where learners could examine, through the context given in the concordance lines, the various functions of the modal *could* (for an overview of how corpora can be used for grammar teaching, see Hughes 2010).

At the level of discourse, corpora can be used to examine features such as response tokens (*mmhm, mm, oh*), where learners can get exposure to interactional language and gain practice in fluency. Furthermore, corpora can be used to investigate register/ genre variation (see Biber et al. 1998); features of online discourse (Klimt and Yang 2004, Riordan 2012, Riordan and Murray 2010, 2012); discourse and pragmatics (O'Keeffe et al. 2011); or indeed, discourse and paralinguistic features using multi-modal corpora[3] (such as Backbone or Sacodeyl).

Corpora can also be used for teaching reading skills, whereby, for example, students can examine the most frequent words in a newspaper article compared to an academic article, and discuss the similarities and differences in the genres, or they can be encouraged to notice structures, features and forms via the written texts. Regarding writing, students can use the corpus as a consultation tool (Chambers 2005, 2007, O'Sullivan and Chambers 2006) or to raise their awareness of features such as cohesion and verb usage (Gilmore 2009). Corpus-based materials can also be used for speaking and listening practice (see Walsh 2010) to teach listenership, highlight the structure of conversation, increase students' interactional competence, and present or reinforce chunks of language (see Braun 2005).

This being said, care and attention must be taken when using corpora to design materials, because the results of corpora may be difficult to interpret (O'Keeffe and Farr 2003) and/or they may not be totally representative of a language (Hunston 1995), and therefore training is necessary (O'Keeffe and Farr 2003, Römer 2011). Other problems include the need for concordancing software (although there are a number of free online resources you can use); the time needed to train learners in using a concordancer and interpreting the results; and the time required for you to develop materials and to sift through concordance lines to get examples of language that meet your needs. Also, DDL is an inductive approach and might not suit all learners, and a lack of knowledge among teachers, as well as teachers having a less central role in the classroom, may pose problems (Gilquin and Granger 2010). There is also a motivational consideration: too many concordance exercises may lead to boredom. On a more positive note, Walsh (2010: 342–3) acknowledges the advantages of corpus-based approaches in that materials 'can be tailored to both the level and the needs of particular groups of students, and . . . students can be more actively involved in the learning process and can develop skills which will help them in their own interactional development' (see McEnery and Xiao 2010 for more on direct and indirect applications of corpora in pedagogy).

A final consideration is that, as the teacher, you also need to decide whether you will design the material and bring it into the classroom or whether you get the students to explore corpora for themselves. I suggest that the former be used in the initial stages to help students become familiar with what corpus-based materials look like (see also Chambers et al. 2011 and O'Keeffe and Farr 2003). To help you, Reppen (2010: 43; see also Farr et al. 2010) offers the following checklist for developing corpus-based materials:

- Have a clear idea of the point you want to teach.
- Select the corpus that is the best resource for your lesson.
- Explore the corpus completely for the point you want to teach.
- Make sure that your directions are complete and easy to follow.
- Make sure that your examples focus on the point that you are teaching.
- Provide a variety of ways for interacting with the materials.
- Use a variety of exercise types.
- Have an alternative plan or activity in the event of computer glitches if you are using computers.

Learner corpora

Before closing this section, it is worthwhile briefly discussing one specific type of corpus which can be used with language learners. This is the learner corpus, which consists of spoken and/or written texts produced by foreign or second language learners. Learner corpora can be used for lexicography (Walter 2010) or to inform language testing (Baker 2010), and, of more relevance here, Nesselhauf (2004) discusses how they can be used for teaching materials. The results from learner corpora can highlight areas of difficulties language learners face, and such features can be included in language teaching materials (see also Flowerdew 2012 on what learner corpora can offer SLA). Corpus-based studies on learner corpora have included a focus on modality (McEnery and Kifle 2002), the passive voice (Granger 2013) and collocations (Nesselhauf 2005), for example.

Perhaps of more relevance to you as a teacher is that learner corpora can be used in the classroom, using DDL, as outlined earlier. Here a feature of language can be examined in a learner corpus and compared against a native speaker corpus in order to stimulate noticing (see Walsh 2010); and features and/or errors in a learner corpus can be examined alone in order for learners to become more aware of their language

1	administration and management will make a bad effect. This will demage Hon
2	g credit card with intelligent can make a best deals on offer. However, fo
3	ly. Some of them, however, want to make a big credit debt. Some of the expe
4	now where the money go in order to make a budget. Students like to posse
5	or not to be, so the customers can make a choice themselves at the same tim
6	smoking in restaurants can help to make a cleaner and less smoky environmen
7	ssionals from China. Then, I will make a conclusion and give my opinion on
8	of students using credit cards and make a conclusion by considering the rel
9	fessionals from China, then I will make a conclusion on the topic. The m
10	topic to discuss and difficult to make a conclusion. Some students lose co
11	moke-free bars and restaurants can make a contribution on improvement of re
12	uy their favourite things and then make a credit debt and need their parent
13	uld use or not. Credit card can make a credit history to the student tha
14	tudents using credit cards easy to make a debts because they have no contro
15	cards. Therefore, parents should make a decision carefully for approving
16	anning smoking in restaurant would make a decline in the number of customer
17	start a deep investigation and to make a detarl consulting studies in thos
18	ery argueable. Even the government make a discision, the discussion will co
19	wn (1999), using a credit card can make a early training in managing the fi
20	Therefore, they should think and make a full financial plan before using
21	hat come from the credit cards and make a good choice when applying. Stu
22	credit card can also help t hem to make a good credit history. One day whe
23	. Students use credit cards can make a good credit history. Credit cards
24	It for the Hong Kong Government to make a good decision on the importing of
25	using credit cards. student will make a good habit to use money more resp

Figure 3.5   Concordance of make in PLEC (via PolyU Language Bank)

use, errors and structures, and to encourage them to notice and indeed appreciate characteristics of learner discourse (see Meunier 2002 and McEnery and Xiao 2010 for more on learner corpora). You as the teacher can either use existing learner corpora which are available (e.g. ICLE or MICUSP) or create a learner corpus from your own learners' language to do this (see Nesselhauf 2004 for more on studies on learner corpora in language teaching).

Figure 3.5 is an example of the verb *make* taken from the PLEC (PolyU Learner English Corpus).Using these examples, learners could examine the nouns used with the verb *make* and check if the collocations are suitable. Learners could use a dictionary and/or a native speaker corpus to check these, which would foster autono-mous learning, language awareness and indeed self-awareness.

As well as this, you can use learner corpora to familiarise yourself with typical errors students make and features of learner discourse for your own professional development (these can be distinguished in terms of L1, language level, speech versus writing etc.), which can then influence your teaching and your own language awareness. You can also browse the websites for the Learner Corpus Association (http://www.learnercorpusassociation.org) and Learner Corpora Around the World (http://www.uclouvain.be/en-cecl-lcworld.html) for further information.

TASK 3.7   CORPUS-BASED TASK DESIGN

Think of an area of language that you want to investigate (a modal verb, a tense, an item of vocabulary). Examine in a corpus of your choice (see Appendix 4) your chosen area of language, and design an activity to practise the language with your learners. Share your findings with your peers. Don't forget to follow Reppen's (2010) guidelines for designing corpus-based activities.

TASK 3.8   CORPORA AND COURSEBOOKS

In 2004, Römer examined how modals were dealt with in a spoken corpus (the BNC) and selected texts from EFL coursebooks. Replicate this study by choosing one coursebook, and within it choose one area of language to see how it is dealt with in the coursebook. Now, examine the same language point in a corpus of your choice. Compare and contrast the findings from the coursebook with the corpus, and share your findings with your peers.

TASK 3.9   EXPLORING THE BACKBONE CORPORA

Go to the Backbone website and load the English corpus (BB English) (http://webapps. ael.uni-tuebingen.de/backbone-search/faces/initialize.jsp). On the top menu, click on the 'Resources' tab and choose 'Exploratory tasks'. Then click 'Show' for a list of resources. Choose one topic you are interested in and take a look through the sample materials and activities that have been designed for learners of English. Try one of the tasks, take reflective notes, and share your findings with your peers. In your own time, you can also familiarise yourself with other resources on the Backbone and Sacodeyl (see Appendix 4) sites, as well as do some corpus-based analysis with the software.

3.5   FURTHER READING ONE

Islam, C. and Mares, C. (2003) 'Adapting classroom materials', in Tomlinson, B. (ed.), *Developing Materials for Language Teaching*, London: Continuum, 86–100.
This chapter by Islam and Mares provides teachers with the knowledge and skills necessary for adapting materials. At the beginning of the chapter, the authors discuss the state of the art in materials adaptation by tracing its historical roots. Here they note that before the communicative approach, the main focus of coursebooks relied on grammar-translation and behaviourism, where structure was at the heart of learning, and language was not seen as a tool for communication (see also Spiro 2013 in this series for more on methodology). Although over time a greater emphasis was

placed on communication, the coursebooks were not reflecting the needs of teachers and learners. The authors review reasons for materials adaptation; for example, McDonagh and Shaw (1993) called for the inclusion of a more systematic approach to grammar, and more complex and authentic material; Cunningsworth (1995) addressed the need to focus on the learners, their styles of learning, their motivation and classroom dynamics; and Candlin and Breen (1980) called for materials adaptation because current materials did not reflect real communication.

From here, the authors offer practical considerations for materials adaptation. They begin by noting the importance of having clear aims and objectives before you start adapting your materials. They refer to McDonagh and Shaw (1993), who argue that materials adaptation can be administered in order to personalise, individualise, localise and modernise, to which Islam and Mares add the following (p. 89):

- Add real choice
- Cater for all sensory learner styles
- Provide for more learner autonomy
- Encourage higher-level cognitive skills
- Make the language input more accessible
- Make the language input more engaging

Therefore, learners should be given a choice in deciding how they want to learn; activities should cater to all styles of learning (the kinaesthetic style is often ignored in coursebooks); learners should be encouraged to learn outside the class and without the teacher. In order to motivate and stimulate learners, activities requiring hypothesising, predicting, inferring, making connections and visualising should be included. The language should be more accessible and engaging, which can be achieved by making materials more authentic, and by changing the forms of materials (for example, making a reading text into an interactive activity). Islam and Mares also offer techniques for adaptation (p. 91):

- Adding: extending and expanding
- Deleting: subtracting and abridging
- Simplifying
- Reordering
- Replacing material

Adding to materials can be done in two ways, firstly by extending the material, whereby the teacher offers more examples of the same type of activity (for example, a coursebook contains ten questions about a grammar point, and the teacher adds a further five). Secondly, expanding adds something which is different to the material (for example, a teacher wants to focus on the pronunciation of past tense regular endings, which the book does not cater for, so the teacher adds practice in this area). While extending is quantitative, expanding is qualitative. Deleting can also be quantitative (subtracting – reducing the number of questions in a task) or qualitative (abridging – removing a whole task if deemed unnecessary). Simplifying involves making the language of task instructions easier, or making the task more manageable. Reordering means that the teacher changes the sequence of activities. Replacing materials means the teacher may use one piece of material over another (for example, a text from another source might be used instead of a text in a coursebook), and is often done with time-specific or culturally specific material. With the above in mind, the authors state that (p. 100):

> Classroom materials need to be adapted in a principled manner to reflect needs within particular teaching contexts, current understanding of second language acquisition and good teaching practices.

Following the aforementioned principles and techniques for adaptation, the authors conclude this chapter by offering three examples of materials adaptation, which I suggest you study before you begin work in this area yourself.

FURTHER READING ONE TASK

1. Once you have examined the three examples of materials adaptation in the Islam and Mares chapter, in pairs, choose one unit from a coursebook that you have used (or will use) with learners (bearing in mind your objectives, as outlined above). Check your materials to examine what (if anything) you would adapt and how you would go about doing this. Use the techniques for adapting your materials outlined above, and share your plans with your peers.
2. The authors offer six reasons for adaptation. Take the following three from their list, and review at least one coursebook to examine how the book deals with these issues:

- Cater for all sensory learner styles
- Provide for more learner autonomy
- Encourage higher-level cognitive skills.

For example, think about the following:

- What type(s) of learning styles are catered for? Are any styles ignored?
- Does the book encourage, or at least provide scope for, autonomous learning? If so, how?
- Do the activities in the coursebook encourage higher-level cognitive skills? If so, give examples.
  Write up your review, and share your findings with your peers.

3.6   FURTHER READING TWO

Chambers, A., Farr, F., and O'Riordan, S. (2011) 'Language teachers with corpora in mind: From starting steps to walking tall', *Language Learning Journal*, 39: 1, 85–104.

This article examines how teachers can integrate corpus-based approaches into classes. The authors begin by giving an overview of corpora and corpus-based approaches in language education, and note (p. 86):

> Researchers involved in integrating corpora into their language teaching and into language teacher education programmes (O'Sullivan and Chambers 2006: 62–3; Farr 2008) discover not only positive reactions from learners and student teachers, such as access to real and up-to-date language use, and uncovering functions and structures not found in grammar books, but also negative reactions or obstacles, mainly relating to the effort needed to master the technology and to analyse the results, and the difficulty in gaining access to appropriate corpora.

Once a number of studies are reviewed regarding corpora and corpus-based materials, the authors offer the following overview of corpus types (p. 89; emphasis added):

> *Large reference corpora* containing a wide variety of written and spoken text types, or *small corpora* containing texts of one genre or a limited number of genres. They may be *monolingual*, or *bi-* or *multilingual* (either *parallel corpora* of texts and their translations, or *comparable corpora* of, for example, academic articles in two or more languages). They may include only texts by *native speakers*, or by *expert non-native speakers*, or texts produced by *language learners*. They may exist only in *written* form, including transcriptions of *spoken* discourse, or they may be *multimodal*, with audio- and video-recordings. They may be *annotated* or tagged in various ways to assist the user, or they may be untagged.

The variety of types of corpora outlined above makes it clear that one of the major issues for teachers is trying to determine which corpus to use to meet their needs, and the authors suggest using free online concordancers (such as the BNC, Lextutor or Sacodeyl) to run a query. To exemplify this, they search for the tokens *nice* and *get back* to show their polysemic natures. The authors conclude that concordance lines may be used (pp. 90–1):

- To enrich the encounter of one example of an expression in an individual text
- To provide additional examples if the expression had proved problematic in a text which was being studied, or
- To simply point out to the learners that the expression does not always have the meaning in the text being studied

As well as freely available corpora, the authors move on to a discussion of using commercial corpora and concordancing software (for example, Wordsmith Tools). They outline a number of corpora to choose from, and exemplify their uses for raising students' language awareness. From the authors' experience (p. 95):

> Getting students to consult with corpus evidence . . . is highly motivational as it reflects their real world, out of class encounters. Such explorations provide data

that can have much potential for the development of materials to compare written, spoken and on-line language, or indeed, when looking at one mode in isolation, for example, spoken corpora, to improve students' awareness and production of spoken language. In addition, the importance of locally contextualised data cannot be [overestimated] in a learning environment for which the variety . . . is not, on the whole, represented in textbooks.

From a more critical and practical stance, throughout the article, the authors offer various pieces of advice, which are summarised below:

- Teachers should be introduced to corpora via a 'graded approach', by beginning with simple activities that demand only basic Internet skills, and once mastered and understood against the backdrop of SLA, more complex activities can be attempted.
- Fuller context is often required (beyond concordance lines), and therefore teachers need to supplement example concordances with texts.
- Teachers need to select examples which are relevant, or ask the software to offer a random sample of a chosen item.
- Teachers need to encourage learners to use corpus data critically, and draw on other resources available to them (and reference works), as well as their own knowledge and intuition.
- Teachers should get learners working with printed concordance lines in the classroom, before moving on to doing their own corpus-based searches.
- Learners should use smaller corpora initially to familiarise themselves with corpus-based searching.
- Results may need to be 'cleaned up' before being distributed to language learners. Tags and coding should be removed to make the material more manageable in order not to distract the learners from the message in a given extract.

FURTHER READING TWO TASK

1. Like the example of *get back* mentioned above, the item *look out* (or other multiword verbs) can also have multiple meanings. Investigate a corpus to find examples of the various meanings of this item (or an item of your choice) that you could present to your learners. Discuss with your peers how you would use the concordance lines.
2. Work in groups of six or more, with one person from each group choosing an area below:
    Corpora and the teaching of:

1. vocabulary
2. grammar
3. reading
4. writing
5. speaking
6. listening

Each member of the group should research their chosen area, and read at least one article. Summarise the article, create a joint report and share with your peers.

3.7 SUMMARY

This chapter has attempted to give you an overview of TESOL materials and issues around their mediation, exploitation, adaptation and evaluation. Mishan (2013: 299) notes that if we want our 'materials to fulfil students' expectations . . . we need to think creatively and to deliver the materials in multifaceted ways'. In relation to this, while there are many caveats to consider when designing and using materials for teaching, I would urge you to:

1. become familiar with available material (published, free, online);
2. always consider your learners and their needs when preparing and using the material; and
3. if you are using a coursebook (or other materials), do not be afraid to adapt it to suit your and your students' needs.

To leave you with some food for thought, I refer to Tomlinson's (1998: 17–21) sixteen principles of materials development, which can be considered when examining your material (see Figure 3.6).

3.8 ADDITIONAL READINGS

Mishan, F. (2005) *Designing Authenticity into Language Learning Materials*, Bristol: Intellect.
A comprehensive overview of SLA factors and authenticity, offering both theory and practical authentic material activities.
Mishan, F. and Chambers, A. (eds) (2010) *Perspectives on Language Learning Materials Development*, Oxford: Peter Lang.
An edited collection including chapters on materials development with corpora, the spoken language, technology and materials development based on learner types and needs.
O'Keeffe, A., McCarthy, M. and Carter, R. (2007) *From Corpus to Classroom: Language Use and Language Teaching*, Cambridge: Cambridge University Press.
An excellent resource outlining the main tools available to corpus users, examples of how corpora can influence vocabulary and grammar teaching, and discourse and listenership.
Reppen, R. (2010) *Using Corpora in the Language Classroom*, Cambridge: Cambridge University Press.
A must-read for anyone interested in using corpora in the classroom. It offers various examples, and advice related to corpus integration.
Tomlinson, B. (ed.) (2008) *English Language Learning Materials: A Critical Review*, London: Continuum.
An edited collection bringing together research surrounding materials design and SLA, different types of materials (for types of classes) and materials in use around the world.

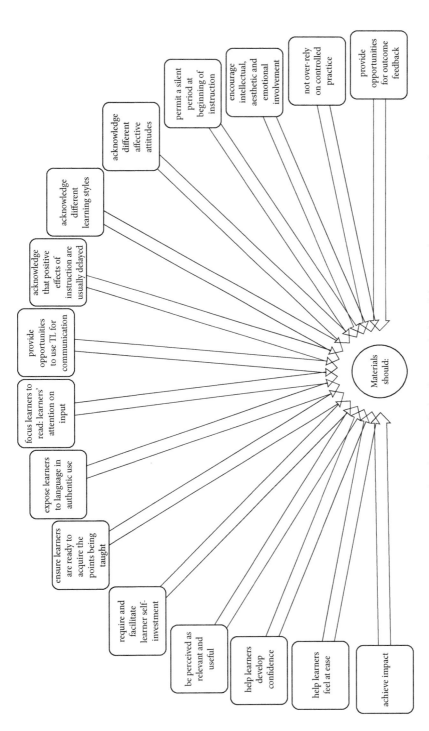

Figure 3.6   Principles of materials development (adapted from Tomlinson 1998: 7–21)

Materials should:

- acknowledge different affective attitudes
- permit a silent period at beginning of instruction
- encourage intellectual, aesthetic and emotional involvement
- not over-rely on controlled practice
- provide opportunities for outcome feedback
- acknowledge different learning styles
- acknowledge that positive effects of instruction are usually delayed
- provide opportunities to use TL for communication
- focus learners to read: learners' attention on input
- expose learners to language in authentic use
- ensure learners are ready to acquire the points being taught
- require and facilitate learner self-investment
- be perceived as relevant and useful
- help learners develop confidence
- help learners feel at ease
- achieve impact

NOTES

1. Coursebook authors are given guidelines concerning appropriacy and inclusivity in terms of being non-sexist and not offending potential readers (for example, by using the PARSNIP model – avoiding issues such as politics, alcohol, religion, sex, narcotics, isms and pork) (Gray 2002).
2. The corpus used in Figure 3.3 was developed at the Universities of Warwick and Reading under the directorship of Hilary Nesi and Paul Thompson. Corpus development was assisted by funding from BALEAP, EURALEX, the British Academy and the Arts and Humanities Research Council. Available at: http://ca.sketchengine.co.uk/open.
3. A multimodal corpus has 'transcripts that are aligned or synchronised with the original audio or visual recordings' (Lee 2010: 114; see also Knight 2011).

4

OBSERVING TO LEARN

4.1   INTRODUCTION

Under what are known as craft-based or apprenticeship approaches to education, learning takes place almost exclusively through watching, learning, assimilating and emulating what is observed. There are cultures where education is not institutionalised but assimilated into other aspects of social and cultural activities. Singleton (1989) details traditions of severe discipline, learning through unobtrusive observation, and a total absence of didactic instruction in Japanese folkcraft pottery apprenticeship, for example. In this context, 'the master is seen as protecting his "secrets" and the learner is expected to "steal" them' (1989: 26). Many of you reading this will probably be familiar with similar (possibly lingering, possibly former) practices in some of your own cultural contexts. There was a time in Irish and other societies when becoming a teacher exclusively meant observing and working with a more experienced teacher for a period of time, until the relevant level of expertise was deemed to have been reached, without any other type of training. While we now have a broader approach to teacher education, which acknowledges that observation is only one way in which the art and skill of teaching are acquired, it still occupies a relatively important place in socio-cultural approaches. A socio-cultural approach in language teacher education provides a broad theoretical account to help understand how scaffolded collaboration with more experienced teachers can be potentially beneficial (Freeman 2004), and working with more experienced teachers in observation cooperatives is a good example of this in practice. And of course, even before you come to your teacher education programme you will have undergone what Lortie (1975) has referred to as 'an apprenticeship of observation'. This is the time you have spent informally observing your own previous teachers' practices when you were a student.

> The net result of this highly influential period of observation is that teacher education courses are said by many to have a weak effect on student teachers. This limited effect and the reported tendency for novice teachers, once they have entered the profession, to revert to their default model can lead to teachers teaching as they were taught, hence exerting a conservative pressure on the profession. (Borg 2004: 275)

According to Kennedy (1990: 17), 'Teachers acquire seemingly indelible imprints from their own experiences as students and these imprints are tremendously difficult to shake.'

Essentially, you have all had educational experiences in the classroom and therefore come to the observation of teaching with a set of expectations, which need to be questioned and in many cases destabilised. According to Wajnryb (1992a: 5) these can be 'conscious or subconscious, or a blend of the two; they might be positive or negative . . . whatever the cargo of experiences and expectations that a trainee brings to a training course, one thing is certain – that the classroom has primacy of place in the learning and teaching experiences that lie ahead'. Some estimates suggest that on initial teacher education programmes, student teachers can spend up to 60 per cent of their time in schools acquiring teaching skills (Tilstone 1998: 2). This will generally consist of some combination and often amalgamation of observation and practice teaching. Bearing that in mind, consider the notion of teaching as an apprenticeship (Hawkins 2004) in conjunction with the concept of legitimate peripheral participation as a stepping stone to full professional membership. This framework is present in conceptualisations of professionals operating within communities of practice (Lave and Wenger 1991) with which observation aligns. Against these backdrops this chapter explores observation as an approach to learning how to become a teacher. Given the value of observation as a learning tool, we should not assume that it has a generally accepted meaning and use. Like many terms, it has the potential to be interpreted in numerous ways, and this will be explored in Section 4.2, centring on considerations for you to contemplate in advance of actually doing an observation. You will then be introduced to suitable approaches to classroom observations in Section 4.3, including some possible frameworks that might be used. Here you will also be asked to deliberate the following: learner variables as discussed in Chapter 2 and how these manifest themselves in the classroom; the teacher in the classroom (classroom management, teaching skills and strategies, language and metalanguage etc.); and the materials used in the context of the teacher's overall aims and learning outcomes for the lesson, as articulated in the lesson plan. Section 4.4 address the post-observation period and what this could entail for you as the observing teacher, and will explore some inherent drawbacks of observing as a way of informing novice teachers' practices.

4.2 PREPARING TO OBSERVE

4.2.1 CONCEPTS, FINDINGS AND TEXTS

Bearing in mind that you have already participated in teaching and learning contexts since you began your education somewhere between the ages of 4 and 7, this section will examine the reasons why you might want to be/have to be involved in more formal observation as part of your teacher education programme and in your future professional life. Consider the following scenarios:

1. A school inspector comes to observe teaching as part of an annual school moderation scheme.

2.   A teacher asks a colleague to come and peer observe as part of a personal initiative to discuss and develop his teaching.
3.   A principal goes to observe a teacher because of a complaint from a number of students about inappropriate practices.
4.   A teacher records his own lesson as the basis for a piece of action research (AR) he plans to do on classroom interactions.
5.   A student teacher sits in on a number of classes with a cooperating teacher as part of the TP component of her teacher education programme.
6.   A teacher/researcher seeks permission from a large number of teachers across a region to observe lessons for the purposes of a large-scale funded research project.
7.   A materials developer observes a group of teenagers in class to inform the activities he plans for his next coursebook.

All of these scenarios involve observing teaching, yet their motives, approaches and outcomes may be very varied. Scrivener (2011: 384–5) outlines five types of observation relating to the purpose in each case: training, developmental, assessment, data collection, peer observation. It is possible that you will be involved in situations like those described in scenarios 2, 4 and 5 during your time as a student teacher. We will discuss professional developmental approaches relevant to scenario 2 in Chapter 8, and research approaches in Chapter 9 (see also Park et al. 2010). In addition, the reverse situation where *you* are being observed will be explored in Chapter 7. Therefore, our attention will focus on a context like that described in scenario 5 in this chapter; where you go to observe and learn from more experienced teachers. In this case, the focus should be very much on gathering information in a non-judgemental way for the purposes of your own learning and development, rather than on evaluating the lesson. Admittedly, a type of critical evaluation is necessary in order to make informed decisions and choices about which aspects of the teaching you might like to adopt and adapt, but evaluation and judgement should not be the main purposes. I propose the following working definition for the type of observation being discussed in this chapter:

> The audiovisual collection of information and evidence during live classes for the primary purpose of informing the improved considerations, judgements and practices of the observer, based on what has been seen and understood.

It is also important to remember that although teachers report on the benefits of observation (Crookes 2003: 29), it can influence their teaching behaviour (Zaare 2013) and it may be a daunting prospect, regardless of the degree of formality or the relationship they have with the observer. The following accounts from Crookes (2003: 28) demonstrate some of the potential effects:

> Patrick, an inexperienced male American teacher: Well, I say that I had thought I wouldn't be nervous, but . . . Monday morning before class I began thinking about my lesson and about Lenny watching me, and I began to get extremely self-conscious. I thought about my lesson plan, my assignments . . . I criticized

everything to myself, thinking about what Lenny may see and 'discover' about me . . .

Karen, an experienced female American teacher: This week I had a number of people in observing my classes . . . I feel the most pressure from wondering how students will react.

As well as considering your own position and the predisposition of the observed teacher, you will also need to be prepared for the level of activity and pace of a typical classroom. Wragg (2012: 1) cautions that 'classrooms are exceptionally busy places, so observers need to be on their toes'. Tilstone (1998: 7–8, building on Jackson 1968) suggests that teachers are involved with students in the following ways: giving and exchanging information, making suggestions, requesting, reprimanding, praising, greeting, answering questions, using non-verbal communication, differentiating, counselling, facilitating and empowering. And given the ubiquitous nature of technology and the generic and specific roles it can play in the classroom, this list could extend to all aspects of being involved with pupils through computer-mediated communication (for example, through the use of interactive whiteboards; see Cutrim-Schmid 2016), mobile language learning (Stockwell 2016), and distance and blended learning (Sharma and Westbrook 2016). Preparation is therefore the key to avoid being overwhelmed by the experience. Richards and Lockhart (1996: 22) offer the following practical advice for achieving a positive experience:

1.   Teachers are busy professionals. Classroom observations are not always a welcome intrusion for the classroom teachers involved.
2.   The observation of classroom teachers is serious business; it should not be approached casually.
3.   Learning how to observe in a manner acceptable to all parties takes time, careful reflection, personal tact, and creativity.
4.   An observer is a guest in the teacher's and the students' classroom. A guest in the classroom is there thanks to the goodwill of the cooperating teacher.
5.   A guest's purpose for visiting is not to judge, evaluate or criticize the classroom teacher, but simply to learn through observing.

A very good way to prepare for observing a live lesson is to do one or a number of trial runs on pre-recorded classes. Some of the ELT publishers have produced video-recorded lessons with observation tasks, which you can practise with; there are many classroom clips and full lessons on YouTube; or your training institution may have locally produced materials, which may be even better as they will reflect more accurately the physical and cultural context in which your real observations will take place. In any case, purposely watching some of these materials will help you to appreciate the complexity of the classroom and to consider focal points for your live observations. Wragg (2012: 79) suggests:

It is a useful exercise for trainees to watch a good video of one or more teachers at work in their own classroom. The opportunity to stop and start . . . speculate about consequences, or discuss outcomes . . . can raise important matters of principle and practice. The development of various forms of interactive technology is an extension of this, offering a high quality of picture, as well as the ability to hold or 'freeze' a single frame and study a still life picture of the classroom.

There is also a growing body of research on teaching interactions in face-to-face and online environments. The dedicated journal *Classroom Discourse*, published by Routledge, is an invaluable source of information, which gives glimpses into language teaching and learning around specific research questions. Even a glance over the journal's contents for the last few years will help you to understand the kinds of issues and investigations experienced teachers continue to have in their own contexts. Ultimately, your live viewing might be based on what you perceive your own needs to be or on what you have found interesting or intriguing in the video-recordings and readings, or, most probably a combination of both. In any case, the time spent watching video-recordings, discussing them and preparing for your live observations will serve you well when it comes to learning from what you see, hear and assimilate.

TASK 4.1   OBSERVATION GUIDELINES

A.   What is your reaction to the advisory guidelines listed at the end of the previous section from Richards and Lockhart? Do you agree/disagree with any aspects?
B.   Would you add any further guidelines to the list? Discuss what these might be.

TASK 4.2   OBSERVING FRAMES

A.   Look at the frames in Figures 4.1a–4.1f for 30 seconds in total. Write down everything you notice.
B.   What assumptions can you make from what you have observed (context, emotions, events etc.)?
C.   Are there any other possible interpretations that could be equally valid?

TASK 4.3   THE PRE-OBSERVATION MEETING

Think about the pre-observation meeting with the cooperating teacher. Make a list of what you think should be discussed (think about information you need, agreements you need to make, permissions you need to seek, disclosures you need to make, materials you need to share etc.).

4.3   DOING AN OBSERVATION: THE WHATS AND HOWS

4.3.1   CONCEPTS, FINDINGS AND TEXTS

Now that you have deliberated the reasons for observing and some of the preparatory considerations, I would like to turn to a discussion of what actually happens when

Figure 4.1a   (Image courtesy of photostock at FreeDigitalPhotos.net)

Figure 4.1b   (Image courtesy of Ambro at FreeDigitalPhotos.net)

Figure 4.1c   (Image courtesy of stockimages at FreeDigitalPhotos.net)

Figure 4.1d   (Image courtesy of Paul Gooddy at FreeDigitalPhotos.net)

Figure 4.1e   (Image courtesy of Paul Gooddy at FreeDigitalPhotos.net)

Figure 4.1f   (Image courtesy of supakitmod at FreeDigitalPhotos.net)

you are embarking on one or a number of observations. There are a number of practical steps to follow:

- Contact the cooperating teacher for a briefing and orientation. Agree the details of the class to be observed and the approach that will be taken.
- Keep the cooperating teacher informed of any change of plan, for example, if you are unable to attend.

- Arrive at the class ahead of time.
- Try to be as unobtrusive as possible when in the classroom (before, during, and after the observation). This will mean sitting where directed in advance by the teacher (the side of the room may be best to make sure you can see what is going on), collecting and recording data appropriately and only in ways that have been agreed in advance (for example, do not record the lesson unless relevant agreements are in place), and not participating in the lesson unless invited to do so by the teacher (this should be agreed beforehand).
- Dress appropriately and behave professionally.
- Try to discuss the lesson with the cooperating teacher at the first possible opportunity after the observation, especially to interrogate further some of the motives and methods apparent during the observation.
- Be appreciative and polite and thank the teacher for the opportunity.
- Keep any commentary about the class and the teacher anonymous in any follow-up formal or informal accounts. Sensitivity and discretion are important.

The techniques and methods associated with classroom observations have been discussed in some detail by experts such as Tilstone (1998). Wragg (2012) has discussed the use of quantitative and qualitative methods, many of which have been associated with research orientations but also have potential for evaluation and teacher learning (see also Chapter 9 in this volume, and Brown 2014 in this series). Others, such as contributors to the Howard and Donaghue collection (2014), focus on the various approaches to observation specifically for evaluation purposes in teacher education programmes and ongoing teacher appraisal contexts. All of these have something to offer a context where you are observing others teaching for the purposes of learning and informing your own developing practices, but we can take a somewhat simpler approach in the first instance. The remainder of this section will use the broad framework proposed by Wajnryb (1992a), which focuses on observing the following: the learner, language, learning, teaching skills and strategies, classroom management, resources and materials. You may decide to direct your attention to one or two of these during any one observation, and it may take some time to be able to observe a number of them successfully at once. Even the very skilled observer may have difficulty having a truly holistic orientation without having recourse to a video-recording of the lesson to complete the picture post-observation. The principle of the Wajnryb framework is to use it as part of a process of reflective practice (see Chapter 8), in which you take what you see and critically consider how you can learn from it, what you would like to exclude from and include in your own developing model of teaching, and how. The principle is not to assume that everything you observe is the 'best' model of teaching for you or for other contexts. There are many good models of teaching from which we can all learn and which we can potentially aspire to, and that may necessarily be different for you and for others (Edge and Richards 1998). In the light of this, you are an active participant and the observation experiences are part of your journey to becoming a teacher, for which you are ultimately responsible. The following account does not attempt a reproduction of the tasks from Wajnryb but includes a brief discussion of the important variables and their components which you may want to consider as part of your observations.

Observing the learner

The way in which the teacher attends to the learner can be of interest and can happen in verbal and non-verbal ways. This has strong potential to influence the affective learning environment and the creation of a positive atmosphere in which learners feel comfortable enough to take risks which will help the learning process. Much has been written about the importance of affect in language learning (Arnold 1999), with some drawing heavily on counselling and other approaches from psychology such as neuro-linguistic programming (Revell and Norman 1997). Overt indicators of attending behaviour can be been found in eye contact and expression, touch, facial and body expressions (nods, smiles, frowns, reprimanding looks, silly faces, hand movements and gestures), response tokens, using students' names etc. It may be interesting to see if any attending patterns are influenced by variables such as seating arrangements, student aptitude, age, sex, ethnicity, motivation and engagement, and other factors. The nature of the attending behaviour of the teacher may be a strong indicator of their methodological affiliation(s), as some teaching approaches within the humanistic tradition in particular attribute much importance to this aspect of teaching (see Spiro 2013: ch. 2).

Learner motivation has been found to be a complex phenomenon (Dörnyei 2001, Dörnyei and Murphey 2003) but one which can influence classroom behaviour and dynamics. The belief that instrumental motivation (wanting to learn to achieve a particular goal such as getting a job, passing an exam etc.) is more effective than integrative motivation (wanting to learn a language because of a desire to interact with its people(s) and culture(s)) has been questioned. Some research now suggests that it is the level of motivation rather than the type of motivation which is more influential: 'what has emerged is that whatever the basis of the motivation of the learner, its level (high/low) has an impact on expected learner roles. Highly motivated learners are more likely to synchronise their roles willingly with the teacher's role; and are more likely to co-operate with the teacher in the various processes involved in classroom learning' (Wright 1987, cited in Wajnryb 1992a: 31). As individual student motivation is not always readily apparent, it may be necessary to discuss this with the cooperating teacher in advance or to focus on this aspect for students with whom you are familiar. That way, learning behaviour might be correlated with motivation to discern any emerging patterns. You might need to be careful about making too many assumptions and may need to speak with the students directly to understand their motivations and behaviour better.

Learner engagement in terms of being actively involved and doing things in the lesson is worth observing. Problem-based, inquiry-based and task-based learning (Bygate 2000) recognise that learning is more effective when students are active and responsible for their own learning. This learner engagement can be cognitive, affective and physical, and patterns around all of the associated types of behaviours are worth observing. Think about what the tasks ask of the students in terms of each of these: what sort of thinking is required of the students; whether there are emotional dimensions; and whether they are expected to engage physically in any way. The tasks can then be linked with what you think the teacher's intention is in each case in terms of engagement and cognitive demands. We now consider learning outcomes in terms of cognitive, affective and kinaesthetic as recognition of the importance of these three realms of learner engagement.

Learner level and aptitude can have a strong influence on classroom interactions. Language teachers recognise fully that even within a predetermined level such as upper-intermediate there can be a wide range of mixed abilities. Homogeneity is more a desirable than a reality for some teachers and learners. In addition, overt signs of level can be problematic and enigmatic, as learners may strategically respond or engage within their established comfort zones, making themselves appear better than they may be in a less contrived environment. As well as trying to identify signs of student ease or challenge, it might also be interesting to be aware of the teacher's strategies in accommodating students of apparently different levels. Such strategies might include speed and complexity of language, wait time, student grouping arrangements, using students as models, reformulating and echoing, differentiated task assignment, scaffolding materials such as indexes, allowing mobile devices and apps to be used etc.

Culture and its relationship with language is characterised by complexity (Kramsch 1998). It can be an influencing variable in language classrooms in numerous ways. Wajnryb (1992a: 40) suggests at least four:

- when learning a language a learner is also learning (about) a culture
- a learner is a cultural being with a cultural perspective on the world, including culture specific expectations of the classroom and learning process
- the cultural dimension of the learner has to be considered and respected
- a positive attitude towards the culture of the target language is a favourable factor in language learning.

It is useful to consider if and how culture seems to have an influence in choice of materials and how they are received, choice of topics and activities, interaction patterns, modes of address, student attitude, levels of verbal engagement and contribution, seating arrangements, levels of cultural accommodation and integration. It is also worth thinking about the different cultural representations of English and the place of the teacher as a cultural artefact or otherwise, and how this influences the lesson.

Observing the language

Although you will have been thinking about certain facets of language when focusing on the learner in the discussions in the previous section, it is worth contemplating the language used specifically and strategically by the teacher for different purposes. Teacher language is addressed in some detail in Chapter 6, and in Chapter 7 with respect to classroom interactions and different teacher modes using Walsh's SETT (self-evaluation of teacher talk) framework (Walsh 2011, 2006) both of which might usefully be read in conjunction with this section.

Teachers typically employ the use of a range of metalanguage when teaching. This can be in the form of language used to organise the classroom and manage activities (Wajnryb limits it to this in this context), as well as the language used to explain technical aspects of grammar or language use. It can include instructions, explanations, responses to questions, corrections, echoing, instructions and directions, praise and criticism etc. Your observation might focus on the actual words used by the teacher, their communicative purpose, and how it differs from how one might communicate the same message to native speakers in another context. It might be worth recording precisely the words used by the teacher to ensure you have an accurate record on which to base your awareness-raising reflections. Observing a wide range of levels, student groups and ages allows a broader perspective on how this aspect of language use can be appropriately modified for the different contexts. The question of how the authenticity of language is balanced against the need for accessibility and comprehensibility is an interesting one and worth some discussion with your peers.

Many questions are raised in language classes, the vast majority of which are typically initiated by the teacher. There are various lenses through which questions can be examined. Extremely influential is the work of Bloom and colleagues. From 1949, Benjamin Bloom co-ordinated a group of educational psychologists who developed a hierarchical classification of intellectual behaviour important in learning contexts. The original 'taxonomy', as it is known, was published in 1956 (Bloom et al. 1956) and consisted of carefully developed definitions for each of the six major categories in the cognitive domain: knowledge, comprehension, application, analysis, synthesis and evaluation. These range from simple to more complex and from concrete to more abstract in terms of cognitive demand. A revised taxonomy was published in 2001 (Anderson et al. 2001), in which the classification of cognitive process presents three lower-order thinking (LOT) dimensions: remember, understand, apply; and three higher-order thinking (HOT) dimensions: analyse, evaluate, create (see Figure 4.2). The taxonomy can apply to tasks, activities, questions, assessments and other components of teaching. LOT questions are generally easy, attainable in a short period and not dependent on prior learning. HOT questions are more difficult and involve new tasks, problems or situations, which are highly dependent on prior learning. They take more time and effort but are more interesting, are academically relevant and create deep learning.

The teacher has a number of options available in terms of the syntactic question type: wh-questions, yes/no questions, alternative (either/or) questions, declarative questions (declaration with rising intonation). From a functional perspective, in terms of anticipated student response, questions can be classified into display and referential. Display questions are those where the teacher typically knows the answer in advance, and referential those where no such pre-knowledge exists. Narrow display questions are those to which the teacher knows the answer and there is only one anticipated response in terms of either content or form. Broad display questions allow for student choice in terms of content or form from a range of possibilities already known to the teacher (Banbrook and Skehan 1989). So, as well as aiming for a particular cognitive demand, the teacher also has choices that can be made from a range of question types and in relation to the anticipated answer. Of course, there is likely to be a correlation between, for example, LOT demands and yes/no display

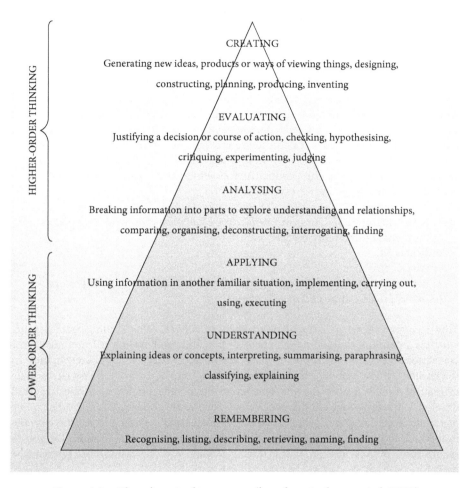

HIGHER-ORDER THINKING

LOWER-ORDER THINKING

CREATING

Generating new ideas, products or ways of viewing things, designing,
constructing, planning, producing, inventing

EVALUATING

Justifying a decision or course of action, checking, hypothesising,
critiquing, experimenting, judging

ANALYSING

Breaking information into parts to explore understanding and relationships,
comparing, organising, deconstructing, interrogating, finding

APPLYING

Using information in another familiar situation, implementing, carrying out,
using, executing

UNDERSTANDING

Explaining ideas or concepts, interpreting, summarising, paraphrasing,
classifying, explaining

REMEMBERING

Recognising, listing, describing, retrieving, naming, finding

Figure 4.2   Bloom's revised taxonomy (based on Anderson et al. 2001)

questions, but this may not always be the case. You will need to think carefully and
devise/use some sort of classification system to observe questioning in the classroom
and the demands that different question types make of students. It is also interesting
to try to trace the relationship between question types and student response in terms
of quantity and quality.

Another aspect of language use is the way in which teachers follow up in relation
to students' contributions. Here I depart slightly from Wajnryb's classification around
feedback on errors and broaden the discussion to include a number of ways in which
teachers can follow up on the language and/or context of what a student has said.
The point of departure in many discussions on this topic will inevitably be the IRF
(initiation, response, feedback/follow-up) exchange structure first formally recorded

on the basis of the results of a large-scale study carried out by Sinclair and Coulthard in 1975 examining classroom discourse. Teachers have a number of options, partially determined by whether the student-produced content contains errors or not. If it does contain errors, the way in which teachers respond will influence their progress, but needs to be handled carefully so that it does not cause anxiety or embarrassment, which can have a negative impact on motivation. It needs to be framed in a positive way and as an incentive for students to improve. Error feedback is most effective when it goes beyond highlighting the error to include opportunities for the student to discover the correct answer from a narrow range of choices. It will also be interesting for you to observe the teacher's attitude to errors as apparent in facial and body gestures, and to notice how errors may be approached during different types of activities and at different stages in the lesson. The following extract from Cullen (2002: 120) contains an example of an IRF exchange:

> T: Now what kind of man is he? What do we call such men who have pistols and point them at pilots? Yes, please?
> Indicates S4.   *I*
> S: We call a robber.   *R*
> T: *A robber? Yes. A thief you mean? Yes, if this was happening on the ground, it could be a thief, but this man's in a plane.*   *F*

This exchange shows us a linguistic correction (*robber – thief*), and a teacher echo, which is a defining characteristic of teacher talk and can have many functions (error correction, repetition for others to hear, clarification check etc.). The evaluation of the content of the response as being incorrect (*Yes, if . . .. but . . .*) also performs a discoursal function allowing the teacher to build on students' contributions and develop a meaning-focused dialogue. The F turn in this dialogue is a good example of a multifaceted response which corrects, evaluates and negotiates meaning with the individual and group of students involved. It would be a useful exercise for you to record some of these IRF exchanges during a lesson you observe and use them as the basis for some small-scale analysis and discussion.

Observing the learning
To say that learning is complex is absurdly simplistic. However, there are aspects of the learning environment and process that can be observed to form the basis for some inferences and assumptions, bearing in mind that these may not always be accurate, as learning as a cognitive process cannot be directly witnessed. We spoke in earlier sections about the importance of affect in language learning, and the classroom context can play a part in the creation of a positive environment. Factors external to the students, such as the lighting, temperature and ventilation in a room, the seating arrangements, the comfort levels (seating, flooring etc.), the acoustics, the visual attraction (pictures, posters, shape, colour etc.), the teacher and other students (appearance, voice tone and quality, physical movement etc.) and what can been seen through windows, all contribute to the affective ambience of a lesson. Focusing on one student over a sustained period of 10–15 minutes may provide insights into their affective

state at a particular time. Think about how they look, move, behave and respond, and examine whether there are any potential links to any of the factors listed above.

There is no guarantee that because teaching is happening learning is taking place. For this reason a core responsibility and role of the teacher is to check student learning. There are generally a number of reasons why a teacher engages in checking at various stages during the lesson: students appearing not to understand, the end of an activity or the transition to another, in response to a query from one student or similar mistakes from a number of students. It is also worth considering what is checked and how this is done, noticing also times when a teacher did not check but you feel it might have been a good idea to do so. The students can also play a role, either in checking with each other, or indeed by the way in which they respond either emotionally or in terms of achievement and improved performance (immediately and later in the lesson).

The lesson plan is the instrument through which the process of learning is clarified and formulated, and as such is an effective yardstick against which to measure what happens in the classroom, while bearing in mind that flexibility is a key component of a good plan (see Chapter 5 for a full discussion of the lesson planning process). The starting point for plans is usually the articulation of aims/objectives, or what the teacher hopes to achieve during the lesson (for example, language learning aims, task-based aims, social aims). Many now also use frameworks around ELOs (expected learning outcomes). This is especially true in the European context of higher education since the introduction of frameworks emanating from the Bologna Process (see, for example, http://www.ehea.info/article-details.aspx?ArticleId=119) and in my experience is trickling down to other educational arenas also. Essentially, it is a move away from a focus on what students do during a programme of study to looking at what they will be able to do at the end of it using what they have learned, assimilated, applied, created etc. as part of their activities in and out of the classroom. ELOs are generally categorised into three domains when planning individual lessons or course components: cognitive (related to understanding and processing information), affective (related to emotions and values) and kinaesthetic (related to movement and touch) (for further discussion see Section 5.3 on the written lesson plan). Irrespective of which mechanism is used by the teacher you are working with, the aims and outcomes can be used as the basis for measuring student learning throughout and at the end of the lesson. In other words, it is good to consider the aims and outcomes, if and how they are made explicit to the students and whether they are achieved (using evidence you observe from the lesson). This will necessarily involve two discussions with the teacher – one before and one after the lesson. These discussions can focus on a number of questions around the planning process, such as:

- What is the teacher's attitude towards planning and the implementation of the plan?
- What part do individual student-related factors such as learning styles and aptitudes play in the overall scheme?

- Which components had been planned, such as vocabulary teaching, and which emanated from the unpredicted but natural development of the lesson?
- To what extent are openings, closings, phases and transitions planned and in how much detail?
- To what extent are instructions and classroom management aspects of the lesson planned?
- How does the teacher measure the success or otherwise of the particular lesson plan and its implementation?

It is a good idea to make some notes, based on your observation around the questions you plan to discuss, and to reflect on how accurate your interpretations were and why. The potential or eventuality of misunderstanding, breakdown and repair can also be an interesting dimension to consider, even if it does not happen in a lesson you observe. Consider the reasons why it might happen and reparation strategies that might be useful to overcome an impasse and move forward with the group and the lesson.

Observing teaching skills and strategies

The focus on observing skills and strategies relates to those parts of the lesson when acquiring content is the specific aim. This may be around a specific point of grammar, vocabulary or pronunciation and may be orchestrated in a teacher-centred way (traditional presentation phase of a lesson) or in a student-centred way (inductive, discovery-type tasks and problems to be completed). A simple way of approaching the task of observing skills and strategies is by looking at what the teacher does and what the students do in a specific instance of content-oriented teaching. Factors such as the physical arrangement of the classroom, the teacher and the students as well as those relating to their voices, audibility, clarity and comprehensibility are important to notice. The context used to exemplify the language being presented can determine how clear the forms and usage patterns are to the students as well as how conducive to generating further practice. The medium or media used are related to this; for example, is the language embedded in written, oral, online, visual, auditory, kinaesthetic artefacts? How effective was this choice and what impact did it have?

Elicitation is a key strategy used by teachers to engage students and prompt active learning. It can be used for a number of reasons: as part of a 'warm-up' to get students thinking about the topic of the lesson, to check understanding, to encourage peer interactions or to address disruptive behaviour, to name a few. The relationship between the purpose and the elicitation prompt (question, calling by name, gesturing etc.) is interesting to explore, as are the suitability and success of any strategy in specific contexts. The success might be evaluated from the student response, the teacher follow-up (as discussed in the previous section on the language of questioning) and completion of the specified activity or task.

Observing managerial modes

There are many times in the classroom when the teacher has to take a lead role in setting up and managing various activities and student interactions. This increases

Table 4.1   Managerial mode in the SETT framework (based on Walsh 2003)

Mode	Pedagogic goals	Interactional features
Managerial	To transmit information To organise the physical learning environment To refer lear ners to materials To introduce or conclude an activity To change from one mode of learning to another	A single, extended teacher turn which uses explanations and/ or instructions The use of transitional markers The use of confirmation checks An absence of learner contributions

teacher talking time (TTT) and is therefore one of the contributory factors to disapprovals around the quantity of TTT relative to STT (student talking time). Researchers such as Walsh (2002: 3) have been critical of those who take a quantitative approach to TTT:

> Communication in the ELT classroom is a highly complex, complicated and elusive phenomenon: a 'problematic medium' (Cazden 1986: 432). For many years, educators and researchers have been concerned to analyse the communicativeness of the classroom by comparing it to communication in the 'real world'. Teachers have been criticized for their excessive TTT . . . and trainees on initial and in-service courses have been advised of their need to reduce talking time. Put simply, the focus has been on the quantity rather than quality of teacher talk, a position which is clearly both simplistic and unrealistic.

In fact, he argues that the classroom is a unique social context which must be investigated on its own terms. Walsh's SETT framework is outlined in more detail in Chapter 7, but I give in Table 4.1 a description of the types of talk he includes when teachers are in managerial mode.

Teachers are usually in managerial mode when they are giving instructions and directions (see Chapter 6 for further discussion); managing error, patterns of interaction, pair and group work, time and pace, and teaching and learning roles. This is a relatively diverse grouping, which comes with associated teacher power, and so may need to be broken into more wieldy units for the purposes of observation.

Observing resources and materials
There are a number of useful learning resources that can be used in any teaching context. Thinking of traditional classrooms, the black/whiteboard is an obvious example, which has stood the test of time. Interactive whiteboards and other types of technology (Farr and Murray 2016) now form the backdrop for many modern classrooms, allowing access to a range of information and interactive resources not previously available, although they bring with them their own limitations (see next section for a fuller discussion). Another resource is the learner, and according to Wajnryb (1992a: 124) 'It has become a maxim of education to acknowledge that the greatest resource the teacher has is the learners themselves.' This is important as

the very nature of language learning demands active participation by the students, drawing on their own and other resources. However, it is worth observing whether there are times when the learners are not used as a resource, why this might be and what the impact is.

Good materials are often considered a vital element of a successful lesson. Mishan and Timmis (2015) emphasise the need for materials to be principled, motivating, affectively and cognitively engaging, challenging, with suitable input and opportunities for appropriate output. In the world of TESOL, the issue is more often a question of evaluating and selecting appropriate materials rather than creating them from scratch. We work in a profession abounding with very high-quality materials, both commercially available and some freely available as open educational resources. In this scenario, your observational role will most probably focus on the suitability of the materials considering the following factors: goals, input, activity, teacher and learner roles, context and setting. Notice also any adaptations that the teacher may have made to the materials (to provide more choice, autonomy, accessibility, challenge, or to remove inappropriate content etc.) and how they worked. The expectations of students functioning in the digital age for the materials they use in class are worth considering. The other side of that argument is that we have become too focused and reliant on producing and using materials with high production standards, to the detriment of good quality and a focus on the learners. Thornbury (2000: 2), writing over fifteen years ago, makes a convincing argument that we do not necessarily need materials to the same degree that we generally use them. This may be even more convincing today if we consider the further explosion of resources and materials offered in the era of Web 2.0 and soon to be Web 3.0 technologies:

> Along with the quantity (I hesitate to use the word variety) of coursebooks in print, there is an embarrassment of complementary riches in the form of videos, CD-ROMs, photocopiable resource packs, pull-out word lists, and even websites, not to mention the standard workbook, teacher's book, and classroom and home study cassettes. Then there is the vast battery of supplementary materials available, as well as the authentic material easily downloadable from the Internet or illegally photocopied from more conventional sources. There are the best-selling self-study grammar books, personal vocabulary organisers, phrasal verb dictionaries, concordancing software packages – you name it. However, where is the story? Where is the inner life of the student in all this? Where is real communication? More often as [sic] not, it is buried under an avalanche of photocopies, visual aids, transparencies, MTV clips and Cuisenaire rods. Somewhere in there, we lost the plot.

Observing technology-enhanced teaching and learning environments

The potential for online learning has exploded since the time of Wajnryb's book on observation. We now have many options around blended and online modes, many interactive and live (Sharma and Westbrook 2016), and the expectation for you to be able to teach in this technology-rich environment is very real. This will most probably be part of your methodological induction included in your TESOL programme (see Spiro 2013: ch. 8), and it is also highly advisable that you find the opportunity to observe some technology-enhanced learning environments, either in the classroom or in an online mode. All of the different aspects that we have discussed so far in this chapter can legitimately form the basis for these observations but with the added question of how the online or blended environment influences teaching and learning behaviours and outcomes. A basic principle should always be an examination of how learning can be enhanced, rather than an assumption that technology is globally better. Like any other tool or resource, technology has a number of limitations and boundaries (Kern and Malinowski 2016), which need to be judiciously considered as part of your observation agenda (see also Further Reading Two below). The question of digital literacies and redefined roles is an interesting one to consider in this context (Gillen 2014). In terms of observing technology-enhanced learning environments, there are two options. The first is to join the community live as an observer in a physical environment or as a lurker in an online environment (this will need to be negotiated carefully with the teacher due to potential intrusion or disturbance). The second is to examine the artefacts after the live teaching, as a post-event observation (such as viewing the video-recordings, examining the discourse produced in online chats or discussion forums; see, for example, Farr and Riordan 2012, 2015). Options will need to be discussed in detail with cooperating teachers to ensure agreed understandings and practices for observations in these emerging teaching environments.

TASK 4.4   STUDENT LANGUAGE AND ITS IMPACT

Consider the following quotations from Hashim, a North African student taking part in an ESL course in the United States as reported in Kayi-Adar (2013). The following extracts come from group work activities:

> 'Hmm, pay attention. Pay attention.' (addressed to a fellow student)
> 'No, completely wrong.' (addressed to a fellow student)
> 'Just one minute. That's not fair.' (addressed to the teacher)
> 'I've read that in the Physics before. The science.' (addressed to the teacher)

A. What are your reactions to the various extracts?
B. What do you think are the influencing variables in Hashim's choice of language?
C. Can you predict different ways in which the teacher could react in each case? What might be the consequences of each?
D. Kayi-Adar categorises the extracts under the following functions: engaging in teacher-like positions, displaying symbolic capital, confronting the teacher's methodological decisions. Can you attribute each extract to one of these categories?
E. Read the full article and discuss in small groups.

TASK 4.5   CLASSROOM INTERROGATIONS

There are a number of online resources which exemplify and discuss the application of Bloom's taxonomy of questions in the classroom. Find a resource which could be useful as a framework for observing and analysing questioning in the classes that you observe and teach. Compare your findings within a small group.

TASK 4.6   ONLINE OBSERVATION RESOURCES

Critically evaluate an online observation resource site such as Education World (http://www.educationworld.com/a_admin/admin/admin297.shtml) in terms of its potential benefits and uses for teachers involved in observation at various stages in their careers. Share your findings and impressions in a group and write a summary report to be shared electronically.

4.4   POST-OBSERVATION: WHAT DOES IT MEAN FOR ME?

4.4.1   CONCEPTS, FINDINGS AND TEXTS

As outlined early in this chapter, the purpose of the types of observation we have been discussing is to learn and to make discerning judgements about what this learning means for your own teaching. Closing the observation loop requires a detailed consideration of how you are going to allow or not allow what you have seen to influence your own emerging teaching beliefs, styles, strategies and practices. There are some caveats around the process of observation that you should take into account as part of your reflections. Firstly, you are a third-party observer in the classroom and therefore your experiences will be a step removed from those who are participants. Only they are first-hand players and you are, at best, attempting an interpretation, which may or may not reflect their experiences. Secondly, every teaching context and dynamic is different and activities may or may not transfer to other teaching situations with the same level of success. In other words, what works well for me today with one group may not work for me with the same or another group tomorrow, and more importantly, may or may not work for you in your teaching. Thirdly, the presence of an observer has the potential to change the dynamics in any given situation and we cannot know how subtle this might be and how it has influenced your perceptions of the lesson. Fourthly, teacher personality is pivotal to the way in which a lesson unfolds. The teachers you have observed may have very different characteristics from your own. You need to make careful decisions around what will work for you and how this will work within your own developing teacher identity (see Chapter 6 for further discussion). Finally, the samples of data you collect in a classroom are limited and you should avoid making generalisations based on one or two instances that you observe.

Bearing in mind the cautionary notes just mentioned, your first post-observation task is to debrief with the cooperating teacher. You may have specific questions you want to ask or aspects of the lesson you want to clarify and get an insider perspective on. The teacher may also wish to comment on aspects of the lesson. The format and formality of this debriefing will be decided by you and the teacher, and may be influenced by institutional guidelines that operate on your teacher education programme. This discussion will unavoidably be oriented by the fact that the teacher is personally and subjectively involved and you have been a sort of witness to the event. It is important not to enter or be drawn into any kind of critique of the lesson, remembering that your purpose is to gather information and learn, and not to evaluate. It is also useful to have another lens through which your observational outcomes can be interpreted. This can be with peers or may be a more formal part of your teacher education programme in plenary format with one or a number of your teacher educators. These are all opportunities to start looking at the context more holistically and to link some of the practices you have seen with the theoretical frameworks you have been learning about on your programme. Additionally, it is a useful process to allow for other perspectives and to share yours in a safe learning environment.

The next stage in the process is to start to personalise your observational experiences and discussions, and think about what you want them to mean for you. This requires some principled reflection followed by an action and implementation plan. This is the notion of learning as the construction of personal meaning.

> In this view of learning, the teacher [you, in this case] does not learn solely by acquiring new information or knowledge (such as procedures or techniques), but through thinking about new ideas in the light of past experience, fitting new ideas into her or his thinking, and reappraising old assumptions in the light of new information. New information is therefore absorbed in a way that is creative, dynamic and personal and that will mean something different to each person receiving the information. (Wajnryb 1992a: 10)

Following on from transforming your observational experiences into personal meaning, you are now in a position to be able to initiate your own development. You are the one to determine this for yourself, using appropriate supports available to you. An outsider cannot determine this, as the best teacher that you can be is very specific to you. This is where you need to step up, take responsibility and take action for your own development. There is no prescribed route here and you will probably need to tolerate a little bit of trial and error along the way. The guidelines around reflective practice and continuing professional development in Chapter 8 will be helpful in this process.

TASK 4.7   OBSERVATION MATERIALS

Identify a focus for an observation that you are about to conduct from the contents of this section. Find a published template with the same or a similar focus (based on online materials or those available in Wajnryb 1992a). Discuss in a group how it might need to be adapted to your specific needs and focus. Prepare a final version ready to use during your observation.

TASK 4.8   DOING AN OBSERVATION

A. Follow the observation process outlined in this section (preparation of materials, discussion with cooperating teacher, observation, debriefing with the teacher, sharing experiences within your teacher education community). Reflect on what this means for your own teaching and formulate an action plan for development. Share with a colleague or a tutor to get further insights.
B. Conduct a small research project with your peers examining their experiences following the observation cycle in (A). Share your findings in a group.

TASK 4.9   OBSERVATION IN OTHER DISCIPLINES

Gather some information (online, through interviews, discussions, reading etc.) about the roles and procedures around observation in at least one other discipline (for example, the healthcare professions). How does it compare with the frameworks in language teacher education? Can we learn anything from other disciplines?

4.5   FURTHER READING ONE

Classroom Discourse (journal, published by Routledge).
In this case, I suggest picking any article from the journal since it began publishing in 2010 and reading it from start to finish. It will give you a perspective on a practical learning context, much like those you will observe. It will also highlight some of the research questions teachers investigate for their own teaching contexts. This journal:

> Focuses on research that considers discourse and interaction in settings where activity is deliberately organised to promote learning. While most papers focus on the discourse of classrooms, others report research in more informal, naturalistic settings in which, while learning is certainly still taking place, it is not occurring in the typical and 'traditional' space of a classroom. Examples might include online tutorials, peer–peer interactions of work-in-progress, and dialogues between 'trainer and trainee' in a workplace context. (taken from the journal's website, http://www.tandfonline.com/loi/rcdi20)

FURTHER READING ONE TASK

1. Read an article from the journal and, based on the research focus, design an observation task that you can use. Discuss, share and compare with others.
2. Adopt or adapt the task into a mini-research project that you can use to investigate the same topic in a lesson that you teach.

4.6 FURTHER READING TWO

Kern, R. and Malinowski, D. (2016) 'Limitations and boundaries in language learning and technology', in Farr, F. and Murray, L. (eds), *The Routledge Handbook of Language Learning and Technology*, New York: Routledge.

The Kern and Malinowski chapter in this edited volume on language learning and technology focuses on the limitations of technology compared with a traditional face-to-face teaching context. As such, it will help you to identify any differences in approach and focus you might want to make when observing a technology-enhanced environment. The chapter begins with two short accounts of teachers using technology. Nadia is a German teacher being confronted with an institutional change in the learner management system which she will have to use. She is familiar with the existing system and although the new system has added functionalities which have potential for use in language learning contexts, she and her colleagues also have some reservations about the change process they will have to work through. Ayo, the second teacher, is a university instructor of Yoruba in face-to-face classroom settings. He has recently been twinned with an African language programme at a neighbouring institution to offer his class there synchronously with room-to-room video-conferencing. The authors use these two case studies to explore the issues around their new technology-based teaching challenges. They caution from the outset that:

> In recent decades, with the advent of electronic devices and digital communications tools of all sorts, theorists of technology remind us that it is important not just to think about hardware and software but also the linguistic, cognitive, social, and behavioral practices that evolve through, around, and with the use of technologies.

The next section of the chapter seeks to explore definitions around the notions of limitations and boundaries, and the authors suggest that these should be identified in a variety of domains – spatial, temporal, cultural, material, virtual, cultural, and human (among others) – as they can be abstract and subtle as well as physical and material. Examples of Ayo having difficulties with time delays on the oral/aural channel, the inability to zoom in adequately on written materials, the lack of opportunity to distribute handouts in advance or in class, the fact that some parts of the class are not seen within the zoom, the decisions around whether to face the camera or the students in his own physical environment as the camera is mounted on the wall behind him, and misinterpretations of eye movement all form the basis for an exploration of the definition of boundaries. This grounds the following discussion, where the authors:

> Develop a model for visualizing how such boundaries might be dynamically interrelated, with the goal of aiding educators to adopt a critical stance (Feenberg, 2002) toward their technology use. In particular, we suggest that the transcendence or blurring of a given boundary or boundaries needs to be seen in relation to the creation or emergence of other boundaries.

They present a list of the boundaries which can be overcome by technology, including spatial and temporal, linguistic, social and community and role-based limitations. This is balanced against a list of those created by technology, including constraints around the interface, mobility, user skills, the software, bandwidth, compatibility, censorship and keyboard configuration. The authors suggest that the boundaries on each side of the divide can appear and disappear in waves, and suggest a visual in the form of a kaleidoscope to represent this evolution in which the size, shape and complexity of patterns are not static.

It is precisely this kind of dynamic disappearance and emergence among patterns of cultural, temporal, spatial, linguistic, and subjective relations that is brought about through the introduction and use of various technologies for language teaching and learning. Moreover, just as each person who picks up and views the kaleidoscope will see something different from what others see, each language learner will experience the use – and limitations – of any given technological medium in a unique, personal way.

The chapter then moves to a discussion of the relational limitations of technology, which we have probably all been aware of at some time. Some examples include brevity in text messaging and chat rooms, limitations of onscreen keyboards in typing email messages, and the ability to remain anonymous or to lurk in online environments. These all affect the relationship between those involved in the communication in different ways. On the other hand, communication may be improved through the ability to use gestures in video-conferencing, for instance. Access to languages is the focus of a section examining the keyboard; availability of pedagogic materials in various languages; and cultures, genres and styles. The chapter finishes by looking to the future and offers the following advice:

What is crucial for language teachers and learners alike is to adopt a critical stance with respect to the technologies they use and, specifically, to be attentive to:

- how technologies mediate language use and behavior in particular ways,
- what communicative consequences (in terms of understanding and learning) might accompany that mediation, and
- what social consequences might follow the choice of using one form of technology versus another (in terms of who is included or excluded, how participant interactions might be reconfigured, how cultural processes and products might be affected).

FURTHER READING TWO TASK

1. Familiarise yourself with the work of Professor Sugata Mitra in the 'Hole-in-the-wall' project in India (TED talk and YouTube clips are readily available). Discuss the boundaries and limitations blurred by technology in the context of this project with schoolchildren in India.

2. Consider a context in which you were a participant. What were the affordances and limitations of technology in this context? Design an observation task for a TEL environment around one of the focuses discussed in Section 4.3, paying particular attention to affordances and limitations.

4.7 SUMMARY

This chapter has discussed the practice of observing others teaching as a way to learn and inform your own practices. The various purposes of observation along the continuum from research to evaluation to learning are outlined in Section 4.2, which also addresses various types of cognitive and practical preparations needed. These preparations are vital in advance of engaging in an observation for learning purposes due to the complex, busy and fast-moving pace of the classroom, plus the nature of the demands that you will be placing on yourselves in terms of watching, assimilating and gathering information for later reflection. 'Trial runs' by means of watching videos of lessons and/or reading some research accounts of classrooms are suggested as good preparation, as well as considering the process involved in communicating with and working with the cooperating teacher, for which some guidelines are recommended. Section 4.3 concentrates primarily on the options available to you in deciding which aspects of a lesson you might choose to observe. The discussion focuses on the following: observing the learner (affect, motivation, engagement, language level and aptitude, and culture), observing the language (metalanguage, questions and follow-up), observing the learning (environment, checking student learning, and the lesson aims and outcomes), observing teaching skills and strategies (content teaching and learning, and elicitation), observing managerial modes, observing resources and materials, and observing technology-enhanced teaching and learning environments. Finally, Section 4.4 considers the post-observation stages in terms of making the learning experience personal to you as a way of making sense of it and informing your own future teaching development.

4.8 ADDITIONAL READINGS

Harmer, J. (2007) *How to Teach English*, Harlow: Pearson.

Howard, A. and Donaghue, H. (eds) (2014) *Teacher Evaluation in Second Language Education*, London: Bloomsbury.

Scrivener, J. (2011) *Learning Teaching: The Essential Guide to English Language Teaching* (3rd edn), London: Macmillan.

Tilstone, C. (1998) *Observing Learning and Teaching*, Abingdon: David Fulton.

Wajnryb, R. (1992) *Classroom Observation Tasks: A Resource Book for Language Teachers and Trainers*, Cambridge: Cambridge University Press.

Walsh, S. (2011) *Exploring Classroom Discourse: Language in Action*, London and New York: Routledge.

Wragg, E. C. (2012) *An Introduction to Classroom Observation* (classic edn), Abingdon: Routledge.

5

THE LESSON PLAN

5.1 INTRODUCTION

Whilst not directly addressing the question of choice of language teaching methodology, which itself merits a much more detailed discussion than this volume allows (see, for example, Spiro 2013, Thornbury 2011), this chapter on lesson planning will be strongly informed by the broad theoretical school(s) of thought to which you affiliate. This, of course, will most probably change over periods of time and perhaps even between lessons, depending on your specific aims and focus. In order for this chapter to be practically useful for you, however, you should familiarise yourself with the methodological options available, what they offer in terms of the whats, the whys and the hows of teaching. This will give you a strong theoretical and practical toolkit to bring with you to the job of planning a lesson, which is the focus of this chapter. There are many good reasons for investing time in the preparation of a lesson plan. The very act of writing the plan in most cases aids the logical thinking process, in the same way that writing, as a means of articulation, generally helps clarity of thought and allows for active reflection in advance of the event. You will find that seeing the draft plan on paper sometimes prompts you to modify it and edit it in rational ways to help improve the overall coherence. Crookes suggests that 'detailed lesson planning provides a concretization of practice, or at least of intended practice, and as such is also a tool for distancing oneself from practice so as to reflect upon it' (Crookes 2003: 101).

In addition, having a plan in class provides an important reference point for the detailed information that you will need in order to work your way successfully through your lesson. When you begin teaching, the complexities and performance demands of the teaching context can sometimes be distracting and it will be practically reassuring to know that you have a written document to check if or when you require it. I remember when I began teaching I often drew a blank when giving instructions for a particular activity. I would end up going around in circles and sometimes cause great confusion when explaining the way in which a task was to work, the student groupings and what was required of them. For that reason, I would prepare in detail, write all of my instructions into my lesson plan, and follow them very closely at those relevant stages of the lesson, sometimes to the point of almost reading them verbatim. This helped me to develop good habits and eventually confidence around this aspect of my teaching. Finally, there may be an official professional requirement to have lesson plans and larger schemes of work available as formal accounts of what the group has done. This may be important if teachers move in and out between lessons, if a teacher is absent, or as part of the evidence for individual teachers' ongoing professional integrity, and is often required by external bodies such as teaching councils and ministries of education. To me, these are all convincing reasons to prepare and write detailed lesson plans when you begin teaching, along with the fact that I have seen some of my own student teachers' lessons crumble without the detail they obviously needed.

In this chapter, we will address the basic essentials of writing up a plan, having taken all of the influencing variables into account, having selected the materials to be used, and having observed enough (as discussed in Chapters 2–4) for you to feel comfortable delivering your first joint or solo lesson. The elements to be included in the written plan, such as aims, outcomes, learners' prerequisite knowledge and a detailed, timed procedure, will be explored. Following this, issues around the actual delivery of the lesson plan will be considered (openings and closings, making transitions, setting up and managing teaching aids etc.). The last input-based section of this chapter addresses the factors that could cause you to deviate from the lesson plan, and aims to outline contexts when it is potentially useful and appropriate to do this.

5.2   CONSIDERING THE CONTENT

5.2.1   CONCEPTS, FINDINGS AND TEXTS

When studying the habits of effective professionals, two types of thinking have been identified: reflection-on-action and reflection-in-action (Argyris and Schön 1974). The former relates to the type of thinking, planning and critiquing that goes on outside of the event itself, in this case the lesson. The latter refers to the way that professionals think on their feet and react to a changing context in real time. This is usually something that is learned effectively over time. We will discuss this aspect in more detail in Section 5.4 below. The focus in this part of the discussion is on the considered planning that happens in advance of a lesson, when you have time available to get everything in order. Here I am reminded of a Benjamin Franklin quotation, commonly adopted by Irish soccer player and manager Roy Keane, which warns 'By failing to prepare, you are preparing to fail.' This could not be truer of the novice teaching context. Good planning is absolutely essential. A good starting point is to remind yourself of the fundamental principles on which all plans should be founded, based on what we know about teaching and learning. Murray and Christison (2011: 20) suggest that instruction should:

- Build on what learners already know.
- Present new information in chunks that learners can digest.
- Include teacher input that is comprehensible to learners.
- Challenge learners to move beyond their current level of language.
- Include opportunities for learners to practice new skills and knowledge.
- Provide feedback (from teachers and/or peers).

- Provide a supportive environment.
- Be responsive to learning opportunities that occur in the classroom.

These authors also remind us of the importance of the classroom as a social as well as pedagogic context. In other words, the choice of content, approach and materials will be realised in a context where the participants come with backgrounds, habits, expectations, opinions, emotions etc. This social context must also be considered, especially if preparing a lesson that might challenge your students in any of these ways. I remember a related recent experience in which I introduced a problem-based learning (PBL) task into one of the courses I teach on our MA in TESOL programme. I had considered the students' expectations and predisposition and decided that because they were used to very inductive and learner-centred approaches when I taught them, this purer form of more formalised discovery learning would probably work well. In most cases it did, but there was a lot of resistance from two particular students, who did not embrace the task as I had hoped. They questioned what the task was asking of them, how they could be expected to have the required information and why I wasn't providing more scaffolding, and a number of other issues arose from my discussions with them. I quickly realised that the social aspects of the learning context were impacting negatively on what we were trying to achieve pedagogically in ways that I had not anticipated would be so apparent. I redesigned the task into three so that there were different levels of student autonomy required. I continue to begin with the 'pure' PBL task but can easily introduce more scaffolding if the same types of socially related difficulties begin to emerge.

The social context also overlaps significantly with the other contexts of the learner. Spiro (2013: 45) presents a useful visual representation of the learner's context in the form of a teaching onion. At the centre of the onion is the learner, surrounded in widening layers by family, school, local community and finally national context. I would suggest that international context is also worthy of inclusion in today's world. Spiro (2013: 44) proposes that 'A classroom is more than simply a physical location; surrounding it is a political, geographical, economic, cultural and social context that impacts on what is happening inside the room. For some teachers what happens outside this room is as important as, or even more important than, what happens inside.'

Another aspect of the teaching context is the professional culture, which has been explored in some detail by Holliday (1994). He categorises this in two ways: BANA (British, Australasia and North America) and TESEP (tertiary, secondary and primary). The BANA culture is typically found in the private and commercially run entities which originally emanated from these countries (privately funded, independent in terms of curriculum choice and teaching approaches) whereas TESEP culture is characteristic of state-run institutions (state-funded, policy-governed, externally determined curriculum etc.). The professional context will have significance for the teacher in many ways, for example, class demographics, resources and materials, teacher–student links, teacher qualifications, relationship with national and international educational policies, and requirements around assessment and examinations.

Having taken account of the important pedagogic principles and the teaching context, you are now in a good position to begin thinking about the content of what you are going to teach. This is directly linked with the aims of your lesson, which will be discussed in Section 5.3 below. Language teaching is unique in the sense that as well as teaching about the language, you are also teaching through the language as a complementary approach which has the overall goal of helping students to become more proficient in their English language understanding and use. The implication of this is that you need to consider the content in terms of the language and the topics that will be used to get the students using the language (Murray and Christison 2011: 21).

The language

Three components of the language content of a lesson need to be considered. These relate to the what (grammar, vocabulary, pronunciation; for example, how questions are formed and their associated pronunciation patterns), the how (the mode, for example, through written, spoken and online pieces of discourse, or through an integrated skills approach) and the where (the linguistic setting in which you will present the language, for example, informal language use from online chat rooms, or formal academic essays). These are not discrete questions and need to be planned in a holistic way. As part of the process of deciding the language focal point, you will need to engage in a certain amount of research so that you are completely confident in your own understanding of what you plan to teach and aware of any potential ambiguities or irregularities which may cause problems for you or your students. This research will involve looking up the grammatical item in a number of grammar reference books or online materials to ensure you understand form, meaning and use (recent grammar reference books such as Biber et al. 1999 or Carter and McCarthy 2006 not only present these aspects but also give a corpus-informed, evidence-based account of real language use in context and in terms of frequency across a range of modes). For lexical items, a thorough investigation in some good, corpus-informed dictionaries is required. In addition, you may wish to consult some corpora yourself (see Chapter 3 on materials) to get a strong sense of actual use and any deviations from the grammar 'rules' that are likely to emerge when students encounter the specific language in less controlled contexts than those often presented in teaching materials. Examine a range of teaching materials focusing on the same language point, see how they approach it and check in any accompanying teachers' guidelines to see if they anticipate any problems that learners are likely to have. It may also be useful to think about the similarities and differences that exist in form or use between English and any other languages your learners know.

The topics

If you are teaching in a TESEP context, the topics that you can use may be limited or predefined by a relatively set curriculum. This may also be the case in some private schools if they adhere to a specific syllabus or teaching methodology or approach. You may, however, have complete autonomy over the topics you select, and in such cases it is prudent to try to find a balance between your learners' needs and their wants/interests, particularly if they do not always seem fully compatible. To take an example, a group of third-level students preparing to study in an English-speaking country as part of a student exchange programme will need to be able to do things such as oral presentations and essay writing through English, but they may be more interested in learning about appropriate small-talk strategies or the vocabulary of a particular sport that they are interested in. Both needs and wants are legitimate starting points for selecting appropriate topics for your lesson plans, and how to balance these may be the most challenging part of your job, particularly in the light of the fact that materials are generally more motivating when they are personal, engaging and sometimes controversial (Mishan and Timmis 2015). And this all needs to be balanced against any cultural considerations that may cause prudent exclusion of certain topics that are considered taboo in that part of the world. In this respect, if you are new to the context, it would be worthwhile discussing your choice of topics with some teachers from the local culture, or some who have worked there for some time. They will be able to offer suitable guidance until you feel more comfortable about your ability to discern which choices might be inappropriate.

Whatever you decide to teach in terms of content for a particular lesson, it will need to be considered as part of a bigger picture, or what many will know as the scheme/ unit of work. This will be what you plan to/need to achieve with your students over a specified period of time such as a term or a school year. Both the content and the sequence will be key considerations here (see Task 5.2 below). I would like to finish this section with a word of pragmatism. During your teacher education programme, lesson planning will necessarily occupy pride of place as a mechanism through which good practices and professional habits will embryonically begin to develop. This is hugely important and not to be undermined. However, if this is also to be the site for the development of sustainable practices you need to be realistic in the way in which you approach your planning. It may not be prudent to invest inordinate amounts of time in, for example, designing vast amounts of authentic materials, as this will probably not be sustainable in your busy teaching careers. Now is the time to find ways of forming good practices which will carry through to the future.

TASK 5.1   STUDENT TEACHERS' ATTITUDES TO PLANNING

The following comment comes from a student teacher cited in Crookes (2003: 109–10):

> Many thoughts ran through my mind as I reflected upon my own experience with the process while teaching last semester. Though I loved my work, lesson planning was always difficult . . . There were two problems that I regularly faced – weekly plans and daily plans. I would try to prepare basic lesson plans for the whole week so that I could know the direction I wanted to take. . .But it was often so difficult for me because while I wanted to maintain the basic 'outline' sometimes I couldn't predict how the class would go . . . And similarly where daily lesson plans were concerned, I had a hard time revising the night before what I had planned for each day of the week. Again, sometimes I felt very unassured about what or how much we would cover the following day. No matter how much I prepared, there was always a feeling of uncertainty lurking in the

back of my mind. In fact, I was so worried and afraid about extra time that I overprepared and overplanned.

A. Do you think these experiences and concerns are shared by many beginning teachers? Are they a necessary part of the process? Can you think of any advice you might offer this particular teacher?
B. What other concerns or issues do you experience with your own planning? Share your experiences within a group and jointly try to develop some strategies to overcome them as far as possible.

TASK 5.2 THE BIGGER PICTURE: SCHEMES OF WORK

In many ways, coursebooks are schemes of work designed for use over a period of time, generally a language level of 80–100 hours.
A. Take a coursebook designed for either business English or EAP and examine the scheme of work that is included at the beginning of the book (usually containing information on language, topics, materials, activities and outcomes).
B. In groups, design a follow-up scheme for a further 20 hours of instruction.
C. Use this scheme as the basis for deciding the aims and content of the first three 2-hour lessons.

TASK 5.3 LESSON PLANNING AND EXPERIENCED TEACHERS

A. Research the attitudes of a small group of more experienced teachers. Interview or survey them in relation to a number of factors relating to lesson planning, such as how they felt about the rigours of lesson planning during their formal teacher education, how they feel about it now in retrospect, how they now approach lesson planning (what works and what doesn't work for them) and any other aspects that you consider relevant to your current stage of development in the area of lesson planning.
B. Compare your findings with those of your peers who researched a different group of teachers. How do your results compare? What can you deduce/ conclude from your findings?

5.3 THE WRITTEN PLAN

5.3.1 CONCEPTS, FINDINGS AND TEXTS

Planning is a cognitive process, or more specifically a metacognitive process, which 'is generally defined as the activity of monitoring and controlling one's cognition' (Young and Fry 2008: 1). According to Crookes (2003: 104):

Planning is a practice essential when we humans, with our limited cognitive capacities, engage in new or difficult tasks. It is conceptually linked with monitoring; the execution of a complex task is problematic if we do not have a sense of the desired outcome and appearance of the tasks against which to judge performance and correct it as necessary; in addition, the execution of a complex task new to the performer is improved by mental rehearsal.

The act of writing a lesson plan, then, is the way in which we physically represent these psychological processes and is ultimately the product of our metacognitive activities. It is therefore practically useful to have some guidance and a flexible framework for the proposed contents of a lesson plan. This section outlines what should be planned and included in the written plan. It is based on my own practices and experiences with student teachers over a number of years and also on previous accounts in pivotal publications on TESOL practice (Gower et al. 2005, Harmer 2007). The various components are outlined briefly below, in the order in which they would typically appear in the written plan.

Preliminary information

Some specific pieces of identifying information should be included at the very beginning of the lesson plan. These serve a number of practical purposes (such as differentiating quickly between plans for different teachers, learners, lessons, days etc., or as a quick reference to the materials to be used during the lesson) as well as conceptually framing the rest of the plan around a specific group of students at a particular time and in a precise context. Information that could usefully be included here is: name of the teacher(s); date, time and location of the lesson; anticipated numbers, age and level of the learners; materials, resources and technologies to be used (and the effect that may have on the learning process; see, for example, Crawford 2013: ch. 8); the place of the lesson in the larger sequence outlined in the scheme of work; and names of any cooperating or supervising teachers, with specific developmental aspects of your practice you would like them to concentrate on during this specific observation. Some regimes with which I am familiar also require a detailed account of each learner, assumptions about their previous knowledge, how the contents of the proposed lesson cater to their needs, and any anticipated difficulties they may have.

Aims and expected learning outcomes

Aims and ELOs are related but not the same: the former focus on what the teacher plans to do and the latter on an articulation of the resultant outcomes in terms of what students will be able to do by the end of the lesson. The relationship between the two is not a simple one; in other words just because I teach does not mean that my students will learn from that process alone, or at all. Rather the ELOs should be considered as the outcome in terms of total student effort, which could consist of engaging with the content of what the teacher teaches, what the activities contain and what students learn from each other, and in all probability will be based partially on previously acquired knowledge also. Aims can be articulated for language content such as specific points of grammar (for example, 'to teach spoken discourse strategies relevant for polite social interactions using . . .') or lexis (for example, 'to teach vocabulary relevant to informal social dining contexts . . .'), and may have sub-aims (for example, 'to teach small talk', 'to teach social introductions and greetings'). They may also be formulated around the development of skills such as reading, writing, listening and speaking, or integrated skills. And the teacher may have personal development aims for a lesson (for example, 'to practise integrating the use of technology into the classroom environment as a pedagogically appropriate aid to enhance reading skills'). Aims should generally be specific enough to reflect the detail of the particular lesson under construction rather than something so generic that it could describe a number of lessons in broadly the same topic area (for example, 'to teach listening skills'). Lesson-level student learning outcomes, as discussed in Chapter 4, are generally designated in three spheres: cognitive (using such verbs as 'understand', 'articulate', 'apply' and 'critique', depending on which levels of Bloom's taxonomy you are pitching an activity at); affective (relating to values, as well as personal and social appreciations); and kinaesthetic (related directly to aspects of physical movement or co-ordination to be learned specifically as part of the lesson). Learning outcomes are generally phrased in the following terms: 'by the end of the lesson, students will be able to . . .'. It is also important to specify an immediate and longer-term assessment strategy, which focuses on measuring the learning outcomes as articulated in the written plan.

Prior learning and anticipated problems
This section will include an articulation of what the students need to have learned already in order to navigate the contents of the present lesson successfully. An example might be knowledge of the present simple tense of the verb *to be* in a lesson that focuses on learning the present progressive. Anticipated problems will be based on both prior learning and the specific contents of this lesson. It may relate to such things as pronunciation difficulties for students from specific linguistic backgrounds, or false cognates between languages, or even cultural content with which they may not be familiar in their own frames of reference. These will be very specific and should not be a re-articulation of the aims, as I have seen in some of the lesson plans I review. Familiarity with the student group as well as the research you do around the language content for your lesson (as discussed above) will help you to identify potential problems and therefore prepare for them should the need arise to address them in the lesson.

Procedure
This is the longest part of the plan in terms of content and will require a detailed account of what will happen at every stage of the lesson. It is often recorded on some sort of predefined template, such as that in Figure 5.1, and will contain information on the stage, the specific sub-aims, the content, the time, what the students will be doing and what the teacher will be doing. It may contain visual representations of classroom organisation and student groups for the stages. This is where you can also plan and write specific instructions you want to use, or lexical explanations and examples, so that they are readily available if you need them. This part of the plan will be very detailed when you begin as a novice teacher.

It is always a good idea to prepare the lesson plan far enough in advance to allow you some mature reflection and final changes before the event, but not so far in

Stage/time	Activity and materials	Sub-aims	Teacher/student activity and grouping

Figure 5.1   Template for the procedural component of a written lesson plan

advance that the cognitive processes and reasoning you employed have been forgotten and the plan looks slightly alien to you on the day of teaching. Usually, two to three days in advance works well, although this may not fit with the formal requirements of your programme, which might insist on the submission of all plans in advance of the entire practice placement period.

As the time approaches there are a number of organisational steps you can follow to ensure the smooth running of your lesson. Gower et al. (2005: 182–3) propose the following:

- Check that you have your lesson plan
- Run through your lesson plan and make sure you have all the necessary aids and equipment listed in the plan
- Check any equipment you are going to use
- Lay out any visual aids and handouts (pictures, worksheets, cue cards, etc.) in the order you'll need them; cue up any audio or video equipment you are going to use
- Make sure the seating is arranged the way you want it
- Check that the board is clean
- If there is anything you can put on the board, do so in advance, so you don't waste time at the beginning of the lesson (electronic presentation software packages are useful here also)
- At the same time, be ready to chat with the students as they come into the class!

TASK 5.4   INFORMATION ON EFFECTIVE PLANNING

View two or three online clips/materials on effective planning. Review them critically and consider aspects you agree/disagree with, things you learned and anything you found impractical or just absurd.

TASK 5.5   CREATING A LESSON PLAN TEMPLATE

A. Find a number of lesson plan templates online or in books on teaching and practice. Use these and the information included in this section to create a lesson plan that best suits you and your needs. Compare with others and refine before use.

B. Using your template, write a lesson plan for a lesson you will be teaching soon
    (go through the stages suggested above). Share the plan with a tutor or colleague
    and ask for their feedback.

TASK 5.6   THE REAL STARTING POINT

Some research findings suggest that despite the fact that educational theory and
teacher education programmes advocate the aims and outcomes as the optimal starting point for planning a lesson, experienced teachers do not always follow this route.
Discuss the following quotation from Housner and Griffey (1985: 45) in groups and
draw conclusions for your own practice:

> Research has shown that teachers plan for instruction using very different
> strategies than those advocated during the last thirty years of educational
> practice. Rather than emphasizing objectives, teacher planning is directed at the
> selection of instructional tasks or activities . . . Tasks are apparently chosen on
> the basis of their ability to engender student cooperation rather than on
> educational relevance (Placek 1983). Usually teachers choose tasks that are low in
> risk and ambiguity as these have less chance of causing disruptions in student
> cooperation (Doyle 1984).

5.4   PRINCIPLED DEVIATION

5.4.1   CONCEPTS, FINDINGS AND TEXTS

At the beginning of this chapter we mentioned two types of planning: one outside of
the event (in this case in advance) and one that happens in action (in this case during
the lesson). So far we have been discussing the processes and considerations of planning in advance with the benefit of reflection time. I would now like to turn to thinking about those in situ events in the classroom which prompt a decision to consider a
deviation from the plan. We know from research that effective practitioners have an
ability to respond flexibly and appropriately to such events in ways that are beneficial
to the learning process (Abbitt 2011, Argyris and Schön 1974). Novice teachers need
to give this some thought so that they have some strategies to cope successfully when
the potential for deviation arises. This thought process will involve you drawing on
the developing types of knowledge that you have as a beginning teacher. Shulman
(1986) introduced the concept of pedagogical content knowledge (PCK), and this has
since been expanded into a TPACK framework to address the growing importance
of digital technologies in education, as well as their transformative potential (Mishra
and Koehler 2006). Abbitt (2011: 282–3) summarises the seven knowledge domains
described by Mishra and Koehler (2006) as follows:

*   Pedagogical knowledge (PK): Knowledge of nature of teaching and learning,
    including teaching methods, classroom management, instructional planning,
    assessment of student learning, etc.

- Content knowledge (CK): Knowledge of the subject matter to be taught (e.g., earth science, mathematics, language arts, etc.)
- Technology knowledge (TK): Continually changing and evolving knowledge base that includes knowledge of technology for information processing, communications, and problem solving, and focuses on the productive applications of technology in both work and daily life.
- Pedagogical content knowledge (PCK): Knowledge of the pedagogies, teaching practices, and planning processes that are applicable and appropriate to teaching a given subject matter.
- Technological content knowledge (TCK): Knowledge of the relationship between subject matter and technology, including knowledge of technology that has influenced and is used in exploring a given content discipline.
- Technological pedagogical knowledge (TPK): Knowledge of the influence of technology on teaching and learning as well as the affordances and constraints of technology with regard to pedagogical designs and strategies.
- Technological pedagogical content knowledge (TPCK): Knowledge of the complex interaction among the principle knowledge domains (content, pedagogy, technology).

These different domains of teacher knowledge are constantly evolving for all teachers, albeit at a faster rate for student and novice teachers. These, combined with your own personal theories and beliefs (teacher cognition), are the basis for the decisions you will make while teaching.

There are two general reasons why a deviation may be called for. The first relates to a situation when the planned lesson is no longer working or is interrupted. This might happen for a number of reasons: the students don't understand the content or materials because they are too difficult or they are alien to them in terms of their own conceptual frameworks; the students have already covered the same topic or material with another teacher or in another course; the timing of the plan was not accurate and you run out of teaching activities; something has just happened in terms of world events which renders parts of your lesson obsolete, irrelevant or no longer factual (I have seen this happen on many occasions where teachers choose to use current affairs topics as the basis for their materials and plan well in advance); a mishap takes place involving one of the students or the teacher. The second prompt for deviation can come from a learning opportunity that arises in the course of the lesson which presents a good improvisation moment. Crookes (2003: 106) suggests that 'within teaching, improvisation falls within the general area of teacher decision making or teacher thinking, and the term may cover a range of possibilities. A simple under-standing of the term could be paraphrased as "thinking on one's feet". Think about a class using technology in which one of the students presents the latest gadget from one of the market leaders which she has just purchased. This is a real opportunity for authentic discussion and exploration around the item and should be encouraged. This teachable moment has been framed as an 'interactive decision' by Richards and Lockhart (1996).

In the case of a lesson plan that no longer works, a teacher is forced into a deviation. In the case of a teaching opportunity, the teacher has a choice. At these interactive decision-making moments, expert teachers succeed in making good decisions because they have a number of previous experiences and understandings of a range of possibilities for how a lesson can potentially proceed. Their well-developed repertoires allow them to continue in prudent ways with a certain level of automation even at such unplanned parts of a lesson. As a prospective teacher, this is something that you can develop over time. Murray and Christison (2011: 20) propose that 'for the novice teacher, in situ decision-making is quite difficult and often teachers fall back on teaching the way they were taught. However, with constant reflection on one's practice, teachers can acquire the ability to reason among the dynamic, complex, moment-to-moment events that occur in the classroom.' I would add that this can be aided by closely watching this aspect of experienced teachers' practices as part of your observation agenda as discussed in Chapter 4. In the meantime, it is useful to consider in advance the approach that you will take if a deviation is needed or possible during each of your lessons. This will allow you to make your decisions on the basis of some predetermined principles, taking a range of factors into account for that specific lesson and group. These might include building some flexibility into your plan, with some choices available to you depending on how the lesson plays out; allocating a maximum time limit around any learning opportunities that arise; having some 'extra' activities ready in case your timing doesn't work to plan; having more basic explanations, examples and activities for more difficult language points you plan to teach; and grading activities for mixed ability classes. In circumstances where you have a cooperating teacher or a practice tutor in the classroom with you, you might want to consult with them discreetly and seek their advice if you have discerned that a deviation may be necessary or advisable. All of this provides for a more professional approach than the 'wait and see' scenario, but no one can be ready for every eventuality; you may need to be prepared to live with the prospect that sometimes things don't go to plan and this in itself will provide you with a rich opportunity for reflection after the event.

TASK 5.7   TPACK AND YOU

With reference to each of the seven types of teacher knowledge discussed in this section, reflect on what you already know in each category, and what you feel you still need to learn. Discuss your deliberations in a small group.

TASK 5.8   DEVIATION DECISIONS

A.   Discuss the following deviation principles and think of two examples of classroom contexts which would cause you to adhere to each of the principles:

- Never move away from the plan.
- Allow the students to determine the content and direction of the lesson completely.
- Deviate only for certain students in a group.
- Always deviate for at least five minutes in a one-hour lesson.

B.   Discuss the potential impacts that each case you discussed could have on social
      and pedagogical contexts.

TASK 5.9   IMPROVISATION

Conduct some research online about improvisation in any one of the creative arts or
performances. What can you learn about successful and unsuccessful strategies in
this context? Is this transferrable to the teaching context? Why (not) and how?

5.5   FURTHER READING ONE

**Schellekens, P. (2007) *The Oxford ESOL Handbook*, Oxford: Oxford University
Press (ch. 6, 'Managing Learning', pp. 145–52).**
The specific section of chapter 6 of this book that I suggest reading relates to planning
and delivering lessons. It begins with a brief discussion of the place of the lesson plan
as 'an essential lifeline' (p. 145) for new teachers and also its importance (reducing
over time) for more experienced teachers. Schellekens then identifies some core components of sound lesson plans:

- challenging tasks which are achievable over time
- tasks which create real interest and communication
- a good variety of well-paced activities and materials
- a blend of activities which involve the four skills
- learning which gradually becomes more complex and which extends the
  learners' skills. (p. 145)

She uses these to evaluate two different lesson plans which she includes in the chapter,
looking at issues like coherency, skill spread and transferability across skills, focus,
challenge and relevance. There is then a discussion about the complex relationship
between lesson plans and learning styles. The danger of confusing instructional
preferences with learning styles is mentioned, as is the lack of evidence for the effectiveness of learning style models and their impact on learning. The chapter then
moves to consider the purpose and intention of schemes of work, where the author
suggests:

> It is undoubtedly useful for teachers to plan ahead, not least because, should they
> be absent, the scheme of work allows substitute teachers to provide continuity of
> learning. However, the status and intent of the scheme of work deserves
> attention. The premise that underpins this book is that the planning of learning is
> guided by the identification of the learners' needs. If this premise is accepted, this
> means that the scheme of work (including lesson plans) can only be a 'declaration
> of intent', because aspects of learner needs may surface at any time. This may
> influence the delivery of the rest of the lesson and even the course. Teachers and
> managers should be aware that projecting a team's work is fine, but that changes
> to the document can be expected. (p. 149)

In a section on teaching and learning, the concept of 'interlanguage' is introduced in relation to the order in which language is learnt. This term, originally introduced by Selinker in 1972, describes the ever-changing language that is produced by adults when learning a new language. It consists of three components: features from the first language, English language features, and features commonly produced by learners regardless of their language background. Although teachers tend to pay much attention to the first feature, it should not become all-defining, and students need to receive positive reinforcement on the successful production of the target language also. The movement between the stages is not linear and fluid, but will have an impact on planning. It may seem that students regress at times but this is all part of the 'unstable' nature of interlanguage. As long as there is evidence of 'instability' then the language has not become fossilised.

This leaves teachers with the challenging job of keeping an overview of the various stages that any of the learners may be going through and using their professional judgement and knowledge of language to assess how they are progressing. In this respect, the learner's interlanguage can provide valuable insight both for the teacher and the learner. (p. 152)

The information provided by paying attention to the students' language production can play a pivotal role in deciding on appropriate aims, learning outcomes and activities to be included in lesson planning stages.

FURTHER READING ONE TASK

1. Evaluate the lesson plan that you developed in Task 5.5 above against Schellekens' core components for good lesson plans. Where are its strengths and weaknesses in relation to these criteria?
2. Read Coffield et al. (2004) on learning style models. What conclusions can you reach about incorporating specific models into your lesson plans? What are the advantages and disadvantages of considering learning styles during your lesson preparations?

5.6   FURTHER READING TWO

Bishop, J. L. and Verleger, M. A. (2013) 'The flipped classroom: A survey of the research', paper presented at the 120th ASSE Annual Conference and Exposition, Atlanta, 23–6 June. Available at: http://www.studiesuccesho.nl/wp-content/uploads/2014/04/flipped-classroom-artikel.pdf.
This research review focuses on a relatively recent phenomenon which has gained a lot of traction and has a huge impact on the way the classroom operates. The idea of the flipped classroom is that what was traditionally done in the classroom in terms of content acquisition now happens at home or elsewhere in advance of the lesson, which instead functions as a focus for active learning and problem solving. Bishop and Verleger (2013: 1) explain:

The flipped classroom is a new pedagogical method, which employs asynchronous video lectures and practice problems as homework, and active, group-based problem solving activities in the classroom. It represents a unique combination of learning theories once thought to be incompatible – active, problem-based learning activities founded upon a constructivist ideology and instructional lectures derived from direct instruction methods founded upon behaviorist principles.

The authors trace the development of the flipped classroom to two related movements that are strongly impacting the world of education. The first is the technological evolution, which has made information available at a low cost for many years and now makes its distribution instantaneous in many cases. This means that almost any information an individual wants is available at the touch of a button, or at least perceived to be. The second movement, also related to technology, is the 'free software movement', which seeks to remove any barriers to access. The authors cite some examples, such as Wikipedia and the significant step forward MIT took in announcing its OpenCourseWare (OCW) initiative in 2001 (another topical example is found in the MOOC (massive open online course) movement). And this is all continuing to happen at a time when university registration and tuition fees are increasing in a way unprecedented since the expansion in the 1960s and 1970s which made higher education more accessible to a larger demographic.

> As a result, the natural question being asked by both students and educational institutions is exactly what students are getting for their money. This is applying a certain pressure on physical academic institutions to improve and enhance the in-person educational experience of their students. Students are not the only ones demanding higher outcomes from educational institutions. There is also increasing pressure from accreditation institutions. (pp. 2–3)

Effective communication, problem-solving capabilities and multidisciplinarity are often demanded by professional bodies and employers and have now become embedded in higher education's discourses around learning outcomes and graduate attributes. The dilemma, then, is how to fit instruction around the development of these into curricula already packed with predefined and rigidly evaluated disciplinary content. This problem has led to a realisation and methodological shift:

> Since video lectures are as effective as in-person lectures at conveying basic information, the wisdom of using student and instructor time for live lectures is questionable. Rather, pre-recorded lectures can be assigned to students as homework, leaving class time open for interactive learning activities – activities that cannot be automated or computerized. This is the key concept behind what is becoming the new buzzword in educational circles: the flipped classroom. (p. 3)

The next section of this paper moves to examining the definitions of what a flipped classroom is in the light of the inside and outside activities. Drawing on the research to date on the flipping, it seems to adhere to student-centred approaches in the class-room, which are reconcilable with the educational theories of Piaget and Vygotsky in relation to constructivism, collaborative learning and scaffolding within the zone of proximal development (ZPD). Bishop and Verleger also outline relevant theories from the literature on learning styles; peer-assisted, collaborative and cooperative learning; PBL; and active learning. They do, however, reject very broad definitions which include reading as opposed to video viewing outside of the classroom.

The authors then relay the results from the research studies published to June 2012 on the flipped classroom as a methodological choice. They located twenty-four studies up to that time, for which they present a tabulated summary of context and findings. The main overall findings show that positive experiences are reported, with some caveats. The following provides an overview:

> Despite differences among studies, general reports of student perceptions were relatively consistent. Opinions tended to be positive, but there were invariably a few students who strongly disliked the change. Students did tend to watch the videos when assigned, and even when they were not. DeGrazia et al. (2012) notes that students supplied with optional video lectures came to class much better prepared than when they had been given textbook readings. This observation is encouraging because although learning gains are high for information presented textually, Sappington et al. (2002) shows that college students don't generally complete reading assignments. Nevertheless, upon recommendation by students, many instructors instituted a required pre-class quiz on the lecture material. This was touted as a highly successful practice. Students preferred live in-person lectures to video lectures, but also liked interactive class time more than in-person lectures (Toto and Nguyen 2009). Shorter, rather than longer videos were preferred (Zappe et al. 2009). (p. 9)

The paper finishes with a short section on future directions that research should take, which suggests more controlled studies examining student performance over a semester, and that future practices and studies leverage what the existing research tells us about out-of- and in-class activities. The authors also encourage researchers to describe clearly the activities they employ in their studies.

FURTHER READING TWO TASK

1. Based on what you have read and by viewing some flipped classroom materials on YouTube (for example, those produced by a colleagues of mine from civil engineering at the University of Limerick; Phillips and Quilligan 2014), what is your opinion about whether a flipped classroom approach would work for language teaching (or is the discipline irrelevant)? Justify your opinion on the basis of evidence from your experience, knowledge and research.
2. If a flipped classroom approach were to be used in your future teaching, what implications would this have for the lesson planning principles and processes detailed earlier in this chapter?

5.7 SUMMARY

The numerous aspects of preparing for teaching in the form of lesson planning have been detailed in this chapter. It begins by outlining the many reasons for planning lessons and the purposes that a written plan can serve. For novice teachers it has been described as a lifeline in their earlier days of teaching. Section 5.2 introduces a number of fundamental principles for planning and teaching, based on what we now know about good pedagogy. The section also discusses in some detail the concept of the classroom as a social and cultural environment, where the learners are the embodiment of all of these, represented appropriately in Spiro's onion model containing layers illustrating learner, family, school and national contexts. Holliday's concept of professional context also forms part of this broad discussion of preparing to write the lesson plan. His TESEP framework considers whether the teaching takes place in a BANA-type context or in primary, secondary or tertiary public education systems, and the various affordances and restrictions that these may bring. In addition to contextual variables, the content of the lesson is centrally important, and here the language and the topics feature equally, as the nature of this discipline means that language is both the medium and the product of teaching. In Section 5.3 a framework for writing the lesson plan is presented, consisting of the following: preliminary information; aims and learning outcomes; prior learning and anticipated problems; and a detailed procedure of the stages of the lesson. This section concludes with a brief list of practical and organisational steps to follow before you go to teach the prepared lesson. Emergent situations in the classroom which call for a deviation from the lesson plan might include students not understanding the activities or the content, or might manifest in the form of a positive learning opportunity leading to authentic language use. These are discussed in Section 5.4. More experienced teachers have developed strategies to negotiate these contexts successfully, but beginning teachers need to reflect on and prepare in advance for the potential of finding themselves in these situations, while at the same time accepting that not all things can be planned for and sometimes you need to be willing to 'go with the flow'. With effective critical reflection around such incidents you will develop successful strategies and approaches as you become a more experienced teacher.

5.8 ADDITIONAL READINGS

Abbitt, J. T. (2011) 'Measuring technological pedagogical content knowledge in preservice teacher education: A review of current methods and instruments', *Journal of Research on Technology in Education*, 43: 4, 281–300.

Harmer, J. (2007) *How to Teach English*, Harlow: Pearson.

Housner, L. D. and Griffey, D. C. (1985) 'Teacher cognition: Differences in planning and interactive decision making between experienced and inexperienced teachers', *Research Quarterly for Exercise and Sport*, 56: 1, 45–53.

Shulman, L. (1986) 'Those who understand: Knowledge growth in teaching', *Educational Researcher*, 15: 2, 4–14.

Spiro, J. (2013) *Changing Methodologies in TESOL*, Edinburgh: Edinburgh University Press.

6

IN THE CLASSROOM

ANGELA FARRELL

6.1 INTRODUCTION

Diversity and change are the key words that describe what practitioners face in the modern English language teaching profession, where we find different and unique environments and contexts in which the language is being learned, and traditional and new approaches to how it is taught (see Spiro 2013: 35–56 for a detailed discussion of different EFL/ESL learning cultures and contexts, and teaching approaches). With the shift in language teaching towards a more learner-centred approach, the role of the English language teacher has become more rewarding. However, contemporary communicative language teaching (CLT) and task-based language teaching (TBLT) methodologies have brought new challenges and demands, not least the requirement for high levels of peer interaction and target language use, which are considered essential for language learning to take place (Oxford 1997: 443). As a result, practitioners must develop the types of practical expertise in classroom management practices and professional language use which they may be unfamiliar with from their own previous learning experiences, if they are to create the kind of supportive environment in which learning can flourish. Against this backdrop of changing trends and needs, it is not surprising that for new teachers who lack experience and skills, the modern English language teaching classroom can be a daunting and unsettling environment, even for the most competent and confident users of the language.

Carter and Nunan point out that while language pedagogy is nowhere near developing an agreed-upon set of 'rules of the game', there is a rapidly growing knowledge base which student teachers can draw on to gain a more developed sense of professionalism (Carter and Nunan 2001: 5). Good TP today means that in addition to acquiring knowledge of linguistic and pedagogic theory, which is the hallmark of the language teacher's professionalism, you will need to develop insight and strategic competence in areas such as the psycholinguistic, psychological and socio-pragmatic dimensions of teaching and learning English, to cope with the new demands which have arisen in the classroom for teachers and learner alike. Throughout your professional career, it is possible that you will teach learners from backgrounds and cultures whose experiences, expectations and beliefs may differ fundamentally from your own (Jenkins 2007). How well you deal with this further challenge will depend on your ability to develop the type of intercultural sensitivity and strategic expertise that enables us, as practitioners, 'to move sensitively and intelligently from one cultural context to another' (Byram, cited in Spiro 2013: 191). Like professionals in other contexts and fields, teachers require and use a metalanguage to enable them to 'speak the same language'. This allows them to share and discuss ideas and concepts related to education, teaching and learning and classroom practice with colleagues, and in their practice. You will meet/revisit some of the concepts and terms which form part of the English language teacher's metalanguage in this chapter. To facilitate the discussion in this regard, a linked review and glossary are provided in Appendices 5A and 5B.

6.2   TEACHER IDENTITY AND TEACHING APPROACH

6.2.1   CONCEPTS, FINDINGS AND TEXTS

One of the greatest challenges facing teachers in their professional careers is the need to develop a teaching approach which takes account of the individual identity of the teacher, as well as meeting the needs of learners and professional standards. Brown observes that teaching approach, also commonly referred to as teaching style, is almost always consistent with personality style and, like personality, can vary greatly from individual to individual (Brown 1994: 74). It is also likely to be influenced by teaching method(s) and underlying beliefs and principles, whether conscious or not (Bell 2007: 140) (see Spiro 2013: 1–56 for a detailed discussion of teaching approaches, methods and roles). The teaching approach/style we develop is important as it impacts on the rapport we establish with learners, the levels and types of interaction which occur between teachers and learners and amongst peers, and teacher and learner roles; it also sets the classroom climate (Brown 2001: 202–4). As English language professionals embarking on careers in the post-methods era (Kumaradivelu 2006), you are encouraged to adopt an 'enlightened eclectic approach' (Brown 1994: 74). This means gaining a critical knowledge of different methods and techniques, and learning how and when to use them effectively and appropriately to create an optimal learning environment, while remaining sensitive to the culture in which learning is taking place and the culture of those you teach.

Assuming a confident teacher identity
Teaching has traditionally been viewed as a profession characterised by the individual nature of the work and a lack of a shared professional identity (Lortie 1975). However, more recently, there has been a shift towards teachers working collaboratively to create professional learning communities based on shared values and beliefs (Farr and Riordan 2015, Vásquez 2011). Research in the field of education (Mitchell 1997) indicates that how teachers represent themselves in the classroom in terms of their appearance and image, their professional training and qualifications, and the levels of dedication they bring to their work are all strong markers of teacher identity, with perceptions and practices in these areas likely to be influenced by social, cultural and individual orientations towards professionalism. Mitchell's study of teachers' attitudes towards professional identity and role, undertaken in the US secondary school context, found that practitioners were concerned with communicating appropriate levels of familiarity and respect within the teacher–student relationship and demon-

strating the importance of education through appropriate dress, modes of speech and the modelling of a positive and productive lifestyle (1997: 6–7). A trend observed in the findings was that older and more experienced teachers were often strongly critical of colleagues, often younger, who did not place the same value on their appearance and classroom discipline as they did, as in '[A] lot of those [younger teachers] don't seem to know how to dress . . . [T]hey wear just about anything and everything into the classroom' and '[Younger teachers] don't know how to discipline students. It's always been my understanding that as teacher, you were the role model' (Mitchell 1997: 7).

Many teacher educators have observed that new teachers can find it difficult to reconcile the perceived split between themselves as 'teachers' and themselves as 'persons', which can lead to anxiety and uncertainty about aspects of their teacher identity and role, in such areas as self-image, assuming a position of authority,, and their ability to build rapport with those they teach (see, for example, Gatbonton 2008, Rodgers and Raider-Roth 2006, Vásquez 2011). A challenge facing all teachers is the need to maintain their professional standing in the eyes of learners, colleagues and employers, which means being aware of institutional expectations as to behaviour and personal appearance. Brown advises English language teachers to be aware of, and respect, the values of the cultures in which they teach in areas such as appearance, proxemics (distance) and touching (for example, a friendly pat on the shoulder or arm) which may vary from one socio-cultural setting to another; otherwise they may risk embarrassing and offending learners, and losing their respect (2001: 195). I have also heard anecdotal accounts of learners criticising the tendencies of some teachers to drink tea in the classroom while teaching, or to sit informally on the teacher's desk swinging their legs. In all of these cases, this type of behaviour or body positioning was considered to diminish the authority of the teacher in the eyes of learners.

Developing a confident teacher presence

A key factor involved in our developing sense of professional identity is our *teacher presence*. This is a central concept in a person-centred view of teaching and is defined by Rodgers and Raider-Roth (2006: 265) as 'a state of alert awareness, receptivity, and connectedness to the mental, emotional, and physical workings of both the individual and the group in the context of their learning environments, and the ability to respond with a considered and compassionate next best step'. In this sense, it involves practitioners developing two types of awareness in relation to their role: the first is being fully aware of what is happening in the classroom, and the second involves awareness of the ways in which a teacher's behaviour and actions can influence the classroom climate and relationships. Developing a strong teacher presence helps us create a positive and dynamic learning climate. It also enables us to focus on and include all our students to ensure that everyone in the classroom is following the progression of the lesson, rather than becoming confused or disengaged. For teachers to be 'present', they must have a deep understanding of the subject matter and learners, and a repertoire of pedagogic skills (Rodgers and Raider-Roth 2006: 279). Although vital, and widely acknowledged to be so, teaching presence is not often explicitly taught in teacher education programmes (Garrison and Rud 1995).

Table 6.1   Strategies to establish good teacher presence (adapted from Brown 2001: 196–200)

Using students' names to establish good classroom rapport and better control of interaction
Being pleasant, respectful and upbeat in mood, which is vital in every lesson
Attentive monitoring; this involves moving discreetly around the room and really listening to what students are saying
Clear diction to aid comprehension; avoid mumbling
Good voice projection so that the person sitting farthest away can hear clearly
Using body language and facial expressions to enhance meanings; this is particularly important with younger learners and students at lower proficiency levels
Central positioning so all can see you when you are giving important information
Frequent eye contact with all students in the class
Confident posture; avoid folding arms across body as it can appear defensive

New teachers from all backgrounds are often preoccupied with issues and concerns relating to classroom management and their perceived lack of knowledge (Nunan 1992a). Medgyes reminds us that pedagogical knowledge is accumulated over years of practice, and therefore it is not surprising for anxiety and a lack of confidence to be felt by any beginning teacher, whether native or non-native (1984: 318). Difficulties in establishing good control can sometimes arise when inexperienced teachers feel uncomfortable with their position of authority, especially in situations where they find themselves teaching learners who are similar in age, or older. As a result, these teachers can find it a challenge to project a confident teacher presence with particular learner groups, which in turn impacts on their ability to give effective instructions and deal efficiently with classroom procedures. Where learners lack confidence in a teacher's competencies and skills, they may lose interest or become resentful, which can put a further strain on teacher–student relationships and hamper the progress of the lesson. To maintain effective classroom management practices and good rapport with those we teach, practitioners need to become familiar with and draw on a wide range of strategies, such as those listed in Table 6.1.

Developing an informed and flexible teaching approach

The shift in language teaching towards learner-centred approaches means that there is now a stronger emphasis on the views of learners themselves (Garrett and Shortall 2002). It is of paramount importance, therefore, that as teachers we investigate the ways in which the expectations, beliefs and preferences of learners may differ from our own, so that we can develop suitable pedagogic responses. The differences between western, non-directive language TPs and more traditional, authoritarian approaches have been well documented in the research literature in SLA and educational sociolinguistics (see, for example, Butler 2004, Holliday 2005).

Given the fundamentally different orientations towards teaching and learning which prevail in different learning cultures, it is not uncommon for conflicts and misunderstandings to arise in the classroom in areas such as teacher and student roles, interactional patterns, and learning focus and goals. Studies have shown that students who are used to seeing the teacher as a figure of maximum authority, expected to control not only what learners do at every moment of the lesson but also when they speak and the types of language they use, can find less directive, socially oriented lessons based on student–student interaction unfamiliar and confusing (Horwitz et al. 1986). This may lead to reluctance on their part to participate in peer and group tasks. Where teachers lack intercultural sensitivities, their silence can be mistakenly interpreted as boredom or indifference, as is illustrated in the following classroom experience from Diana, assistant director of EFL studies in a private school in Perth, Australia:

> We have lots of Chinese learners and I used to find it hard getting them to join in tasks. I just thought they found my lessons boring or were not that interested in learning English. Then I met an ex-student who told me he had found my lessons really interesting. When I asked him why he didn't speak in class he said that Chinese students were just not used to airing their views in public. They preferred being allowed to sit in the group, listen and quietly reflect on what they were hearing, which fascinated them. I was more tolerant of their silence after that.

Pennington draws attention to the importance for teachers of tolerance towards a variety of perspectives on teaching (1990: 134–5). Meanwhile, linguists concerned with the socio-cultural dimensions of teaching and learning a second or foreign language remind us to be careful not to interpret what is happening in the classroom solely on the basis of our own stereotypical cultural views, as what we think is happening may be quite different to what is actually happening (Byram 1997, Kramsch 1998). O'Neill points out that the value of student-centred activities depends in part on the students' judgements of the learning benefits and on their preferences, and that therefore we should actively explore their perspectives and try to take account of them where possible; otherwise we risk alienating those we teach (O'Neill 1991: 293–304). By being better informed in relation to learners' expectations and opinions, and adopting a more open and flexible teaching approach, we can learn to anticipate and resolve issues of potential conflict in order to maintain positive classroom relationships, while at the same time ensuring that important learning goals are met. This requires being seen to take account of learners' views and making sure they are made fully aware of the *purpose* of pedagogic tasks, so they can appreciate their value in terms of the learners' own learning requirements.

TASK 6.1   TEACHER REPRESENTATION

A.   Read the following accounts in which teachers, students and an employer provide snapshots of the practices and protocols for English language teachers in different institutional contexts and socio-cultural settings, in relation to appearance and conduct:

1. Director of language school in Ireland
We ask teachers to bear in mind the expectations of international students in relation to classroom appearance and professional conduct, and to dress and behave conservatively.

2. Liam: 29 years old, EFL teacher in private language academy in Seoul, Korea
When I got the job, I was asked to buy a suit as I'd be teaching English to adults from professional backgrounds. I was glad they told me as I'd have turned up dressed casually and I would have felt embarrassed.

3. Tao: 31 years old; EFL student from China studying in Ireland
In China, when the teacher is well-dressed, we believe they are qualified teacher and we are happy they teach us. Teachers must have dignity and students must have respect.

4. Marie: 26 years old, ESL teacher in state secondary school in Ireland
I was actually surprised by how smartly dressed the teachers in my school are and how seriously everyone takes the discipline and rules. I mean we're nice to the kids but everything has to be done by the book. In a way it makes our lives easier as there are systems in place for everything and there's a lot of respect for the teachers. We're committed, too.

5. Alice: EFL teacher in a private secondary school in Abu Dhabi, United Arab Emirates
I work in a Muslim country so we're expected to dress and behave 'with modesty'. That means wearing long skirts and dresses and covering our arms and legs. Foreign women don't have to wear the veil. Male teachers are also expected to look respectable with long trousers and shirts. Outside the classroom you have to be mindful of the customs and try not to attract attention. It's something you get used to. I actually love teaching here.

B. Design and carry out an attitudinal survey among three teachers you know from different teaching backgrounds to investigate their views as to how teachers should look and behave in the classroom, and the reasons. Use Appendix 6 to guide you, and to note the findings.
C. What is the influence, if any, of age, culture and institutional context on the findings?
D. Compare the opinions from your survey with the views expressed earlier, and in Mitchell's (1997) survey. In what ways are they similar or different?
E. With a colleague from a different cultural background, discuss the extent to which teachers are role models for their learners.

TASK 6.2   TEACHER PRESENCE

A.   In the following accounts, two student teachers discuss some of the difficulties
     they experienced trying to establish a confident teacher presence. Read their
     accounts, and answer the following questions:
     1.   What types of difficulties were experienced in each case, and why?
     2.   How did it impact on the learning environment?
     3.   Which pedagogic strategies from Table 6.1 would help address these types of
          issues?

Classroom experience 1: Connor, 22 years old, teaching adult EFL students
I was really nervous about teaching the advanced class as I knew they knew a lot
more than I did about grammar so I just rushed through the lesson plan in case
they asked questions. That meant I wasn't able to develop a rapport with learners
the way the other student teachers did. The atmosphere was really tense and I felt
like they were waiting for me to make a mistake. I don't know who felt worse, me
or them.

Classroom experience 2: Anna, 24 years old, teaching adult EFL students
I'm quite small and I speak quietly so I couldn't get the students' attention or stop
them talking which meant I ended up giving instructions over and over again
and they kept getting confused. I used to just stand there feeling stupid. I knew I
needed to feel more confident, more like I was the teacher.

B.   Compare your suggestions with the strategies the student teachers later intro-
     duced (see Appendix 7).
C.   Think back to a teacher you remember who had good teaching presence and try
     to remember how it influenced your learning experience.
D.   Write down some concerns you may have in terms of establishing a confident
     teaching presence.
E.   Which strategies from Table 6.1 could you introduce into your teaching to help
     address these issues?

TASK 6.3   TEACHING APPROACH

A.   Read the following account in which a teacher makes some mistaken assump-
     tions which lead to her teaching approach being strongly criticised by her
     students:

*Classroom experience 3: Mary, 46 years old, teaching EFL in a private language
school in London*
I was teaching university students from Korea. We had a great rapport and used
to chat a lot. They had poor fluency so I got colleagues to bring other student
groups into my class so they could discuss different topics using questionnaires
and survey type tasks I had designed. Meanwhile, I kept a discreet distance when

they were talking so not to inhibit them. They seemed really happy so I was shocked when I read what was written on the end of course teaching evaluation surveys.

B.   In what ways do you think the teaching approach failed to meet the expectations of the learners?
     This is what the students wrote: 'teacher did nothing', 'we learned nothing'.
C.   How would you feel if a group disapproved of your teaching approach?
D.   What future advice would you give to this teacher?
E.   Compare the previous account with the following classroom encounter in which a potential clash between learner preferences and teaching focus is successfully averted due to the open and flexible teaching approach adopted by the teacher, which allowed for negotiation and shared decision-making.

Context: Multicultural EFL class in third-level setting in Ireland
Teacher: So as the essay on the Harry Potter novel is due in next week it might be useful for you to discuss it today in small groups.
Student (Jorge): I prefer you give the points for the essay and we do at home.
Teacher: Well, in the course outline it says you write it individually and get an individual grade but it might be useful to brainstorm areas you are unsure about or need to do some work on now. Are you enjoying reading the novel, Jorge?
Student (Jorge): I read before in Spanish.
Teacher: That's great because this time you can focus more on the language. Do you think it would be useful to discuss it Jorge?
Student (Jorge): (silence)
Teacher: OK. will we ask the others about what they prefer so we can decide as a class?
Student (Jorge): Maybe.
Teacher: Why don't you all take a few minutes in pairs to talk about how you want to do this and then we can brainstorm areas you feel you need to focus on, OK? So will we say five minutes and then we'll decide. Are you happy with that, Jorge?
Student (Jorge): No problem.

Now, read Garrett and Shortall (2002), available at: http://ltr.sagepub.com/content/6/1/25. Note the following points:

•   The benefits of pair and group work, according to earlier studies
•   Learners' views in this regard as documented more recently
•   Recommendations made to enable teachers to reconcile misunderstandings and conflicts in this area successfully.

6.3 CLASSROOM ENVIRONMENT AND RELATIONSHIPS

6.3.1 CONCEPTS, FINDINGS AND TEXTS

The affective dimensions of classroom teaching and learning, including the relationships between students and teachers, the quality of learning experiences and the psychological state of the teacher and learner, have been attracting increasing research attention amongst educators since the emergence of humanistic learning philosophies in the 1970s ('affective education is effective education'; Moskowitz 1978: 14). Within SLA, this has led to a shift away from analyses of classroom processes based only on the 'observable' factors, such as teacher language input and interactional language use, towards studies which explore the 'unobservables', such as the influence of teacher and learner beliefs, attitudes, motivation, learning styles and cultural norms, and the psychological challenges involved in learning and teaching a second or foreign language (Tsui 1995: 121).

As far as the psychological difficulties for language learners are concerned, the well-known model of language acquisition proposed by Krashen suggests the notion of the *affective filter*, which acts as a psychological block to learning when learners feel stressed or anxious (1985: 3). By contrast, when students feel confident and at ease, the filter is low and they are more likely to acquire the language (see Spiro 2013: 11–16 for a detailed discussion of hypotheses and theories of SLA). The belief that stress can impact negatively on learner progress is now a commonly held one in the field of SLA. Studies which have investigated this area have revealed that it is not uncommon for learners to face debilitating insecurities and anxieties about their learning (Horwitz et al. 1986). For instance, research undertaken in ESL-type contexts in mainstream education, in parts of the world where the learning of English typically takes place in monocultural groups with non-native speaker teachers, suggests that pupils often dread being asked questions, or are reluctant to speak English in front of their peers due to inhibitions and fear of derision and making mistakes (Shamin 1996, Tsui 1996). As a result, they can become disengaged from the process, and even disruptive. These types of psychological difficulties have also been observed in multicultural classroom settings in many English-speaking countries, and are thought to be exacerbated in these contexts by cultural differences which lead to a greater potential for misunderstanding and conflict (Walsh 2006).

As a result of the insights gained from research in this area, making student teachers aware of the underlying psychological dimensions of teaching and learning has become an important area of focus in language teacher education (Tsui 1995). The aim here is to enable teachers to develop good interpersonal skills so that more positive and less stressful learning experiences can be promoted. For this to be achieved, teachers must acquire a high level of pragmatic expertise across both social and linguistic dimensions, so that they can deal efficiently and appropriately with sensitive pedagogic areas where issues of power and face are involved, such as when asking students questions, checking understanding and correcting errors (N. Murray 2010, Walsh 2011). By developing a range of face-saving strategies which they can draw on in these situations, teachers ensure that positive social relationships and communication practices are maintained while still attending to important pedagogic goals, such as promoting a high level and quality of learner participation and engagement in the lesson. This type of socio-pragmatic expertise also helps practitioners to become better prepared psychologically for their role in the classroom in terms of attending to their own face needs, and learning to become more confident and comfortable with their position of authority.

Encouraging learner response and participation

Promoting learner participation and engagement in the classroom to encourage a high level and quality of target language use is considered vital for language learning to take place, from a CLT viewpoint (Swain 1985). This leads teachers to employ a range of questioning techniques and strategies to elicit students' answers, opinions and questions. However, getting students to respond to questions can be a major problem. Research has shown that when faced with reticent students, teachers feel uneasy with the silence, and rush in to answer the question themselves (White and Lightbown 1984: 229). The phenomenon of a very short wait time after questions is also common in language learning classrooms as a result of institutional pressures to cover the syllabus and of teachers' fear that a longer wait time may lead to disruption. Tsui's research (1996) carried out in the secondary school context in Hong Kong suggests a further cause: the misconception amongst some teachers that effective teaching involves teachers talking all the time (see Further Reading One below). In the following classroom encounter we observe what happens when a teacher fails to give students sufficient wait time to process and develop their responses. As you read the transcript, notice the teacher's use of language, and its impact on the classroom climate:

Context 1: Adult EFL class, multilingual group, intermediate level
Teacher: So, what's the difference between the two tenses on the board? Alberto?
Students: (silence)
Teacher: Alberto?
Student (Alberto): (silence)
Teacher: Well? Paolo?
Student (Paolo): (silence)
Teacher: OK, Claire?
Student (Claire): Maybe the time? . . . I am not sure
Teacher: What about the rest of you? Do you understand?
Students: (silence)
Teacher: You're not getting this are you?
Students: (silence)

Even though we are not present, we can sense the mounting tension as the teacher becomes frustrated and impatient with the students' poor response. When we compare this incident to the following encounter in a similar EFL-type class context, we observe a teacher with considerable socio-pragmatic skill, who draws on a range of interactional strategies to achieve a higher level and quality of learner response and engagement. As you read, notice the teacher's polite and respectful language use, pleasant manner and easy rapport with the learners:

Context 2: Adult EFL class, multilingual group, intermediate level
Teacher: So we are going to do some work on grammar now. If you'd like to look at the slide there are some examples from the reading text. In each sentence there is a different structure. Take a few minutes and try to work out what the structures are and talk to your partner. Will we say a few minutes? And then we can check together.
Teacher: (waits 2–3 minutes while students talk in pairs) We're going to check now so who would like to tell us their answer?
Student (Carlos): In the first . . . is past and the second is perfect . . . present perfect because there is auxiliary verb 'have' so 'have been' but for the first there is only 'saw'.
Teacher: Exactly, well done. Did you all hear? Do you all agree with what Carlos said?
Students: Yes
Teacher: OK, to make sure, go through the explanation again in your own words with your partner and I'll come around in case anyone has a question before we move on just to check everyone understands it. OK?
Students: (students repeat the answer in their own words)
Teacher: Now are there any questions about these verbs before we talk about the different meaning?
Student: Why it is 'have been' and not 'have gone' for the first?
Teacher: That is actually a very good question so I'm glad you asked.

We will return to explore some of the strategies used by the teacher in this excerpt in Task 6.4, given their importance for good teaching and communication practices in the classroom.

Validating learners' responses

To facilitate the construction of genuine learning experiences, students must feel their ideas and opinions are valued and respected. Belenky et al. (1986) highlight the importance for teachers of the capacity to connect with their students, at the heart of which is trust. We bring this notion to the classroom by responding with interest to learners' answers and contributions and remembering to acknowledge the effort made, even if the answer is not the desired one, and to do so without sounding totally unnatural or patronising. A further point which has been raised by linguists who seek to promote critical English language pedagogy is that teachers must be careful to avoid imposing their own worldviews on those they teach (see, for example, Kumaradivelu 1999). This kind of problem can arise when teachers lack awareness of the assumptions and beliefs they carry into the classroom and of the impact of their actions, and it can be exacerbated by the poor intercultural sensitivities, as occurs in the following classroom incidents:

Context 3: Multicultural EFL class with adult learners
Teacher: So what did you do in Dublin?
Student: We visited the Trinity College and the Book of Kells.
Teacher: OK but you went for the craic* too . . . you know the pubs . . .
Guinness?
Student: No alcohol . . . he is Muslim.
(*Craic* means fun in Gaelic.)

Context 4: Multicultural EFL class with adult learners
Teacher: I want you to think about some of the biggest problems facing the
world today.
Student: Maybe the globalisation?
Teacher: Seriously? I would have said world poverty was worse than that.

Spiro, amongst others (for example, Kramsch 1995), stresses the importance of language teachers' developing their own social, pragmatic and intercultural knowledge
and expertise as global citizens 'to be able to live and work comfortably beyond the
comfort zone of the familiar' (2013: 192).

Dealing efficiently and sensitively with errors

The ability to manage errors efficiently while at the same time attending to the face
needs of learners (Brown and Levinson 1987) is a vital pedagogic skill which takes
time to perfect. Correcting every language error made in the lesson is both unrealistic and undesirable in terms of the time it would take and the impact it may have on
learner confidence and willingness to take risks. For these reasons and others, teachers differentiate between important errors that need immediate attention, and those
which can be dealt with at another time, or ignored. Listed in Table 6.2 are a number
of strategies that teachers can use to manage errors. However, there are important
issues and considerations surrounding error correction which teachers need to be
aware of if they are to attend to errors efficiently and sensitively. The types of knowledge and expertise you will need to develop in this area will be further investigated
in Task 6.5.

Dealing with difficult students

There will be times in your professional career when you will encounter difficult
students, and have to deal with discipline problems over and above the general management of the classroom. This can be stressful and challenge your professionalism.
To maintain good classroom control and the respect of your students, it is essential
that these types of problems are dealt with efficiently and appropriately. The types of
difficulties and issues which can occur are listed in Table 6.3, and further investigated
in Task 6.5.

The extent to which you can expect to meet these types of problems will depend
on factors such as learner age (children and young teenagers can be more difficult
than adults); motivation (whether the students are willing learners or are obliged to
be in class); size of class (the larger the class, the more difficult to maintain control);

Table 6.2   Strategies for error management

Strategy	Example of use
1. Provide opportunity for learner to self-correct and guide them	
2. Get student to repeat corrected version	
3. Reformulation (repeating correctly in a natural way)	
4. Correct immediately	
5. Note error for later pedagogic focus with learner/class	
6. Write correct version on a piece of paper and discreetly pass to student	
7. Elicit peer correction (with tact and sensitivity)	

Table 6.3   Discipline problems and suitable responses (adapted from Gower et al. 2005)

Problem	Suitable pedagogic response
1. Students who are unwilling to participate in tasks and activities	
2. Students who refuse to work with other students	
3. Students who are attention seeking and over-dominant	
4. Students who refuse to do homework	
5. Students who are persistently late	
6. Students who are disrespectful towards you or other students	
7. Students who cheat in tests	
8. Students who attend erratically	

atmosphere and ethos of the institution, in terms of rules and degree of strictness; and learner respect for teachers in general, and for you as a teacher in particular (Gower et al. 2005). This is an important aspect of classroom management which will be explored in more depth in Task 6.6 and Appendix 8, where possible pedagogic solutions to these problems are listed.

TASK 6.4   ENCOURAGING LEARNER RESPONSE AND PARTICIPATION

The left-hand column of Table 6.4 lists some of the strategies used by the teacher in the classroom incident in Context 2 above to achieve a higher level and quality of response and participation from the learners. These are important classroom techniques which you should introduce into your own teaching, in addition to developing socio-pragmatic sensitivities and expertise in relation to your social and organisational language use in the classroom. For this task, re-read the classroom

Table 6.4 Strategies to encourage learner participation and response to questioning (adapted from Brown 2001: 169–73)

Strategy	Example of use
1. Giving students plenty of wait time to process and work out their answers	
2. Eliciting learners' ideas and opinions	
3. Encouraging students to discuss and check their answers in pairs to reduce stress and gives opportunities for target language use	
3. Validating the student's response	
4. Creating opportunities for learner questions	
5. Encouraging students to ask questions	
6. Checking comprehension	

encounter to identify an example of each strategy listed, and complete the right-hand column of Table 6.4.

TASK 6.5 SPOKEN ERROR MANAGEMENT

A. To raise awareness of the causes of errors, the different types, and the issues and considerations involved in their effective management, read Gower et al. (2005), which provides valuable information in these areas. Following this, complete the right-hand column of Table 6.3 above, with details of the pedagogic considerations and learning value of each of the strategies listed.

B. Now watch a teaching video online (at http:www.teflvideos.com) and identify the types of errors made by learners, the ways in which they are dealt with by the teacher, and the extent to which you think effective error management is achieved.

C. With a colleague, discuss any concerns you may have about correcting errors, and the strategies that you intend to introduce into your own teaching to try to deal with errors more efficiently and sensitively.

TASK 6.6 DEALING WITH DISCIPLINE PROBLEMS

A. Listed in Appendix 8 are some options available to teachers to deal with the types of discipline problems which were outlined in Table 6.3 above. Read the options there and match each to one of the discipline problems listed in Table 6.2. Then think about situations where you may have witnessed or experienced the use of these strategies by teachers to deal with discipline problems in the classroom.

B. Design a survey in which you ask three colleagues from different cultural backgrounds to select a suitable responses or responses for each of the discipline problems listed in Table 6.3 above, from the options provided in Appendix 8.

C.   Compare and contrast their views. What, if anything, has surprised you about their opinions? To what extent do you share their views?

D.   Think of a specific discipline problem you witnessed as a learner. To what extent was it dealt with efficiently and appropriately by the teacher? How would you respond if you were faced with a similar problem in the classroom today?

6.4   TARGET LANGUAGE USE AND COMMUNICATION PRACTICES

6.4.1   CONCEPTS, FINDINGS AND TEXTS

The ability to teach English effectively through the medium of English is a crucial skill and requirement for English language teachers, especially in contexts and settings where English is taught for communicative purposes (Oxford 1997). Difficulties in relation to target language use can arise for teachers from all backgrounds, native and non-native speaker alike. For instance, native speaker teachers typically struggle to pitch the target language correctly, according to the language proficiency level of different learner groups. They may also lack awareness of issues relating to the intelligibility and 'appropriacy' of different varieties, registers and styles of language use. As a result, they fail to modify their speech in ways which scaffold target language use to make it more accessible or acceptable for classroom use (Tsui 1995, Walsh 2006). For non-native speakers different challenges arise, such as acquiring the required competence in English and the ability to sustain its use with confidence throughout the lesson (Copland et al. 2013). This is notwithstanding the superior knowledge of the target language system which many non-native speaker teachers typically gain through studying it formally over many years. It is not uncommon, therefore, for new teachers to struggle with different aspects of their own target language performance in the classroom and feel a lack of confidence in this regard (Walsh 2006).

Part of the knowledge base that language teachers need to acquire is concerned with the psycholinguistic processes involved in the acquisition of language, such as the order, speed and rhythm at which acquisition develops and how the pace of learning may differ from one learner to another. This type of competence helps practitioners to identify the linguistic needs of learners, and to adjust their teaching accordingly. For instance, practitioners can learn to select language content which is appropriate as target language input for learners at different proficiency levels, and modify their teacher talk accordingly. This provides student teachers with opportunities to become familiar with the types of strategic expertise which teachers typically gain through classroom practice, and also gives them insight into the range of interactional strategies through which they can learn to tailor their target language use systematically to suit different learner groups and different classroom microcontexts; for instance, the effective use of repetition, comprehension checks, and the avoidance of imprecise, ambiguous and overly informal registers (Walsh 2006, 2011). This is of particular importance when asking questions and giving instructions, which are key functions where the careful framing of language use is essential (Long and Sato 1983, Tsui 1995). In these ways, teachers can ensure that the target language is used in more meaningful and effective ways to reinforce understanding.

A further important consideration in relation to teacher talk is the suitability of the language that teachers use with learners as a target language model (Jenkins 2007). Providing learners with exposure to authentic language use is vital for communicative language learning purposes; however, the benefits must be weighed against factors such as the degree of intelligibility of the language for the learner(s) involved, and its perceived 'appropriacy' for classroom use (Carter and McCarthy 2006, Prodromou 1992, 2003, 2008). Native speaker teachers often lack awareness of the difficulties that foreign language learners experience in understanding colloquial English. This type of language features idiomatic expressions, slang and non-mainstream grammar which students are unfamiliar with, and where the meanings are often culturally rooted and therefore difficult to decipher (Carter and McCarthy 2006: 82–91). A further related issue which arises in relation to teacher talk is the acceptability of the use of non-mainstream structures and lexis by English language teachers, given that this type of language has traditionally been excluded from the language learning classroom on prescriptive grounds. While attitudes in this regard are subject to change, as a growing number of linguists reject the prevailing native speaker standard English status quo in favour of an alternative model, this issue remains controversial (Jenkins 2007).

Giving effective instructions

Giving clear and precise instructions is essential for effective classroom management, especially when the target language is used as the main means of classroom instruction (Walsh 2001, 2006). To establish good control and avoid confusing students, a firm, directive manner is necessary; however, teachers must also remain polite or they risk offending learners. Achieving the correct balance can be difficult for teachers who lack confidence in their authority, or may be unaware of the socio-pragmatic dimensions underlying language use in the classroom (N. Murray 2010). Socio-pragmatic knowledge involves an understanding of social and cultural norms and practices in areas such as politeness, levels of formality/informality and power relationships, and being able to make suitable choices in terms of the types of language we use in different social, cultural and professional contexts, and with different people (Lakoff 1973). Giving teachers opportunities to gain awareness and expertise in this area by exploring and discussing real classroom experiences and data is important if we are to develop good communication and management practices in the classroom (Walsh 2006, 2011).

TASK 6.7   THE LANGUAGE OF INSTRUCTIONS

A.   For awareness-raising purposes, analyse the language used by the teacher in the following excerpts, and decide whether you think the correct balance between giving clear direction and politeness has been achieved, taking into account the contextual information provided. Rewrite any instructions you feel are imprecise or inappropriate, to make them more suitable:

Context 1: Multilingual EFL class' adults' intermediate level
Micro-context: The teacher wants to set up a group work task in which the

students will discuss any fears and phobias they may have, as a lead-in to a reading exercise based on this theme.
Teacher: OK, so guys feel free to have a chat about it for a few minutes.
Student: We talk together?
Teacher: Yeah, if you like.

Context 2: Multilingual EFL class, adults, intermediate level
Micro-context: The teacher wants the students to compare their answers to a grammar exercise with a new partner.
Teacher: Listen up now. I want you to move to a different place and compare your answers. Now, off you go . . . is there a problem?
Student: I prefer to stay . . . I am tired.
Teacher: You'll live.
Student: (silence)

Context 3: Multilingual EFL class, adults, intermediate level
Micro-context: The teacher wants to end a group speaking task to elicit feedback.
Teacher: OK everyone, that's great, but we need to stop talking now so we can make sure everyone hears the different opinions. Is that OK, everyone? Are we all ready, as the group over here is going to start . . . OK, Jacinta?
Student: Sorry, I don't hear.
Teacher: That's OK; we're listening to this group so we need to focus, OK?

TASK 6.8   PEDAGOGIC STRATEGIES FOR INSTRUCTIONS

Having become more aware of the type of language teachers need to use to give instructions in a suitably authoritative and respectful manner, we can proceed to investigate the range of pedagogic strategies that teachers should draw on in their teaching to ensure that instructions are effective.

For this purpose, read Gower et al. (2005), and in the right-hand column of Table 6.5 add important details and the rationale for each of the strategies listed there.

TASK 6.9   INTELLIGIBILITY AND 'APPROPRIACY' OF TEACHER TALK

A.   To explore some of the critical dimensions of teacher talk, analyse the examples in Table 6.6 of classroom discourse from EFL classes at intermediate proficiency level, and pick out any aspects of grammatical and lexical usage by the teacher which you consider to be unacceptable because of lack of intelligibility and/or lack of 'appropriacy'.

B.   Decide where modifications need to be made to teacher talk, if at all, and write them in the right-hand column of Table 6.6.

C.   Now check the online version of Carter and McCarthy (2006), available at www.cambridge.org/elt/cdrom, to see how the grammatical items in Table 6.6 are categorised and evaluated by these authors, in terms of mainstream/non-mainstream and formal/informal usage, and of their pedagogic acceptability.

Table 6.5   Strategies for effective instructions (adapted from Gower et al. 2005)

Strategies	Details and rationale
1. Making sure you have the attention of all students and they can hear you	
2. Using a lower level of language than the language being taught	
3. Avoiding overly informal and imprecise language (e.g. 'feel free to . . .')	
4. Being careful not to treat adults like children (e.g. 'off you go')	
5. Giving the instruction in stages, as and when required	
6. Providing visual support such as gestures, pictures and object	
7. Being consistent	
8. Checking students have understood by asking them to re-tell the instruction to peers	
9. Giving a demonstration of what has to be done	

Table 6.6   Evaluating teacher classroom discourse

Teacher talk	Modifications (if required)
1. I know it's hard to concentrate on a Friday afternoon as you're all wrecked . . . I might be able to let you off early . . . just don't let on.	
2. Was the listening OK or were you thrown off by the accent? Will I play it again?	
3. When you're done you can move on to the grammar exercise in the box.	
4. Are you heading off anywhere nice this weekend? I'm going to a stag in Carlow.	
5. Well lads, you've been brilliant . . . I'll probably hit into you around the campus next semester if you're staying on.	
6. How long are you living in Limerick?	
7. The place is still a bit of a kip . . . but they've done it up by the river . . . have you been down there?	
8. We need to wrap it up now as some of you have oral exams today.	

D. Do likewise for the lexical items in the *English COBUILD Dictionary* online, available at dictionary.reverso.net/English-cobuild.

E. What have you learned from this research task that you can apply to your own classroom teaching in relation to your own classroom language use?

6.5 FURTHER READING ONE

Tsui, A. B. M. (1996) 'Reticence and anxiety in second language learning', in Bailey, K. M. and Nunan, D. (eds), *Voices from the Language Classroom*, Cambridge: Cambridge University Press, 145–67.
This is an insightful account of research which has important findings for our TPs. It describes a study undertaken by the author, Amy Tsui, to investigate the problem of student reticence in the context of mainstream secondary schooling in Hong Kong. We noted in our earlier discussion (see Section 6.3) that many teachers experience difficulties getting students to respond to their questions, and consider this a major pedagogic challenge. Tsui's study explored teachers' perceptions of the causes of this problem, and the effectiveness of the classroom strategies they drew up and employed to try to encourage the pupils they teach to respond more fully to their questions. After outlining the aims and methodology of the study, the author explains the rationale for her research, situating it in the field of SLA, and in relation to previous related studies. Earlier accounts by Chaudron (1988) and the author herself (1985) suggest that while student reticence is a common problem in many school settings, it is particularly acute amongst Asian learners, who are generally more reserved and less willing to contribute than their western counterparts. Tsui then highlights the pedagogic significance of this problem:

> Although one should avoid making the sweeping generalization that talking equals learning (see Allwright 1980), and forcing students to participate when they are not ready (see Allwright and Bailey 1991: 144), one cannot deny that participation is very important in language learning. When students produce the language that they are studying, they are testing out the hypotheses which they have formed about the language. When they respond to the teacher's or other students' questions, raise queries, and give comments they are actively involved in the negotiation of comprehensible input and the formulation of comprehensible output (Swain 1985) which are essential to language acquisition. From a pedagogical point of view, contributions from students, as pointed out by Katz, help to create the content of the lesson. (p. 146)

Tsui's study revealed that 70 per cent of the participating teachers identified student reticence as one of their greatest classroom challenges. This research is important, therefore, because it investigates a very real pedagogic problem which impacts negatively on the everyday practices of many teachers and on the progress of learners, and diminishes the quality of the teaching and learning experience. The teachers identified five causes for student reticence: low English proficiency, fear of mistakes and derision, teachers' intolerance of silence, uneven allocation of turns and incomprehensible input. The types of strategies the teachers devised and implemented to try to address this problem included: lengthening wait time, improving questioning technique by modifying speech, accepting a variety of answers, peer support and group work, focusing on content, and establishing good relationships. As far their effectiveness is concerned, some were more successful than others, and a few were found to have little or no impact. Lengthening the wait time did not always have the desired effect, and at times embarrassed students, further leading the teachers to conclude that insensitive lengthening of wait time can exacerbate the anxiety rather than alleviate it. Modifying questioning to include more referential and open-ended answers also largely failed to generate better responses. However, allowing students to prepare and write down their answers first was seen to be more effective. Additional strategies considered to be effective were teachers being flexible in accepting variations in students' answers, and giving student opportunities to check their answers with their peers. Introducing activities which focused students on content rather than form also seemed to motivate students and generate a higher quality of response, as did involving them in discussions about their feelings to build greater trust. The author concludes the study by advising us to be realistic and not expect to be able to solve this problem overnight. However, teachers should persevere, given the importance of making language learning a more enjoyable experience for learners.

FURTHER READING ONE TASK

1. *Learner needs*
In what ways has reading this article helped you to become better informed about the needs of learners?
Observe an EFL class to investigate the behaviour of the teacher and the learners in relation to the types of psychological and pedagogic issues raised in the above research by Tsui (1996).
Use the reading as the basis for a discussion about this problem with the teacher involved, in relation to the lesson you observed (see Chapter 4 on observations).

2. *Learner attitudes*
Design and carry out a study of *learners'* attitudes towards the causes of student reticence, amongst EFL/ESL students from different learning backgrounds, to explore similarities and differences in opinion.
Compare your findings with the conclusions reached in Tsui's research.
Write up your research in report style, including the following areas: background, rationale, aims, methodology and findings. Give the research report to three colleagues to read and discuss with you.

6.6   FURTHER READING TWO

Copland, F., Garton, S. and Burns, A. (2013) 'Challenges in teaching English to young learners: Global perspectives and local realities', _TESOL Quarterly_, 28: 4, 738–62.

This article describes an important research project carried out by these researchers in 2011 to investigate some of the pressing challenges which have emerged in the teaching of English to young learners in different EFL/ESL contexts and settings worldwide, in line with the growth of English as a lingua franca. The study builds on previous accounts which have highlighted the unsuitability of imported, western-style CLT and TBLT approaches in many countries, due to large class sizes, a lack of resources, inadequate teacher training, and fundamental differences in educational ethos and 'cultures of learning' (e.g. see Littlewood 2007). Using a mixed methodological approach comprising surveys, observations and interviews, the study explores the perceptions and practices of more than 4,000 primary school teachers in 142 countries.

The main areas of challenge identified were teaching speaking, discipline, motivation, differentiation, teaching writing and teaching grammar. The overall findings were that large class sizes, lack of time, differentiation, classroom management and the lack of motivation, in particular, were areas where the greatest concerns and difficulties arose:

> The worst thing that a teacher could experience is when he has no motivated students. [The problems are] particularly acute for teachers new to teaching young learners whose expertise is in language learning and teaching rather than in primary school pedagogy. (p. 11)

The report also notes some teachers' concerns about their own levels of English. Some of the main conclusions reached were that:

> Teacher education should focus on strategies for maintaining discipline, managing large classes, and developing motivation in the context of teaching young learners, and that greater consideration may need to be given to the use of local languages for classroom procedures despite the central tenet of CLT that classes should be conducted in English. (p. 11)

This research is likely to be extremely valuable and relevant to your future teaching, given current and future learning and employment trends in the EFL/ESL industry and profession (Graddol 2006). It is also important because it highlights an issue which is a common concern for all teachers: how to motivate learners. Some of the issues raised will be further investigated in the following tasks, and in the additional readings in Section 6.8 below.

FURTHER READING TWO TASK

1. *Motivating learners*

The research discussed in the previous reading highlighted the problem of low motivation and teaching speaking to young learners. Watch Annie Hughes, an expert in the field of teaching English to children, as she talks online about teaching speaking: https://www.ed2go.com/Classroom/Lessons.aspx?classroom=1k%2f wxFs%2fZrBYAhLuxCGMh24%2bWIVXvNAQ4qoRuekvWZw%3d&bc=Lessons& lesson=1.

Summarise the points she makes about how to motivate and engage young learners. Write down some activities and strategies you think would be useful to try with young learners.

2. *Teaching young learners*

On the basis of Annie Hughes' talk, design a fun and motivating lesson (see Chapter 5) for young learners at a low proficiency level (i.e. elementary) to practise speaking skills. Use materials that are suitable for the age, level and culture of the students, as discussed in Chapters 2 and 3.

Add the lesson plan and materials to your portfolio of lesson plans for future use.

6.7 SUMMARY

This chapter has looked inside the contemporary English language teaching classroom to highlight some of the challenges which lie at the heart of the everyday practices of English language professionals, and which can have a profound impact on their work. The chapter has also drawn attention to the personal qualities, knowledge and skills that modern-day practitioners need to acquire to be able to respond to these challenges successfully. Through the exploration of authentic classroom experiences and data which served as stimuli for awareness raising, discussion, reflection and evaluation of aspects of good practice, it is hoped that a multidimensional picture has been provided of what really happens in the classroom and how teachers and learners feel.

The journey towards a more developed sense of professionalism is represented in Figure 6.1.

6.8 ADDITIONAL READINGS

Cameron, L. (2001) *Teaching Language to Young Learners*, Cambridge: Cambridge University Press.
This is essential reading for teachers in EFL/ESL primary and secondary school contexts.
Dobbs, J. (2001) *Using the Whiteboard*, Cambridge: Cambridge University Press.
This book provides useful tips and suggestions to help teachers use the classroom chalkboard or whiteboard more effectively and efficiently. It is designed to cater for a wide range of age groups and proficiency levels and includes more than 130 activities.
Macaro, E. (2003) *Teaching and Learning a Second Language: A Guide to Recent Research and its Applications*, London and New York: Continuum.
In chapter 5 of this book, the author synthesises relevant and valuable research in this area.

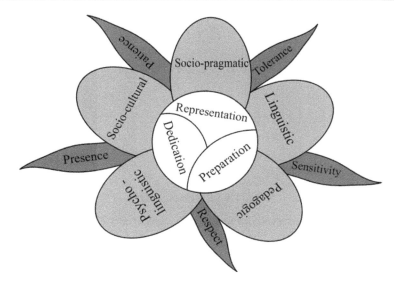

Figure 6.1   The professional journey towards a confident TESOL teacher identity

Walsh, S. (2006) *Investigating Classroom Discourse*, London and New York: Routledge.
The author provides an authoritative account of theoretical issues and considerations surrounding interactional language use by language teachers, together with a practical framework for teacher self-evaluation (SETT). (See also Walsh 2013.)

7

TEACHING PRACTICE FEEDBACK

7.1 INTRODUCTION

By now, you will have observed others teaching, prepared your plan and taught your own lesson. Although it may feel like the hardest part is over, and it probably is, the TP cycle is not complete. Indeed, it is the last stages (of the process that we spoke about in Chapter 1) which often make the most difference in how successful you will be as a qualified teacher. In this chapter, we begin to consider the critical review of your teaching performance, which aims to help you make informed decisions on possible modifications and adjustments for the next lesson, and the lessons after that. Such decisions are often best made with some sort of input from others who have more experience, although your peers can also be a valuable resource in this respect. Tutors, lecturers, course leaders or co-operating teachers are all good people to discuss your performance with, as well as more general issues you feel may be affecting on your practice.

This chapter focuses mainly on the type of face-to-face spoken feedback found in many TESOL programmes. Many of you may never have encountered this as it usually happens in private with only a tutor and the relevant teacher(s) present. It is not easily observable by third parties, for a number of legitimate reasons, and therefore needs to be dealt with in a more overt way in this book. The first section in this chapter focuses on the potentials of both immediate and mature teacher reflection in preparation for the feedback conference with the relevant tutor, and the importance of documenting these with reference to actual evidence from the lesson under review. The SETT model (Walsh 2006), introduced in earlier chapters, is outlined in detail here as a structured way for teachers to analyse and interpret their recorded classroom discourse. The nature of typical types of talk that can be anticipated from the feedback session is investigated using a framework previously developed (Farr 2011), which includes the following: direction, refection, evaluation and relational talk. Finally, the responsibility of the teacher as collaborative participant is given some thought in the light of the inherently uneven distribution of authority normally found between the participants in this context.

7.2 PREPARING FOR FEEDBACK

7.2.1 CONCEPTS, FINDINGS AND TEXTS

Feedback with another person will be most effective if you prepare for the meeting in advance. There are two (overlapping) stages in this preparation: reviewing the evidence, and reflecting in a purposeful way.

Reviewing the evidence for evaluation purposes
There are numerous types of evidence that you can use to evaluate your own lesson:

- audio or visual classroom recordings (for which learner consent must be obtained in advance)
- feedback from the learners (see Harmer 2007: ch. 3 for suggestions on how this might be done)
- work that learners have produced during the lesson
- informed discussion with any of your peers who observed the lesson or who team taught with you
- evaluation of the achievement of your learning outcomes
- materials from grammar reference books to check points of language teaching
- materials from methodology reference books to check points of teaching performance.

It is next to impossible to review, in any detail, all components of the lesson. Therefore, as mentioned in Chapter 5, it is good to have decided in advance of teaching, if possible, but certainly in advance of feedback, which aspect(s) of the lesson you would like to focus on in the discussions. When you have made your decision, then you can select the most appropriate type of evidence to use. For example, if you are interested in reviewing the way you give instructions or elicit from students, then classroom recordings work well. Analysing the classroom interactions (verbal and non-verbal) as the basis for more teacher-centred, objective and focused discussion during feedback has been advocated. The fields of discourse, conversational and interaction analyses are evidently influential here. Such an approach usually involves the use or adaptation of a pre-existing categorical matrix such as the Flanders or the FLint system (Moskowitz 1971), the Teaching Appraisal for Instructional Improvement Instrument (TA III) (Hunter 1984), Fanselow's FOCUS (1990) or the SETT reflective scheme developed by Walsh (2001) (see also Davies and Parkinson 1994, Nunan 1989). Often, the analysis of classroom transcripts is an integral part of such methods. They typically aim to provide a descriptive/diagnostic tool, ultimately to be used by teachers independently of an observer.

Analysing classroom interactions can encourage more teacher-centred, objective and focused discussion during feedback. There are many frameworks and templates that can be used to analyse classroom interactions (for example, the SETT model by Walsh 2006). To use this effectively, you can either transcribe relevant excerpts from the recordings, or simply work directly from your recordings and find examples to

Table 7.1   The SETT grid (Walsh 2003: 126)

Mode	Pedagogic goals	Interactional features
Managerial	To transmit information To organise the physical learning environment To refer learners to materials To introduce or conclude an activity To change from one mode of learning to another	A single, extended teacher turn which uses explanations and/ or instructions The use of transitional markers The use of confirmation checks An absence of learner contributions
Materials	To provide language practice around a piece of material To elicit responses in relation to the material To check and display answers To clarify when necessary To evaluate contributions	Predominance of IRF pattern Extensive use of display questions Form-focused feedback Corrective repair The use of scaffolding
Skills and systems	To enable learners to produce correct forms To enable learners to manipulate the target language To provide corrective feedback To provide learners with practice in sub-skills To display correct answers	The use of direct repair The use of scaffolding Extended teacher turns Display questions Teacher echo Clarification requests Form-focused feedback
Classroom context	To enable learners to express themselves clearly To establish a context To promote oral fluency	Extended learner turns Short teacher turns Minimal repair Content feedback Referential questions Scaffolding Clarification requests

illustrate the relevant categories. Walsh suggests that a 15-minute lesson extract can be effectively analysed using the SETT framework in about 45 minutes, which is a reasonable amount of time to spend preparing for feedback. Table 7.1 presents the SETT grid. Using this, you can use your recordings/transcripts to identify one or a number of the four modes listed in the first column (managerial, materials, skills and systems, or classroom context). The aims or goals relevant to each of the modes are found in the second column, and illustrative features that you will find in the classroom interactions are listed in the third column. So, for example, if you as teacher are in managerial mode, your aim will be to transmit information or refer learners to materials, and evidence of this in the classroom talk will manifest itself in any of the interactional features listed (use of confirmation checks, transitional markers etc.).

Reflecting in a purposeful way

Reflection is something that permeates every part of the TP process. However, we need to consider briefly what reflection is before exploring how to do it. Reflecting, simply put, means thinking. It can be about past, present or future events. John Dewey (1859–1952), an American educational philosopher and reformer, was among the first and most influential to differentiate between two types of thought. He defined 'routine thought' as automatic and unconscious, and 'rational thought' as active and considered (Dewey 1933). In reflective practice, we are concerned primarily with rational thought. However, rational reflection is not enough. As a teacher you must not only reflect rationally but ensure that this reflection includes a good deal of criticality (van Manen 1977). In other words, you must focus; question; hypothesise; relate reflections to theoretical, social and ethical concerns; and translate the outcomes of such critical reflections into future actions. This is a process which your tutor will guide you through until it becomes more familiar to you (see also Chapter 9 for a full account).

It is also useful to recognise that immediately following TP, your reflections and reactions are likely to be more emotional than rational. You might feel thrilled that you have survived the experience, disappointed that you did not do as well as you had hoped, or annoyed at yourself, the learners, the tutor, even the technology. These are all very legitimate feelings, and are a natural part of the process. We are, after all, emotional beings. It might be good to record or share these feelings in some way as 'red-hot reflections' immediately following your lesson. This can help to get matters off your chest, so to speak, and to make way for more mature and rational reflection. I fully acknowledge that there is not a simplistic divide between the emotional and the rational part of our being. However, you need to ensure that emotions do not have too much of a negative impact on the feedback discussion. Having done some 'red-hot reflecting', allow some time, gather the appropriate evidence and begin your more mature, rational reflection. You might do this in the form of notes or a diary/ blog, or using a template with some leading questions. It should be in writing so that you can bring it with you to your meeting. After identifying your focus for feedback, gathering the relevant data and taking some time to reflect critically, you are now ready for the feedback session with your tutor. It is recommended, for a number of reasons, that such sessions take place within a reasonably short period following the lesson under review. Up to three days after the event has been suggested to be most appropriate and preferable (Farr 2011: 169).

TASK 7.1 DIFFERENT TYPES OF REFLECTIONS

The following extracts come from blogs, which are essentially written thoughts recorded in web diaries.
A. What are the differences and similarities between them? Discuss in terms of purpose of the blog, written style and language, audience, anticipated outcome and any other factors you may notice.

B.   What are the pros and cons of writing your reflections?

C.   What are the pros and cons of sharing your reflections?

Blog A: Phatire video
Last Sunday, while riding at Sprain Ridge Park I took some footage with my iPhone (3GS). This involved perching my phone atop rocks and logs, held fast by small twigs and pebbles. An iPhone tripod would have been really nice although goes against my low-tech intentions. Once I had the phone precariously balanced, I'd grab my bike, ride through the scene, and double back for the camera. I did this about ten times until my battery was just about dead. To make the most of my footage I added the 'out takes' and camera grabs.
Source: http://phattire.blogspot.com

Blog B: Student teacher reflecting on the day's events
Yesterday was our last class of my elective. It was a make-up class because Sarah couldn't come last week, so it was held in BX345. Nobody knew where this room was located, so Canela and I sat in the canteen pondering what to do. Then Sarah walked by, and she didn't know where it was either. Then Sandra came by and she knows everything, so she told us where it was.

There are only 4 of us in the class, and Canela, Fatjack and I went with Sarah to the mystery classroom, which was freezing. Joe was missing as usual. Then Fatjack's mobile phone started ringing every 5 minutes, and it was Joe trying to find out where we were. The class started with Sarah criticising my project, which I turned in last week. Ouch! Nothing like a public attack on your homework. It made me very nervous because now I'm sure I got a horrible mark on it, and it's 30% of my grade. Anxiety again. The whole class seemed to be structured around the weaknesses in my project, which did nothing to lower my affective filter, Mr. Krashen.
Source: data collected by and used with permission of Dr Elaine Riordan, University of Limerick

Blog C: Student teacher reflecting on a TP lesson
Teaching on Friday went well. Was a bit anxious about the class as I've only taught the Advanced level up to now and I was worried I would be speaking too quickly for them etc but everything seemed to go OK. I enjoyed the class and so I hope the students did too. Also I had built up a nice rapport with the two Advanced classes and now with new students I was worried it would take time, that we don't have, to get to know the Ss and for them to get to know me and my style. However, the Ss were very nice and it'll be good to finish the term with them.

I had a new partner to teach with on Friday. I'll be teaching with this new person for the next few weeks. I know that when the observer is in the room it's hard not to double check explanations with them, but this person had some phrases back to front and their pronunciation can be wrong at times. I'm not an

expert but if this person is still double checking the meaning of new words and their pronunciation with the supervisor how is that fair on the Ss and on the rest of the MA class? They are a good teacher though!
Source: data collected by and used with permission of Dr Elaine Riordan, University of Limerick

TASK 7.2   PRE-FEEDBACK REFLECTING

A. Create a template for yourself to help focus your reflections after your TP but before you meet with your tutor. What form would it take? What would you include? Discuss with your peers to get further ideas.
B. Compare what you have created with the template used on your programme. How are they different? Was yours more general or specific? Which aspects are good/bad in each?

TASK 7.3   USING EVIDENCE FROM YOUR LESSON

A. Transcribe 5–10 minutes of part of your lesson you would like to focus on during reflection and feedback. Using the categories from the SETT grid in Table 7.1, label and tag the various stages of the interaction by *mode* and *interactional feature.* Use this to reflect critically on how effective this part of the lesson was and why.
B. Are there other types of evidence you could use in addition to the SETT evaluation during feedback? Consider those mentioned in Section 7.2.1 above and others that may be appropriate.

7.3   THE DISCOURSE OF TEACHING PRACTICE FEEDBACK: WHAT CAN I EXPECT?

7.3.1   CONCEPTS, FINDINGS AND TEXTS

It is useful to know what to expect in advance of your first feedback session, in terms of the type of discussion that might typically take place. Previous accounts suggest that there are a number of different approaches that tutors adopt during feedback. By understanding what some of these are, you will be better able to anticipate what is to come. Traditionally, drawing implicitly on older educational philosophies that see the teacher as the expert and the student as someone to be filled with knowledge, directive supervision was common. Here the tutor informs, acts as a model and evaluates. Such encounters can often be very prescriptive and negative. This approach has been criticised (Gebhard 1990), not only because it can be stress-inducing for the observed teacher, but because it is based on what many now believe to be a false assumption that good teaching can be easily defined, when in fact it is highly variable and context-dependent (Korthagen 2004). Hopefully, you will not encounter such an approach in its pure state, but it does still exist among some educators and in institutions that are more conservative. Interestingly, it is often incited by more novice teachers who feel they are adrift in the classroom and want to be told what to do to make them perform better next time. The problem is that the advice given may not apply to the context of the next time and the teacher is then left with no alternatives, as none has been considered.

This leads us to a second approach that can be found in supervision, which consists of providing alternatives (Freeman 1982). This can also be directive but is more supportive as it explores, in a more collaborative way, a limited number of feasible alternative courses of action, different from that actually chosen during TP. Such explorations equip teachers with a broader range of pre-considered options for future scenarios, should they need to draw on them. Collaborative supervision aims to create an equal relationship between the teacher and the tutor, as they are joint participants in solving problems. Clinical supervision, which has its foundations in medical sciences, often adopts this approach (Gaies and Bowers 1990).

The non-directive approach stems from Rogers' client-centred counselling (Freeman 1982), where the observer listens and echoes the teacher's own thoughts and opinions in the context of a trusting relationship. It is very therapeutic and similar to the type of classroom approach advocated by Curran in community language learning (Richards and Rodgers 1986: 113–27), which typifies some of the educational thinking of the 1970s in particular. As with language teaching methodologies, we are now in a more creative or eclectic era, where tutors will draw on a range of appropriate styles and strategies, depending on the context and on the stage of development of the teacher. So, do not be surprised if you find that the initial direction and support that were used to scaffold in the first weeks of TP are slowly taken away as you become capable of thinking more independently about your own practice, on which, after all, you have an insider's perspective.

In previous research, drawing on a corpus of approximately 160,000 words of spoken and written feedback, I identified the types of discourse that occur in one-to-one tutor meetings. Table 7.2 illustrates these. Reflection happens in both focused and more general ways. The tutor gives direction on the management of the lesson (instructions, elicitation etc.), the content, materials, and what the teacher might do to improve future performances. Evaluation takes place in terms of teachers being praised or criticised. This can come from both parties and often teachers are particularly critical of themselves. Finally, depending on the influencing variables, amounts of talk can be dedicated not only to building and maintaining good relationships (greetings, small talk etc.) but also to explicitly addressing some affective issues. This might relate to teachers who are nervous or lack confidence while teaching, or even to personal circumstances which might be affecting their teaching, for example, family bereavements, relationship break-ups or coping with being a single parent while studying full time, among others.

The amount of time that is devoted to any one of these types of discourse will depend exclusively on the variables in play at the time of feedback. These variables might include influence from institutional or national educational policies. You must remember that feedback is an interaction just like any other, where it is the

Table 7.2   The discourse of teaching practice feedback: a framework (Farr 2011: 73)

Reflection	Open reflection Focused reflection
Direction	Management direction Content direction Performance direction
Evaluation	Praise Criticism
Relational and cathartic talk	Small talk Addressing emotional incongruity Apologising Irony

participants who determine what will unfold, and the contents of which can never truly be known in advance. Politeness and face-saving strategies are usually very important, as the teachers are considered to be in a vulnerable situation because they are under review and evaluation. The teachers are also careful, as they do not want to challenge, insult or contradict the tutor, who is in a position of knowledge and authority in this institutional setting. Nonetheless, there is a task to be done as part of the developmental process of the teacher, and so the parties are expected to engage fully in the various types of talk which typify this sort of interaction.

TASK 7.4   YOUR PREFERRED APPROACH

A.   Thinking about the approaches outlined in Section 7.3.1, what type of approach would you prefer your tutor to take during your feedback session? Why did you choose this approach?
B.   Is it the best approach for your development as a teacher at this point in time?
C.   Is your preference likely to change over time? If so, in what way?

TASK 7.5   ANALYSING FEEDBACK DISCOURSE

The following extract on planning and vocabulary teaching comes from a feedback session which takes place in an Irish institutional setting.
A.   Using Table 7.2 above as a framework, identify the various kinds of talk that occur.
B.   Consider especially the balance between the transactional language (reflection, direction, evaluation) and the interactional strategies (emotional and cathartic). Do they interact well to achieve successful interaction?

Teacher: Em, you know, in terms of planning it, I mean, I, you know, I I should have been more realistic, I mean, when we discussed it last week, em, you know, there was a lot of vocabulary there, a lot to take in and I should have been, in the plan itself, been more realistic about how many of those exercises I was going to get through . . .

Tutor: Yes, but I would, on the other hand, say it's always better to over plan than . . .

Teacher: Yeah.

Tutor: . . . under plan, you know, so I I wouldn't fault you really on that, I think that was okay. Okay what else Jim? What other sort of comments did did you make?

Teacher: Em.

Tutor: What else were you happy about? What were some of the other good good features of your teaching?

Teacher: Em I mean I <pause> I wasn't, when I was planning, I wasn't sure about how much vocabulary to pre-teach . . .

Tutor: Yeah.

Teacher: . . . and I . . .

Tutor: It's always difficult in vocab lessons, isn't it?

Teacher: . . . you know, I, we had last week discussed actually pre-teaching more than I did but when I looked at it I felt that to pre-teach too much was going to take the point away . . .

Tutor: Yeah.

Teacher: . . . for some . . .

Tutor: Gives the game away, doesn't it?

Teacher: Yeah and I I did point that out to them.

Tutor: Yeah and . . ..

Teacher: So, I I think, I think that did, that did work quite well because they had to think about it more . . .

Tutor: Yeah.

Teacher: . . . and I think that it's no, I don't know, I put a question mark here somewhere about did they have to think about it too much, but I thought, you know, I don't think it's any harm . . .

Tutor: You can't think too much you know <laughing> you can never think too much.

TASK 7.6   FEELINGS ABOUT FEEDBACK

A.   How would you have felt if you were the teacher in the extract in Task 7.5?

B.   Consider the following list of emotions. Which do you predict you are likely to feel during or after feedback? What might cause you to feel this way?

encouraged	happy	relaxed	confident	secure
respected	satisfied	defensive	upset	surprised
indifferent	unsure	lost	uneasy	discouraged
frustrated	angry	annoyed		
Other:				

C. Now do the same from the perspective of the tutor. How might they feel and why?

7.4 THE TEACHER'S RESPONSIBILITY AS COLLABORATOR

7.4.1 CONCEPTS, FINDINGS AND TEXTS

Under socio-cultural models, now in widespread use in language teacher education programmes, all interested parties are expected to contribute and be active in their own learning. Despite this, feedback continues to be an area where the tutor tends to contribute much more to the talk than they believe is good or necessary for the development of the teacher. Results reported in previous research suggest that tutors typically talk for approximately 60–65 per cent of the time, with teachers contributing only about 35 per cent (Farr 2005, Vásquez and Reppen 2007). This can be very frustrating for tutors and teachers alike. Tutors typically want the teachers to contribute more, and teachers may feel they do not have a voice in such scenarios. There are a number of other factors which can affect TP feedback. I have discussed these in detail elsewhere (Farr 2011: 24), but will summarise the most important here. In each case, I am suggesting ways in which you can contribute to ensuring the feedback meeting will be a productive one.

1. *Conflicting agendas.* This is essentially when you and the tutor have different ideas about the approach to be taken during feedback or about the content of what is to be discussed. To avoid this, prepare for the meeting (as discussed above), and negotiate the approach and content in advance, or at the beginning of the meeting.
2. *Anxiety.* If you are especially upset or anxious about the lesson under review, or indeed about the feedback meeting, it is likely to have a negative impact on how effective it will be. Do some 'red-hot reflecting' (as discussed above), or vent with some friends/colleagues in advance, to provide an outlet for some of these negative, though legitimate, feelings.
3. *Idealism versus reality.* The feedback meeting can sometimes be a little too idealistic in a context where you feel that the advice and ideas being discussed will not easily translate into the reality of the classroom. This can lead to a feeling of 'it's all good in theory, but the practice is different'. Raise this during feedback if you are worried about it and negotiate with the tutor how the ideas may need to be modified in the light of practical constraints.
4. *Skills, attributes and behaviours of the tutor.* The relationship between tutor and teacher is really important. If either party says or does anything to break the relationship of trust and respect during feedback, this has the potential to impact negatively on the whole process. Some tutors are amenable to being asked to comment on their style and approach, and this may be a way for you to raise issues around interpersonal behaviour. If this is not their practice, then you have the right to raise any misgivings with the tutor during feedback, or indeed to take more formal action by speaking with your course director or lodging a formal complaint. Remember, your development as a teacher may be at stake.

Although I mention some of the things you can do to lessen any negative impact because of these factors, I fully acknowledge that a lot of the responsibility also lies with the tutor. They are the more authoritative professional in this context and should know how to negotiate feedback meetings successfully. An important thing to remember here is that your immediate experience of your lesson is primary, and you therefore have the right to contribute fully and freely to the feedback discussions. The tutor will have his or her own legitimate sources of knowledge, but you have practical and experiential knowledge of the lesson under review to draw on.

TASK 7.7   COMPARING GENRES

Compare and contrast the following extracts. The first comes from a casual conversation between university student friends, and the second from a TP feedback meeting.
A.   Comment on the different interaction and contribution patterns in each and explain why these differences might occur.
B.   Are there any features of the casual conversation that would not be appropriate or acceptable in TP feedback, or vice versa?
C.   What would have helped the teacher in the second extract to contribute better?
D.   What might prevent teachers from contributing more during feedback?

Ciara: What did who say?
Tina: What did Lorna say about the thing?
Ciara: She said.
Tina: Where did she go?
Ciara: Oh she went to the party, em, and she said that ur Barry Roche em, no, Liam Ryan, went back to O' Connoll's and she, ah, she said it was a good night. She was just asking me about the, eh, how we got on.
Tina: Did Lorna go back to O Connoll's? No?
Ciara: Lorna. No, no. She, ah, went to this party in, ah, of a friend in her, of her classes.
Tina: Oh.
Ciara: Yeah.
Tina: Who, eh, who was it you know?
Ciara: Aoife, you know, she kinda got a round face.
Tina: Round face.
Ciara: Kinda a pudgy face, you know.
Tina: I think I know her all right, actually.
Ciara: Yeah, yeah, em, so she said she got on good. She was going on about how crap the party was. <snigger> I must actually ask her.
Tina: 'Twas rubbish actually.
Ciara: It was rubbish. It was really bad, em.
Tina: Mm.
Ciara: But, em, that's, em, I don't know ur, 'twas a good night.
Source: data from the Limerick Corpus of Irish English (Farr and O'Keeffe 2004)

Teacher: It was terrible.

Tutor: Did you ask?

Teacher: I think I did . . .

Tutor: What did you ask?

Teacher: I said did anyone know what PC is.

Tutor: Yeah, and somebody did, didn't they?

Teacher: I don't think they did actually . . .

Tutor: Yeah, but one guy was nodding at you, that you didn't see, I don't think.

Teacher: I think I got two answers.

Tutor: Yeah, you got somebody to define political correctness, didn't you?

Teacher: Yes, I, em, but I am not sure that they defined it correctly.

Tutor: What did they say? Can you remember?

Teacher: I'm lost. I have no idea.

Tutor: Okay, I can't remember either but I am just wondering if it was . . . I thought that you got a reasonably satisfactory definition from them and remember it is not that easy to define. It is examples that you might need to look for. Can you give me an example of when the explanation that you gave at the end could have been switched around into questions and then they would have been very specific and then maybe they would have been able to answer a bit better? Would you think?

Teacher: Yeah.

Tutor: Yeah, okay, yeah. I have at this point 'be careful of yes no questions'. Did you think you were slipping into 'does anybody know what political correctness is? Yes? No?' em 'What is PC?' you said first of all. That was your first question, which is fine, but then following it up with 'Does anybody know the other meaning?' or something like that . . .

Teacher: Okay.

Tutor: . . . em you were making an effort, I think, to ask more discursive type questions but you still need to work on that, I would say, because some of them tend to be a little bit closed, yeah, do you agree?

Teacher: I'm not sure . . .

Tutor: <laughing>

Teacher: . . . I thought that, em, that some of the questions they could have answered them a bit more.

Tutor: Yeah, but why didn't they then? You need to ask yourself and, I mean, there are a number of reasons for that. You need to look at the question type. You need to look at all the different things we spoke about last week and see what, perhaps, was going on . . . But, you know, you have to just keep battling at it, which you did, in fairness to you. You did do that and you kept questioning and you asked very sort of, em, deep level questions when you tried to pick up on specifics and things when you went through, which is good, okay. What else did you have?

Teacher: That's about it <laughing>

Tutor: That's all you had? <laughing>

TASK 7.8   EXAMINING YOUR CONTRIBUTIONS DURING FEEDBACK

Record one of your feedback meetings (with permission from your tutor). Listen to it a couple of times.

A.   How would you assess the contribution you made during this feedback meeting?
B.   Note some very specific ways in which you could increase the quantity and quality of your contribution.

7.5   FURTHER READING ONE

Crookes, G. (2003) *A Practicum in TESOL: Professional Development through Practice*, New York: Cambridge University Press. Chapter 2, 'Writing, observing, interacting, and acting together'.

According to Crookes, the aims of this chapter are for teachers to consider the benefits of working collaboratively with other teachers during a practicum, the personal and interpersonal practices needed to do this, and the problems that might occur and how these might be prevented. A concern about the brevity of the TP component on many teacher education programmes motivated the writing of this chapter. In the light of the restrictions on what can be achieved in teacher education programmes, it is an attempt to encourage the types of collaborative practices that will benefit teachers in their future careers so that they will continue developing. Crookes describes teacher development groups as follows:

> Teacher development groups are small-scale, informal gatherings of teachers to work together on their professional concerns. They may be meetings organized to share experiences or they might involve discussing readings, books, articles, and so on. Under favourable circumstances they might include discussion and feedback based on mutual observation. These groups work against the individualist conception of teaching dominant in Western educational systems that prevents teachers from gaining assistance from those most immediately able to offer it – their fellow teachers (cf. Shimahara [1998]). I believe that teachers, for the sake of their own continued professional development, and possibly for the sake of their own mental and emotional health in a demanding business, should become aware of and capable of participating in and running teacher development groups. (p. 21)

The underlying purpose of such an approach is to enable support and reflection as facilitators to development so that teachers do not simply relive the same experiences repeatedly. Crookes discusses three mechanisms through which reflection can be achieved: writing, observation and feedback, and group discussions and investigations.

Writing

In this section, various types of personal writing as a support for professional growth are introduced. An initial distinction is made between logs, diaries and journals, with journals being identified as most suitable for professional development. A journal, which will typically include some facts as well as personal thoughts recorded comprehensively and systematically over time, is suggested as something to be shared between the teacher and the supervisor. In other words, the teacher writes the journal, shares it, and the supervisor responds. The chapter then moves temporarily to a more theoretically elaborate discussion of the place of journal writing as a manifestation of narrative.

> The keeping of personal reflective writing has a wider and increasingly influential theoretical context that should be considered as well. Personal reflective writing that goes on over time is a form of narrative; and narrative has been identified as both an archetypal type of knowledge (e.g. Bruner, J., 1986) and as a way we represent ourselves, that is, a way we figure out who we are or who we are becoming. Given my emphasis on the congruity between self-development and teacher development, personal narrative seems particularly important in this light. During a practicum, participants may be making a particular effort to review their values, their reasons for being a teacher, and so on, for which, again, journaling can be very useful. (p. 24)

The importance of narrative for personal growth is discussed and it is considered as a way of making sense of one's life, and caring for oneself. If journals are shared then they can contribute to professional knowledge also in a number of ways: helping colleagues, contributing data for research purposes etc. This section concludes with some practical tasks and an illustration from a teacher–supervisor email journal exchange, which highlights the informal and open nature of such dialogues.

Observation and feedback
This section begins with two teacher narratives outlining their experiences of being observed by others. Both stories tell of initial nerves and anxiety, which were quickly replaced with feelings that are more positive. The focus in this part of the chapter is on mutual peer observation for development purposes, and not supervisor observation and feedback. In this context, Crookes specifies:

> Subsequently, egalitarian, descriptive, and relatively non-judgemental observation would be the target. The objective of such observations can be to share perspectives, provide general feedback, or, subsequently, to provide data on specific aspects of practice which may be nominated by the individual teacher, or of concern to the group as a whole. (p. 30)

The second part of this section discusses the important issue of ground rules and procedures for the observer, as outlined by Master in a 1983 *TESOL Quarterly* article. These include the following: allowing time for the teacher to develop rapport before starting observations, sitting at the side of the room and not the back or front, checking if the teacher would like you to take an active role in the lesson if needed, minimising note-taking as it is a distraction, and giving immediate feedback after the lesson. A summary of advice offered in later articles is also provided, with some attention given to peer observation systems as advocated by Nunan and Lamb (1996) and Peters and March (1999). This section again concludes with some discussion and practical tasks for teachers to do collaboratively.

Talking
Group discussions are described in some detail here, with the various roles of the participants outlined (keeping notes, timing, starting topics, nominating speakers etc.). The notion of a rotating chair is explored as a remedy when individuals under-participate because of gender, cultural backgrounds, language levels and other factors. A list of potential pitfalls given includes hogging the show, defensiveness, negativism, self-listening, avoiding feelings, speaking for others, and more. The dominance of native speakers over non-native speakers is given some space at the end of this section and leads into the discussion and practical tasks.

The remainder of the chapter explores the process of AR as a framework for experimenting and sharing one's experiences, and the collaborative aspect of this is emphasised. AR is presented as an essential part of a teacher's development, and some of the rationale and procedures are outlined.

FURTHER READING ONE TASK

1. On a trial basis, start to keep a blog/journal about your practical teaching experiences and share it with a friend/colleague. Agree the ground rules in advance.
2. After a week or two, discuss how you found the process with your partner.
3. Allow someone to observe your class or a recording of it. Share your feelings about the experience with that person without doing formal feedback on the content of the lesson.
4. Think about how you typically participate in meetings (level of contribution, role, reaction to others etc.).
5. Write down a self-profile for this context.
6. Ask a close friend/colleague to do the same for you.
7. Compare and discuss the results.

7.6   FURTHER READING TWO

Copland, F. (2010) 'Causes of tension in post-observation feedback in pre-service teacher training: An alternative view', *Teaching and Teacher Education*, 26: 3, 466–72.
This article focuses on the potential that feedback has to cause tension and disquiet, particularly in pre-service education contexts. Traditionally, such tension is blamed on the possible conflict between the supervisor's role as facilitator and assessor (see Section 7.1 above for further discussion). However, in this article Copland explores alternative reasons for such tension. She begins by outlining a typical teacher education context in the UK and many parts of the world, where tutors observe and meet the practising teacher for a post-teaching feedback session. The data used in the study

comes from a pre-service TESOL programme. On privately run 120-hour certificate programmes, such as the one reported here, a key component is 6 hours of TP. These 6 hours are typically taught in 30-minute slots, shared with other trainees in a 2-hour lesson. There is a lot of pressure on the trainee teachers, as they do not usually have the opportunity to re-teach lessons that go wrong, and they must pass this part of the programme in order to pass overall.

The context for the study is explored in a section entitled 'The feedback session', where the nature of the multiparty meetings is detailed. Up to five teachers discuss their lessons with the trainer, usually for about an hour. Trainees, therefore, have an audience when they discuss their own lessons, and they are expected to feed back to their fellow teachers in relation to their performance. Copland views this as some-what problematic for beginner teachers who find it difficult to reflect in a critical way on their own teaching and may feel very uncomfortable, as novices, commenting on others. The chosen methodology for the study is linguistic ethnography, which she defines as follows:

Linguistic ethnography is an emerging discipline in sociolinguistics research which brings together linguistic and ethnographic tools of data collection and analysis (Creese, 2008; Rampton, 2007). Situated within 'the new intellectual climate of late modernity and post-structuralism' (Creese, 2008: 1) linguistic ethnography foregrounds a reflexive approach to data collection and analysis in which the researcher is rigorously accounted for and where 'truth claims made by the research' are informed by the role the researcher has played in this research (Tusting and Maybin, 2007: 579).

The data for Copland's study consisted of audio- and video-recordings of the feedback sessions, plus her own observer's field notes, collected from two separate courses. Four trainer and nine trainee interviews are also part of the dataset. The recordings were transcribed and coded according to what she calls 'phases', refer-ring to Waite (1993), such as 'self-evaluation, peer feedback, and trainer feedback' (Copland 2010: 467). A more detailed system was then applied to each of these phases, where speech acts such as 'praising' or 'suggesting' were tagged. Some very specific extracts were also subjected to fine-grained micro-analysis using frame-works from conversation analysis. The researcher was not involved in the running or any aspect of the courses and was not working at the institute where the data was collected.

Having considered previous studies of the feedback context and discussions around the assessment and facilitator role tension, Copland goes on to discuss two different types of tension which she identified in her study:

Tension arising from peer feedback
The first cause of tension to be discussed arises from the peer feedback role that all trainees were required to perform in feedback. While many groups in my experience cope well with delivering peer feedback, others struggle with negotiating the rules of the game of this discourse practice. (p. 468)

Tension arising from reflection on practice
Once again, tension can be traced back to the participatory structures that are imposed on trainees. The art of reflecting does not come easily to some (see Korthagen, 2004) and understanding the norms of self-evaluation discourses in this context may have eluded or challenged Hannah (one of the trainees) . . . It may be that Hannah is similarly unsure of what she is supposed to say or how she is supposed to say it. (p. 470)

These tensions are discussed using data from the feedback recordings and applying appropriate theoretical frameworks. The article concludes with two recommendations on how tension might be reduced in such contexts. The first suggests putting in place a formal induction specifically about the feedback session, so that trainees can at least begin to think about what will happen in terms of process and purpose. The second advocates the use of a variety of frameworks during feedback, so that trainees will feel comfortable at least some of the time (for example, peer, trainer led, pairs, groups, formal, informal etc.).

FURTHER READING TWO TASK

1.   What are the main benefits and pitfalls of one-to-one feedback with a tutor versus group and peer feedback?
2.   In relation to what is said and done in feedback, is there any unacceptable type of behaviour? Discuss what they might be and why.
3.   How comfortable would you feel giving feedback to your peers on their TP? Why? Think about approaches you would use if in this situation.

7.7   SUMMARY

It is natural for you to feel vulnerable and exposed at times during feedback, so the interaction works best if your collaborator is someone you trust and respect, and whose input and opinion you value enough to be able to use it actively to shape your future teaching. If you believe there are relationship issues, then you should try to resolve them or take the necessary steps to ensure that you work with someone else for review purposes (remembering that you also have some responsibility for building and maintaining good relationships). This is usually possible by speaking with your course director. Much research in educational settings suggests that positive relationships between mentors/teachers and their students have a significant impact on both emotional and academic achievement (Barduhn 2002, Chamberlin 2000, Hoover et al. 1988, Koerner et al. 2002, Woodward 1997). Edge (1992: 63), in the framework of what he calls 'co-operative teacher development' between peers, highlights respect, empathy, and honesty, as the three essentials for success (see Chapter 8). He suggests that these are necessary to replace the traditional educational culture of discussion and argumentation where the point is to win and not to understand. Feedback encounters should be about understanding and developing, not simply about winning the arguments.

In the even more relevant setting of practice teaching Koerner et al. (2002) high-light the relatively high priority teachers in training give to the personal qualities of cooperating teachers and trainers. Woodward (1997: 5) suggests that 'when you ask teachers what they like and remember about their trainers, many will mention personal qualities such as sensitivity, flexibility, and a sense of humour rather than strategies and techniques used and often rather even than the content or knowledge passed on'. Significantly, Barduhn concludes that the three factors she mentions have been empirically proven to have positive benefits not only for students' emotional but also for their academic success. If this is the case, it increases the formal obligation on teacher educators to develop the necessary skills and traits which will help them to achieve their goal more effectively and affectively.

A second factor which has the potential to impact negatively on feedback ses-sions relates to contexts where tutors are required to assess the TP lesson formally, in percentage or grade terms. This can create problems for both the teacher and the tutor. For the tutor, there is what I have called elsewhere a 'paradox of facilita-tor roles' (Farr 2011: 26). In other words, they are required to play the part of both helper and assessor. These dual roles require them to support and encourage, but also to be objectively judgemental while assessing. The conflict between development and assessment duties is often difficult for tutors (Copeland 1980), and they can feel a sense of betrayal and disloyalty towards the teacher. This is something that they must find ways to overcome as assessment has been identified as one of the general reasons for observing (Orland-Barak 2002). Teachers such as you often see it as being a very important part of the process, and some published research and discussions have reported on a type of grade-obsession among those being evaluated. This pre-occupation with 'what grade did I get?' can be counterproductive during feedback (Mann 2003). It can lead to an argumentation around the grade, in other words, force a summative agenda, as opposed to a discussion which promotes more formative development. As I claim elsewhere, 'This can have a detrimental effect on professional development, mainly if the grades are poor or if the student teacher is particularly sensitive or highly competitive' (Farr 2011: 27). The best way to avoid such a scenario is to receive your grades using a different system; for example, I email teachers grades on their written feedback reports after I have met with them for a face-to-face discus-sion. They know this will happen and therefore one of the ground rules of the feed-back session is that grades are not discussed. They can freely use other procedures if they want to understand the grading process or outcome better, or to challenge it. Once you have resolved these issues, and considered the other issues discussed in this chapter, you are ready for feedback discussions.

7.8   ADDITIONAL READINGS

Copeland, W. D. (1980) 'Affective dispositions of teachers in training toward examples of supervisory behavior', *Journal of Educational Research*, 74: 1, 37–42.

Edge, J. (1984) 'Feedback with face', *English Language Teaching Journal*, 38: 3, 204–6.

Farr, F. (2011) *The Discourse of Teaching Practice Feedback: An Investigation of Spoken and Written Modes*, New York: Routledge.

Orland-Barak, L. (2002) 'The impact of the assessment of practice teaching on beginning teaching: Learning to ask different questions', *Teacher Education Quarterly*, 29: 2, 99–122.

Phillips, D. (1997) 'Teacher training: Observation and feedback', in McGrath, I. (ed.), *Learning to Train: Perspectives on the Development of Language Teacher Trainers*, Hemel Hampstead: Prentice Hall, 82–8.

Vásquez, C. and Urzúa, A. (2009) 'Reported speech and reported mental states in mentoring meetings: Exploring novice teacher identities', *Research on Language and Social Interaction*, 42: 1, 1–19.

8

REFLECTIVE PRACTICE AND CONTINUING PROFESSIONAL DEVELOPMENT

8.1 INTRODUCTION

Very often, on graduating to the workplace, novice teachers are completely sub-merged in the chaos of educational institutions and the restrictions of a full teaching schedule. You may have experienced this yourself. I certainly have, and so have most of the teachers I have met over the years. In times when resources are not plentiful we feel this even more acutely. In such a context teachers can be so preoccupied with short-term planning and coping that their own professional development inevitably takes second place (Borg 2009). In this chapter I hope to provide a strong founda-tion for motivating and mobilising you towards engaging in reflective practice (RP) as part of your ongoing professional development when you finish your teacher education programme and begin teaching as a qualified teacher. Given the rate at which skills and knowledge date, continuing professional development (CPD) is no longer optional for teachers, and many national teacher standards and councils now require teachers to engage fully and show ongoing evidence of how they do this in meaningful ways. In these circumstances, it is important to maintain ownership of your CPD and manage it in ways which benefit you and your particular needs and wants as your career progresses. This can only be done by taking full account of your learners and your context(s) of teaching. The more personalised you can make your reflection and development, the more likely it is to have a positive impact on improving your practices, and this will also make it more motivating for you to engage with and sustain.

Other than being obliged to do it, there are compelling reasons for planning and orchestrating a CPD programme, either individually or within institutional struc-tures. Among other reasons, it can help:

- solve problems you encounter in your teaching
- give a sense of community among teachers
- you to try new ideas and approaches, and to keep abreast of new developments and thinking
- challenge and/or reaffirm your educational beliefs and values
- share ideas with others
- trace your thinking and development over time
- others to benefit from your experience

- maintain a sense of confidence and pride in your work
- your learners to follow by example and see you 'practise what you preach'
- you to make more informed decisions and choices about your learners, your teaching and even your career path.

In this chapter I start by examining the dimensions of RP, drawing primarily on Zwozdiak-Myers' (2012) framework and discussing what it can mean for you in real and tangible ways. In the second core section a typical RP cycle is outlined procedurally (following Schön 1987 and others), and combined with discussions of AR, which will be elaborated on further in Chapter 9. You will move through the various stages of RP with concrete examples from your own and others' teaching. In Section 8.4, various other techniques and tools that are useful for professional development are critically discussed; all of these incorporate reflection, so that you can begin to build your own toolkit as you move through your professional career.

8.2   THE DIMENSIONS OF REFLECTIVE PRACTICE

8.2.1   CONCEPTS, FINDINGS AND TEXTS

Dewey (1933) has often been credited with establishing the roots for RP, especially in his notions of the importance of social context; an interest in and ownership of a problem to be resolved; the use of systematic procedures, observations and experience; testing ideas through practice; and the implementation of new courses of action. More recently Schön (1983) provided an elaborate framework for professional contexts, and targeted its suitability and use for teaching and learning in two of his later books (Schön 1987, 1991). So: what does RP mean? Wajnryb (1992b: 9) defines it as a dynamic process in which the 'teacher is actively reflecting and exploring'. It is believed that teachers, both prospective and practising, learn through the construction of personal meaning, and through the constant reassessment of their thinking in varied situations. Novice teachers reflect on what they have experienced and then generate their previous knowledge to make informed decisions and subsequent changes to their own teaching. During teacher education programmes, tutors typically coach the student teacher or initiate peer coaching, and this is often carried out through reflective journals, personal stories and group discussions, some of which have been explored in earlier parts of this book. There are a number of underlying assumptions which exist in the implementation of such a model in teaching. Richards and Lockhart (1996: 3–5) outline the five which they consider to be core in their approach:

- an informed teacher has an extensive knowledge base about teaching;
- much can be learned about teaching through self-inquiry;
- much of what happens in teaching is unknown to the teacher;
- experience is sufficient as the basis for development;
- critical reflection can trigger a deeper understanding of teaching.

TASK 8.1   QUESTIONING UNDERLYING ASSUMPTIONS

Read through Richards and Lockhart's assumptions carefully (refer to the original text if you wish) and consider two things:

- to what extend you agree with each assumption
- what evidence you have from your own or others' teaching to support your beliefs in relation to each one.

8.2.2   A REFLECTIVE PRACTICE FRAMEWORK

In her 2012 book *The Teacher's Reflective Practice Handbook*, Zwozdiak-Myers gives extensive coverage to the entire range of theories and practices around RP. She defines it as '[a] disposition to enquiry incorporating the process through which student, early career and experienced teachers structure or restructure actions, beliefs, knowledge and theories that inform teaching for the purposes of professional development' (2012: 5). She also formally presents her framework of RP, which was developed in 2010 as part of her PhD research. The framework presents nine dimensions of RP which can occur in a non-linear way for any individual teacher. These nine dimensions will be presented and explored briefly here.

Dimension 1: Teachers study their own teaching for personal improvement
Dimension 1 relates to the teacher's ability to change role, from being the actor to being the critical observer, in what is known as 'experiential learning' (Kolb 1984). It is the ability to detach yourself from the context in order to evaluate objectively, yet to retain the insider's understanding you gain from being a primary participant in that context. To study your own teaching effectively demands the capacity to structure your reflections in a way that can usefully guide improved practice. The means of achieving this may be individual and context-dependent. A useful distinction here is one originally presented by Schön (1987) between 'reflection-in-action' and 'reflection-on-action' as discussed earlier. Reflection-in-action refers to the immediate actions taken by teachers on the spot as problems actually arise during practice. This necessitates simultaneous thinking and doing, and comes more easily with extended experience. Reflection-on-action, on the other hand, is a more mature, retroflective process and takes place in a more extended timeframe. This is the type of reflection that usually happens after TP and during feedback, as discussed in Chapter 7, and makes explicit what you do on the basis of what you implicitly know. When studying your teaching it is important to ask questions about the context, what the learners are doing, what they are thinking and what they are feeling (Korthagen and Vasalos 2005), in order to get a comprehensive understanding on which to base modified future actions.

Dimension 2: Teachers systematically evaluate their own teaching through classroom research procedures
Dimension 2 refers to the task of structured appraisals of what happens in your classroom. This is where you become a critic of your own practice in relation to the goals

you set for your lessons. This aspect of RP incorporates models of AR, which will be explored in more detail in Chapter 9. Essentially, it is where you identify a practice-based problem, define it, assess it, devise an action plan to improve practice, implement the action, evaluate the action and then make a final decision on whether the results are satisfactory or whether further action and evaluation are necessary. Each phase is systematically recorded and documented as part of a research study, and it is therefore often more structured, data-informed and formal than the processes described in Dimension 1.

Dimension 3: Teachers link theory with their own practice

Dimension 3 discusses how teachers can relate various relevant theories with actual classroom practice. Theories can take different forms, and as well as the more formal or 'espoused' theories (of SLA, language etc.; see Spiro 2013) generally found within the profession, it is now recognised that teachers also draw on procedural and tacit knowledge which comes from experience (Freeman 1991). Researchers and writers have discussed the importance of personal practical knowledge (Golombek 1998) and some, such as Edge (2011), have strongly questioned the usefulness of any theory which does not easily map on to practice. There are generally agreed types of theoretical knowledge that teachers are required to have. Shulman (1986) outlines seven types: content knowledge, pedagogical knowledge, curriculum knowledge, pedagogical content knowledge, knowledge of learners and their characteristics, knowledge of educational ends, and knowledge of educational contexts (see also Chapter 5, Section 5.4, for a discussion of the TPACK framework, to include technological knowledge). Much of what you will know about each of these aspects will come from a combination of your familiarity with espoused and practical theoretical knowledge, learned during your teacher education, your practical experience and your ongoing professional development activities. The key to this dimension of RP is the ability to apply and implement these various kinds of theoretical knowledge appropriately during your teaching. According to Shulman (1987), this application involves the stages of *teacher comprehension* (a full understanding of what is to be taught from several perspectives), *transformation* of this understanding into appropriate content for the learners, providing good *instruction* in class, *evaluating* understanding both formally and informally, *reflecting* back on the experience, and achieving *new comprehension* through analysis, discussion and documentation. Some research would suggest that the application of different types of theory to practice is a complex process, especially for teachers in training (see, for example, a longitudinal study by Cheng et al. 2012).

Dimension 4: Teachers question their personal theories and beliefs

Dimension 4 deals with another aspect of a teacher's theories, that of individual beliefs, opinions and values, all of which combine to shape personal professional cognition. These are highly personal and you may not even be aware of some of those which influence your teaching. On the basis of research since the 1980s, Zwozdiak-Myers (2012: 84) summarises the main findings on teachers' personal beliefs and theories:

- student teachers come to teacher education programmes with pre-existing beliefs based on their own school experiences (as a result of what Lortie (1975) calls their own 'apprenticeship of observation'; see Chapter 4 above for further discussion)
- they are highly resistant to change
- they act as filters for new information, by matching this new information against existing beliefs and, on that basis, deciding whether it is to be accepted
- they are often implicit and tacit, which makes them difficult to articulate.

This all serves to highlight how important it is to try to understand your own beliefs, and to challenge and question them. This is often best done with the help of a trusted 'outsider' who may be able to see things that you don't in your teaching, things which reflect some of your subconscious assumptions and opinions.

TASK 8.2   EXAMINING PERSONAL THEORIES AND BELIEFS

A.   Web search for a short video clip (10–15 minutes) of a real classroom in action. From what you see the teacher doing with the learners, what can you say about the teacher's personal beliefs and assumptions? Is there more than one possible interpretation of any of the actions you have examined?

B.   Work with a partner. Video-record one of your lessons and select a 10–15-minute excerpt. View your partner's excerpt. From what you see them doing with the learners, make some notes about what you think your partner's personal beliefs and assumptions about teaching are. Do the same for your own extract. Have a conversation with your partner and compare notes. What did you learn about yourself from this task?

Dimension 5: Teachers consider alternative perspectives and possibilities

Dimension 5 has to do with situating learning in real-world contexts and considering numerous perspectives on how things can be done. As a teacher you will find more alternatives available to you as you develop and gain more experience. Additional possibilities are also explored through conversations and activities with other teachers (peers and those with more experience), who may have different perspectives and experiences to share. You may wish to engage with a mentor or involve yourself in peer observations in order to gain insights from others. And of course getting the learners' perspectives through feedback from them will also inform your practice and is likely to offer numerous suggestions that you may not have thought of. All of these activities need to be done in a structured way to be of most benefit (see Zwozdiak-Myers 2012: 100–7 for suggestions).

Dimension 6: Teachers try out new strategies and ideas

Dimension 6 is where teachers move towards the full and active engagement of all learners. This can be done by drawing on a number of techniques: drawing on previous knowledge, challenging, cooperative group work, scaffolding, and deep and surface learning, among others. Methods of presenting, explaining and eliciting need careful consideration if they are to engage your learners actively. As well as challenging learners cognitively, you will need to consider the range of learner styles (see Chapter 2) in your classroom and vary techniques to try to reach the widest possible audience. Dimensions 5 and 6 seem to be closely linked, with Dimension 6 being more action-oriented.

Dimension 7: Teachers maximise the learning potential of all their students

Dimension 7 is about what learners are entitled to and ensuring an environment of inclusion in educational systems. This is a big challenge for teachers, as they have a range of factors to consider: cultural backgrounds; social, emotional, intellectual and special needs; and a range of learning styles, motivations and aspirational influences and levels. This is not an easy task and can be daunting for many teachers, especially novice teachers. For this reason, how you plan to achieve this needs due thought and planning as part of your RP. You may need to draw on a range of strategies, and in particularly demanding circumstances you may need to consult with others from a range of professional backgrounds.

Dimension 8: Teachers enhance the quality of their own teaching

Dimension 8 addresses the very complex issue of teaching quality. Much research has been done into what constitutes good-quality teaching and teachers, and also into learners' perceptions of quality. For a number of years we spoke of 'best practice' and in many cases still do. In 1998, Edge and Richards published a very interesting article entitled 'Why *best practice* is not good enough' (italics in original), in which they argue that the best can be the enemy of all of the good practice of teachers. In other words, an exclusive focus on a best model can undermine the many examples of good and very good practices that teachers can successfully use in their classrooms.

In present times, information and communication technology is also an essential component of good teaching, and some countries have published standards in relation to its integration (for example, Healey et al. 2011). A quick web search will give you many definitions and papers on what constitutes good-quality teaching. It is your responsibility as a teacher to reflect continuously on the quality of your teaching, with the ultimate aim of enhancing it. You might like to avail yourself of some of the very useful tools developed during the ITQ (Identifying Teacher Quality) European research project to help you do this in a more structured way. They are available on the project website (http://www.teacherqualitytoolbox.eu/home) in a number of languages under the 'reflection tools' tab on the left, and draw on a range of aids such as observations, standards documents, pictures, movies, metaphors etc.

Dimension 9: Teachers continue to improve their own teaching

Dimension 9 has CPD at its core. It acknowledges that learning to be a teacher is a lifelong process and does not end with initial teacher education (ITE). In fact, most would argue that ITE is merely the beginning of an ongoing process in a changing world. In 2003 an OECD report attributed the complexity of a world characterised by change to three major factors: technology, societies becoming diverse and compartmentalised, and globalisation (summarised in Zwozdiak-Myers 2012: 164–5). All three inevitably have an effect on education and teaching contexts. CPD can happen in a number of ways, many of which have been discussed here and in other parts of this book. Zwozdiak-Myers (2012: 174) identifies three main sources: within the school (induction, mentoring, observation etc.), school networks (cross-school, virtual etc.) and other external expertise (further study, professional associations etc.). A number of key questions need to be asked before and after any such activity and all CPD should be recorded in a professional development portfolio, which will be discussed in Section 8.4.

TASK 8.3   EXAMINING THE FRAMEWORK FOR REFLECTIVE PRACTICE

A.   Consider Zwozdiak-Myers' dimensions and framework of RP and answer the following questions:
Do any of the dimensions overlap? If so, how?
Do you think any of the dimensions are more important than others? If so, which and why?
Do you think any of the dimensions are easier for you to engage with, as a teacher? If so, which and why?
Which of the dimensions are likely to trigger RP action for you? Why?
Can you think of examples of how you engaged with any of these dimensions in the past? What were the outcomes?
Which of these dimensions do you need to continue to develop?
B.   Plan an activity around one or two related dimensions of the RP framework, implement it when you next teach, and write and report the outcomes to a colleague or tutor.

8.3   THE ROLE OF COOPERATION

One criticism that has been made of RP models is that they can promote individualistic and isolated teachers who focus inwardly on their own teaching (see Further Reading Two below for more details). And of course this can happen if teachers direct their RP activities exclusively in this way. However, it is now well known that within professional communities of practice (Lave and Wenger 1991), much can be learned and shared with others who have had similar and different experiences. Models of social constructivism (Bruner 1985, Vygotsky 1978) in education emphasise the central role played by constructing knowledge while engaging with others in joint discussions, tasks or other social activities. So, even when the emphasis is on oneself, it does not mean that we must or should work alone. In fact, perhaps too much of what we do as teachers is individual and unshared experience. I would argue that good reflective engagement should ideally have a balance of both individual and joint undertakings, and an inward and outward focus in order to achieve the best outcomes. As a teacher and an individual you will decide the precise balance which suits you, based on a number of factors such as your own learning style and your professional and cultural contexts. In this section I draw on Edge's discourse framework for continuing cooperative development (CCD) (Edge 2002), which aims to help teachers to listen and respond better during non-judgemental discussions aimed at creative and exploratory professional development. Edge's framework is for teachers interested in continuing to improve what they do in small-scale ways throughout their careers. It relies on equal peer relationships between like-minded teachers who have interests in exploring and enhancing their practice. It may offer you some skills to help you do this, or you may favour other routes to your development. I have found Edge's work interesting and engaging in my own career and have therefore decided to share it in this book.

The basic assumption of CCD is that the starting point for any development is a recognition of where you are and an appreciation of what you do, rather than a sense that you need to move away constantly from this and towards something that you are told or perceive to be 'better'. This acknowledges that as well as an 'external approach' to continuing development we also need an 'internal growth' approach (Edge 2002: 11). In Edge's words, 'the best way for you to teach is exactly the way that you do teach, provided only that you are committed to the development of your teaching in ways that you believe to be sensitive to the needs of your students and yourself' (p. 10). He believes in teaching development in cooperation with others so that we can better understand our own experiences, ideas, attitudes and opinions: 'through cooperation, we have a chance to escape from simple, egocentric subjectivity without chasing after an illusory notion of objectivity' (p. 16). However, CCD relies on a type of cooperation where the other person is not seeking to change you in ways that they think you ought to be changed, but where they will help you see yourself clearly so that you can make your own judgements and decisions about whether and how you want to change. In other words, your development remains within your control. 'Cooperative development is a way of working together with one or more colleagues in order to develop as a person who teaches in your own terms' (p. 18). CCD focuses on learning through conversations where you articulate your thoughts and experiences so that others can understand them. These conversations require the underlying attitudes of respect, empathy and sincerity.

So how does CCD work in practice? It is based on the rotating roles of Speaker and Understander (and sometimes Observer) and on five interactive techniques: attending, reflecting, making connections, focusing and moving towards action. Each of these will be explored in the next paragraphs, with some tasks adapted/adopted from Edge. CCD conversations can take place between two or more people and it is suggested that they be recorded so that you can later review them. It is also a good idea to take notes during the sessions. How often and with whom you do CCD is up to you, but it works best if it is a relatively regular part of your RP.

Attending
Attending or listening supportively to the Speaker is essentially the most important thing an Understander can do. Positive listening is extremely powerful and can encourage increased quality and quantity of speaking. When listening, we communicate our interest and emotions in numerous ways: the way we sit or stand, what we do with our hands, our facial expressions, our eye movements, our interjections and vocal responses (there is a large body of literature on the forms and functions

of minimal and non-minimal response tokens in different contexts; for example, McCarthy 2002, 2003). Even silence says a lot. I am Irish, which means I grew up in a culture where silence in a conversation is almost taboo and every effort is made to avoid the embarrassment caused by a lull in the talk. But while I am not comfortable with silence, in other cultures it is highly valued. Scollon and Scollon (1981) report on the importance of silence in the presence of those considered to be superior among Athabaskan peoples. To speak continuously in this context would be a grave mark of disrespect. In CCD, silence can be important as a space for reflection and articulation, and Understanders should consider carefully when to interject and how. Edge suggests that we need to do two things to help us to attend better. Firstly, we need to become informed about what has been written about body language (see, for example, many writings from the field of neuro-linguistic programming). Secondly, we need to become aware of our own body language and how we behave.

TASK 8.4   LISTENING

A.   List what you think makes a person feel well listened to and not well listened to. Compare your list with others'.
B.   Find people from cultures other than your own. Discuss the role of silence and eye contact in each of your cultures.
C.   Listen to a colleague telling you about a recent difficulty they had while teaching. Allow an observer to watch the interaction, take notes and give some feedback on your attending behaviour. Listen to the observer's and the colleague's accounts of how you listened. How are their accounts consistent with or different from what you think and feel about your attending behaviour?

Reflecting
The second interactive technique that Edge discusses is the more active skill of reflecting, on the part of the Understander. In regular social conversation, you usually interject for two reasons: to signal listenership and to make space for yourself to take the floor. In CCD, the second of these has to give way to a more reflective type of listening where the focus remains firmly on the development of the Speaker. This is often frustrating for the Understander initially but is a technique to be acquired over time. By reflecting, the Understander empathetically mirrors the Speaker's ideas so that they can get a clearer perspective on them. This technique is also associated with certain traditions in counselling. The three main purposes are to check understanding, to encourage progress and to facilitate insight. Checking understanding can lead to more clarity and further insights. The Speaker is encouraged to continue, expand, and take risks if they feel valued because of the Understander reflecting their content in a way that is recognisable as belonging to them. Insight is facilitated when the re-presented picture prompts a realisation or insight that had not been considered before that point in the conversation. There are also additional practical reasons for reflecting, such as giving the Speaker a break from speaking, partially equalising the vulnerability of the context, avoiding Understander memory overload, and checking that there has

been no misunderstanding. Reflecting in a non-judgemental way is not usually an easy skill to grasp, but Edge is convinced of its value, as evidenced when he says, 'it is difficult to Reflect accurately and empathically, but Reflection is of great help to the Speaker and to the relationship on which co-operative development is based' (2002: 67).

TASK 8.5   REFLECTING

A.   Read one of the following reflective blog entries from PhD-level English language teachers, look up from the page, and reflect it verbally to a partner who has read a different entry. You might like to audio-record yourself also. Discuss with your partner the words that you used and your attempt at reflecting.

Blog A: A teacher from Malaysia
Planning is one of the most important things in teaching. I always remember the saying says 'failing to prepare is preparing to fail'. It means that when teacher fails to prepare her/his teaching, she/he is preparing to fail her/his teaching objectives. However, in planning sometimes we do not really know what my students' interests and needs are. In planning, I always try to put myself on the students' position and see the lesson from their point of view. What do I need from this lesson? What do I want from this lessen? And what will I learn from this lesson? In this way, hopefully I have considered my students' needs over my own interests.

During the teaching process where I implement my planning, I usually make changes based on the classroom and students situation. Teaching is very dynamic process that teachers should be able to respond appropriately. In the teaching process, the student's individual learning is my focus. By looking at their responses and engagement in the process, usually I can identify if the students get difficulty and then I modify my interaction to guide the students to be able to learn and achieve their learning objectives.

My reflection on my practice was not something that I did intentionally. I was not really aware of reflecting on my action in term of using reflective practice theories. I did it naturally as an effort for me to improve my teaching. I reflect my teaching based on what was good, what was bad and need to be improved, and how can I improve it if I have to do this class in the future.

Blog B: A teacher from Saudi Arabia
I used to, regularly, see what my students said about my teaching in the forums in regard to teaching/learning objectives, instruction, students input about my delivery, support, guidance, etc. In my country, some of my colleagues asked me about students' evaluation. In fact, students knew that I read their comments, but they did not know that I made adjustments learning from their comments for my own benefits as a teacher. Therefore, I disregarded the students who wanted to be funny.

We, teachers, know that Students talk to their parents and tell them the positive and negative points about us. Students talk to each other and share what they think about their teachers. I see that if teachers know students' evaluation about them, it offers a good opportunity to make amendments to improve teaching learning process. However, a personal and negative action from teachers is not supposed to take place.

As stated by researchers, action and reflection are essential ingredients in the construction of knowledge and in deeper teaching/learning process. Now, you, as a teacher, what would you do briefly if you were in my position and found some of your students made fun of you, and some others mentioned some points as weaknesses of your teaching? How are you going to deal with your students, and how are you going to teach the module you are coordinating? Let us discuss this issue.

B. The Understander may have to interrupt the Speaker in order to reflect. List some phrases that you would consider useful to help you do this, for example, 'Can I just check something with you?'

Making connections
Taking reflecting a step further involves the Understander thematising or drawing links and connections together from what the Speaker has said. Once they have offered the possibility of a link, it is then up to the Speaker to accept this possibility and evaluate it if they wish to. This process helps the Speaker to establish connections and maybe overall coherence in what they have said, and may lead to a larger-scale discovery about their teaching and possible next steps because of the discovery. Edge illustrates how bringing two ideas together can also work in a challenging way. He gives the following example from what he himself said:

Students were wasting their time learning word lists.
Learners learn in different ways and that people should do what works best for them. (p. 80)

His Understander asked how these two statements fitted together, in a move which Edge calls a Challenge, that is, bringing together two ideas that the Understander finds difficult to reconcile (rather than a challenge to the ideas or opinions behind what had been said). This should be understood only as an opportunity for the Speaker to show how their ideas are coherent. Maybe the Challenge can be resolved immediately or maybe it needs more reflection and development work on the part of the Speaker.

Focusing
To avoid talking in generalisations and in order to move towards action, explicit focus points need to be found during CCD conversations. By focusing, a deeper understanding can be reached and this should then lead to conscious action. The Understander facilitates by questioning and pointing things out. The Speaker,

through their own talk and the Understander's help, can evaluate and decide where and how to act on the specifics. It is again important here that the Understander does not try to move the Speaker in a direction that the Understander thinks they should. When to focus and what to focus on should always be within the Speaker's control.

Into action
The final interactive technique outlined in Edge's CCD framework is moving into action. The conversations are only a means to this end of improved teaching, and in order to improve, some planned and conscious action must take place. This may not happen because of every conversation, and often several discussions are needed to explore and evaluate before a focus point for action can be identified. Each teacher and each context is different, and CCD must be used in a way that suits you and how you think and how you work. Ultimately, a particular action will be decided upon and, according to Edge, the motivation for this action:

> Will probably come from one of three types of realisation. Speakers will realise:
>   that they are dissatisfied with what is happening in some area;
>   that some particular success deserves wider application;
>   that one area of professional activity is so interesting as to demand further investigation. (p. 108)

Once the motivation has been ignited through the CCD conversations, it is time to set some goals and plan action for what has to be done. The Speaker decides what to do on the basis of their values, knowledge, experience and goal, and the Understander puts themselves entirely at their service when they are doing this. Small-scale goals are easier to implement and are more likely to be acted upon successfully. The exact classroom procedure for the implementation of the goal can be talked through in what Edge calls 'trialing'. This ensures that all steps have been considered and that they are coherent, and the Understander can bring up points of detail. Once a plan is in place, the Speaker can use it, possibly in a flexible way based on how it materialises in class. The Understander should avoid the temptation to advise at this stage, even if asked. What does not work for one person may work for another and any lessons learned will be the Speaker's.

TASK 8.6   HAVING A CCD CONVERSATION

Find one or two peers or colleagues that you trust and with whom you have a good working relationship.
A.   Select some practice tasks from Edge's CCD book and work through them over a couple of sessions. You might like to select those which practise the skills you feel you need to develop. It would be good to have an Observer role during these activities so that you can get some feedback.
B.   Once you have done the practice tasks in (A), have some real CCD conversations over a few weeks with each of you getting time to play both the Speaker

and the Understander (and Observer if you wish). Set up a shared blog where you can record what goes on in each of the sessions.

8.4   THE PROFESSIONAL DEVELOPMENT PORTFOLIO

8.4.1   CONCEPTS, FINDINGS AND TEXTS

So far in this chapter we have seen lots of examples of RP activities. Some can be done alone, for example, keeping a teaching diary or blog; some can be done with others from your professional communities, for example, CCD conversations; some require you to focus inwards on your own practice, for example, peer observations; and some require an external focus, for example, attending in-service events or conferences. As I mentioned earlier, each of you will find the balance between the various types of RP endeavours that suit you and your teaching context best. And of course technology has made it easier than ever to engage with other members of your community of teachers to advance your RP. There are many websites with teaching ideas, community blogs, shared discussion spaces, freely available software and the opportunity to engage in events virtually from anywhere in the world. There really is no reason or excuse for not being an active reflective practitioner. In fact, if you are like me, the difficulty is not so much the engagement but the follow-up in the form of keeping a record of what you have done and what the outcomes have been. For this reason, RP should be recorded in a professional development portfolio (PDP). This can be as formal or informal as you would like it to be and will grow as you do, so it needs to be flexible. Its purpose is to capture evidence of your growth and development, and it should ideally begin during your ITE. It can take any format that works for you. Mine is a folder on my computer with about twenty different files that have names such as 'philosophy and beliefs', 'experience', 'training events/courses attended' (and another for those I organised), 'conferences attended' (and another for those I organised), 'projects', 'publications', 'talks given', 'online activities', 'MA and PhD supervisions', 'peer observations', 'teaching evaluations' and 'feedback'. I try to update them a couple of times a year and can draw on any of the contents when I need to put together a more formal portfolio that will be read or evaluated by others.

Wolf and Dietz (1998) present the model shown in Table 8.1. This model is necessarily general, as PDPs are very personalised and individual. You decide what goes into it and how it looks. Zwozdiak-Myers (2012: 178–9) suggests the following artefacts which might be included:

- Qualifications and curriculum vitae;
- Syllabi, units of work, lesson plans, reviews of lesson plans and activities;
- Professional development plans and subsequent reviews;
- Feedback from peers, mentors, supervisors;
- Observation and appraisal reports with personal reflections following such events;
- Reflections on aspects of your teaching;
- Reflective log or learning diary;

Table 8.1   Professional development portfolio model

Portfolio model	Professional growth and development
Purpose	To explore, extend, showcase and reflect on teachers' own learning
Processes	Teachers identify their own goals and build portfolios to reflect these goals; self-assessment with assistance from peers or mentors
Audiences	Teacher/colleagues
Structure	Open-ended, teacher-determined
Content	Wide variety of teacher-selected work and records relating to self-selected goals

- Information, handouts, programmes from conferences, seminars and workshops you have participated in and reflections on sessions you have attended;
- Plans for training sessions you have delivered along with participants' evaluations of those sessions;
- Support and guidance given to colleagues;
- Samples of pupils' work and your feedback to them;
- Records of assessing pupils and tracking their progress;
- Notes and letters from parents/carers/pupils;
- Personal reflections on source material you have read and research undertaken.

TASK 8.7   PROFESSIONAL DEVELOPMENT PORTFOLIO TEMPLATES

Spend some time looking online, through publications and through available materials at your institution. Select any templates or models that you would like to use for your PDP.

TASK 8.8   CREATING A PROFESSIONAL DEVELOPMENT PORTFOLIO

Start to create a PDP using the materials from Task 8.7, and add any other content you feel you would like to include. Store it electronically and online if you wish so that you have a permanent working document to add to and change (Google Sites and Mahara are currently popular e-portfolio systems).

TASK 8.9   REFINING YOUR PROFESSIONAL DEVELOPMENT PORTFOLIO

Compare your PDP and its contents with that of a colleague or peer you trust. Are there any changes you would like to make to yours?

8.5   FURTHER READING ONE

Farrell, T. S. C. (2012) 'Reflecting on reflective practice: (Re)visiting Dewey and Schön', *TESOL Journal*, 3: 1, 7–16. The issue is free at: http://onlinelibrary.wiley.com/doi/10.1002/tesj.10/pdf.
In this publication, after many years of engagement in RP, Farrell revisits the original thinking of Dewey from 1933 and then of Schön (1983, 1987). He does this in the light of the following introduction to the article:

> Currently it seems that the terms reflection and reflective practice are so popular in education that they are nearly mandatory terms used in language teacher education and development programs – reflection is mentioned somewhere in these programs. Yes, many language educators still agree that some form of reflection is a desirable practice among teachers; however, the agreement stops there because there is still almost no consensus as to what reflective practice is and which reflective practices actually promote teacher development (Farrell, 2007). Perhaps this state of indecisiveness about what reflective practice in TESOL really means can be attributed to the many different interpretations of reflection and reflective practice that have surfaced in the past. Indeed, much has been written about reflection and reflective practice in many fields, such as education, medicine, and second language education, but there still remains a sense of lack of clarity about what it is and how it can be achieved. (p. 8)

In outlining Dewey's thinking and writing, Farrell draws on the original concern he had with actions arising from routine thinking, which is guided by tradition, impulse or authority. He makes a strong distinction between this and active reflection. Dewey warned of the dangers of teachers becoming slaves to routine if they did not learn how to think intelligently about their work. He outlined five phases of reflective thought, which he considered to occur in no particular order:

1. *Suggestion:* A doubtful situation is understood to be problematic, and some vague suggestions are considered as possible solutions.
2. *Intellectualisation:* The difficulty or perplexity of the problem that has been felt (directly experienced) is intellectualised into a problem to be solved.
3. *Guiding Idea:* One suggestion after another is used as a leading idea, or hypothesis; the initial suggestion can be used as a working hypothesis to initiate and guide observation and other operations in the collection of factual material.
4. *Reasoning:* Reasoning links present and past ideas and helps elaborate the supposition that reflective inquiry has reached, or the mental elaboration of the idea or supposition as an idea or supposition.
5. *Hypothesis Testing:* The refined idea is reached, and the testing of this refined hypothesis takes place; the testing can be by overt action or in thought (imaginative action). (p. 10)

Farrell also refers to the work of Boud et al. (1985), who gave emotion an important place in their model of reflective thought, which has the three broad categories of experience, reflection and outcome. Dewey encouraged the use of systematic reflections with teachers' practical experiences in order to raise awareness. This, he ascertained, would lead to professional development and growth. Thus, according to Farrell (p. 11), 'Dewey was advocating early for a form of evidence-based teaching.'

Farrell next moves to looking at the much later work of Donald Schön (1983, 1987), which draws centrally on Dewey's theory of inquiry. Schön's first book on the topic, *The Reflective Practitioner: How Professionals Think in Action*, focused on practitioner-based knowledge and its distinguishing features. Not referring directly to teachers, he described 'reflection-in-action' (as discussed earlier in this chapter) as how practitioners think on their feet; in order to do this they must possess a level of 'knowing-in-action' based on past ideas and experiences. If teachers did not 'know-in-action' then they would find it very difficult to make the sort of on-the-spot decisions required in the classroom. This mostly happens at a subconscious level, especially for more experienced practitioners. When new scenarios arise then 'reflection-in-action' is required, and this involves a number of stages in order to attempt to solve the problem:

- A situation develops that triggers spontaneous, routine responses (such as in knowing-in-action): For example, a student cannot answer an easy grammar question, such as identifying a grammar structure, that he or she was able to answer during the previous class.
- Routine responses by the teacher (i.e., what the teacher has always done) do not produce a routine response and instead produce a surprise for the teacher: The teacher starts to explain how the student had already explained this grammar structure in the previous class and so the teacher wonders why this is the case. The teacher asks the student if anything is the matter, and the student says that he or she forgets the answer.
- This surprise response gets the teacher's attention and leads to reflection within an action: The teacher reacts quickly to try to find out why the student suddenly 'forgets' a grammar structure the teacher knows the student has no trouble understanding. The teacher can ask the student directly to explain what is happening.
- Reflection now gives rise to on-the-spot experimentation by the teacher: The student may or may not explain why he or she is crying. The teacher will take some measures (depending on the reaction or non-reaction) to help solve the problem: ignore the situation, empathize with the student, help the student answer the question by modeling answers, and so forth. (p. 13)

According to Schön, such a sequence leads to reflection-in-action, which in turn leads to new understandings and actions.

Farrell then considers how Dewey's notion of systematic, mature, intentional 'reflection-on-action' and Schön's notion of on-the-spot 'reflection-in-action' can lead to 'reflection-for-action'. Both Dewey and Schön moved the idea of reflection from simply meaning loose thoughts to one of systematic inquiry, which is rigorous and disciplined. Farrell states:

> For me the implications of both Dewey's and Schön's work is that reflective teaching is evidence based; teachers collect data or evidence about their work and then reflect on this evidence to make informed decisions about their practice. Engaging in evidence-based reflective practice enables teachers to articulate to themselves (and others) what they do, how they do it, why they do it, and what the impact of one's teaching is on student learning. The results of engaging in such reflective practice may mean an affirmation of current practices or making changes, but these changes will not be based on impulse, tradition, or the like; they will emerge as a result of analysis of concrete evidence. (p. 14)

The article ends by returning to some of Dewey's ideas on the attributes of a reflective individual. He highlights four: open-mindedness (a desire to listen to alternative views), responsibility (considering the outcomes of an action), wholeheartedness (overcoming fears to evaluate practice in order to make change) and an attitude of directness (that something is worth doing). This concludes Farrell's consideration of Dewey and Schön's contributions to RP in this publication.

More of Farrell's work can be found at: http://www.reflectiveinquiry.ca.

FURTHER READING ONE TASK

1. Identify an issue/problem from your teaching and take it through Dewey's five phases of reflective thought. Do this in collaboration with another teacher and work through their issue in the same way. Report on the outcome and your experiences of applying Dewey's framework.
2. Write a short blog on a portal of your choice (no more than 1,000 words) about the advantages and disadvantages of following Schön's ideas on RP.

8.6   FURTHER READING TWO

Akbari, R. (2007) 'Reflections on reflection: A critical appraisal of reflective practices in L2 teacher education', *System*, 35: 2, 192–207.
Akbari, in this 2007 article, takes a critical stance during his deliberations on the ideas associated with RP. He starts by describing how the present-day implementation of RP in teacher education began as a direct result of the post-method era and the growth of research into teachers' cognition, beliefs and practical knowledge. Because teacher education could no longer look to one particular method or source for conceptual knowledge, something else was needed. He quotes Halliday (1998: 598): 'it is understandable that the notion of reflective practice has been eagerly seized upon by the beleaguered teacher educators seeking to do something emancipatory and authentic in the act of hostility towards theory, moral deliberation and contextuality in teaching practices'. The article argues that in the chaos of the search, teacher

education moved to the other extreme (RP), without giving enough critical thought to what such a framework might have to offer.

After outlining Dewey's and Schön's contributions to the RP movement, this article considers discussions from Fendler (2003), who considers the term *reflection* as having a Cartesian basis which views knowing about the self or self-knowledge as a valid means of knowledge generation. Fendler also credits the role of feminism in the reflective movement. The basic assumption here is that the masculine nature of knowledge has put women in a subordinate role. In language teaching, the fact that most of the academics are males and most of the practitioners are females (Pennycook 1989) would seem to substantiate this claim. By validating the knowledge generated by practitioners, feminists aim to redress the imbalance. Following this discussion, Akbari introduces the typology proposed by Jay and Johnson (2002):

> They regard reflective practice as consisting of three crucial steps of description, comparison, and criticism. The descriptive stage is the problem-setting stage during which the teacher determines which aspect of the classroom or her practice should form the core of her reflective attention. The second stage, i.e., comparison, is the phase during which the teacher starts 'thinking about the matter for reflection from a number of different frameworks' (p. 78). It is during the comparative stage that the practitioner tries to make sense of other people's viewpoints, or develops a new frame of reference (Schön, 1983) which will enable her to comprehend viewpoints which may run counter to the ones she holds. This ability to detach oneself from the limits of one's experience will enable us to 'discover meanings we might otherwise miss' (Jay and Johnson, 2002, p. 78). The ultimate result will be a more comprehensive understanding of the teaching context and its complexity. The last stage of reflection is what is termed as the critical stage. At this stage, the reflective practitioner evaluates different choices and alternatives and integrates the newly-acquired information with what she already knows. It is, in fact, the decision making stage resulting from careful analysis of the situation and deliberation. This last stage will form the basis for the formulation of alternative ways of teaching or approaching the problem on the part of the teacher. (p. 195)

For the remainder of the article Akbari problematises RP as it happens today in teacher education. He outlines a number of issues as follows:

> A careful reading of the literature shows that there are some major theoretical and practical flaws in the concept of reflective teaching as it is practiced today. From a historical/theoretical viewpoint, there is no common, agreed upon definition of reflection since reflection has been influenced by many trends and philosophies; reflection, as it is promoted by teacher educators in L2 settings, is of a retrospective nature, not paving the way toward creativity; moreover, current reflective models in L2 teacher education lack the necessary critical dimension. From a practical viewpoint, there is no published evidence to show improved teacher or student performance resulting from reflective techniques; the

personality of teachers is a missing variable in almost all discussions of reflection; and finally, too much emphasis on reflective practices and teachers' practical knowledge might result in isolation from the language teaching discourse community. (p. 193)

In the conclusion to the article, Akbari acknowledges that reflection will give practitioners a stronger sense of autonomy, but cautions that teacher educators must be aware of the limitations and misinterpretations of the idea. He suggests that:

From a practical viewpoint, it must be borne in mind that reflection is not an end, but a means to an end; the end sought here is better student learning and more efficient teacher performance. As long as there is evidence that reflective practice is helping teachers to achieve these goals, there would be no objection to its application. However, in the absence of such evidence, caution should be the order of the day, leaving the door open to other possibilities and models of teacher education. (p. 206)

Finally, he advocates for realism in the light of the fact that teachers are limited in what they can do in a class, and questions the impact that the academic notion of *post-method era* has on the everyday lives of teachers. Bearing this in mind, promoting reflective teaching without evaluating its consequences will add to any existing confusion (citing Britzman 2000). He finishes on this note:

At its best, reflective teaching can provide language teachers with a set of techniques to become more conscious of their own actions and feelings in and outside classrooms; at its worse, it can result in isolation from the discourse community. It is good to reflect, but reflection itself also requires reflection. (p. 205)

FURTHER READING TWO TASK

1. To what extent do you agree with Akbari's criticisms, and why?
2. Compare your RP activities (during your teacher education programme or as a qualified teacher) with others in a small group and say how much of what Akbari says is true of your experiences.
3. Jay and Johnson (2003) provide a relatively practical system for doing RP. Decide on a focus for your RP, based on a recent experience, and take it through the stages of their framework. How useful do you find this process?

8.7 SUMMARY

RP is an essential part of your ongoing growth and development as a teacher. Given the rate of social, cultural and technological change which affect what and how you teach, relying on what you learned in your ITE programme to serve you for your entire career is no longer an option. RP takes many forms and has many dimensions, as discussed in Section 8.2 above. Although you will select which work best for you, it is also important to engage in a range and to develop any that you may not be intuitively attracted to. This can be done at a rate that you feel comfortable with. Some aspects of RP can be done on an individual basis, but other practitioners can be of great assistance to you and you to them. Working with trusted colleagues can allow you to gain a better insight into your own practices, and this can be done through developmental conversations in a CCD framework, as detailed in Section 8.3. These can be very motivating and facilitative in developing and implementing a plan of action around aspects of your teaching that you deem it to be important to improve. You can also learn from others through their shared practices, documented accounts, in-service events and other professional events. In order to organise and manage all of your RP activity, a PDP will document aspects of your growth that you consider important. The format and content of your PDP are a matter for you to decide, but it should be a complete and representative account of how you progress through your career. This is primarily a personal document, but you may be surprised at how often you will need to use it for other purposes (for example, job applications, promotions, performance evaluations). Another more investigative approach to RP is AR, and this will be elaborated in some detail in the next chapter.

8.8   ADDITIONAL READINGS

Clarke, A. (1995) 'Professional development in practicum settings: Reflective practice under scrutiny', *Teaching and Teacher Education*, 11: 13, 243–61.

Farrell, T. S. C. (2007) *Reflective Language Teaching: From Research to Practice*, London: Continuum.

Farrell, T. S. C. (2015) *Promoting Teacher Reflection in Second Language Education: A Framework for TESOL Professionals*, New York: Routledge.

Griffiths, V. (2000) 'The reflective dimension in teacher education', *International Journal of Educational Research*, 33: 5, 539–55.

Korthagen, F. and Vasalos, A. (2005) 'Levels in reflection: Core reflection as a means to enhance professional growth', *Teachers and Teaching: Theory and Practice*, 11: 1, 47–71.

Mann, S. and Walsh, S. (2013) 'RP or "RIP": A critical perspective on reflective practice', *Applied Linguistics Review*, 4: 2, 291–315.

Zeichner, K. and Liston, D. (1996) *Reflective Teaching: An Introduction*, Mahwah: Lawrence Erlbaum.

TEACHER RESEARCH ENGAGEMENT

9.1   INTRODUCTION

In Chapter 8, we briefly mentioned research as one of the dimensions of RP, and this chapter will elaborate on that discussion. There are many types of research which are directly or peripherally relevant for language teachers, such as research on language and discourse, research on second language acquisition, research on sociolinguistic variables such as age or gender, and research on assessment (for a full account see Brown 2014). All of these are highly valuable undertakings, and while I would encourage any type of research as a developmental tool for the individual and the profession, I am aware that the demands placed on teachers' time are many, and more pressing priorities often win out over good intentions to conduct research. In my own observations and discussions with teachers I have found that unless research is part of an ongoing academic programme (such as that described in Gore and Zeichner 1991), many types don't normally get done by many practising teachers. This is demonstrated in a more evidence-based way in a study by Borg (2009), where he reports low engagement among his teacher group. In his book *Teacher Research in Language Teaching* (Borg 2013: 2), he extends his discussion and speaks about the paradox 'between the potential value and actual uptake of teacher research in language teaching' and the 'need for teaching to be evidence-based'. I believe that most teachers appreciate the value of research, and my own positive predisposition towards the notion of professionals engaging with it has motivated me to include a specific chapter in this volume devoted to it. In addition, with the changing nature of professional standards, policies and demands, more structured RP in the form scholarship is often specified. Rossouw (2009: 2), in the context of the South African Norms and Standards for Educators, quotes one of the educator roles as 'scholar, researcher and life-long learner', and I am aware of similar requirements in many other parts of the world.

As English language teachers you always have new issues, challenges and problems that you need to solve as part of your everyday practices (for example, the student who won't participate, overuse of the L1, political tensions among mixed groups of students). And you solve these in highly professional and appropriate ways. The role that research plays in finding these solutions can take two directions: reading research publications and actively doing research. In terms of doing research, AR for local inquiry is suggested as a good framework to use when trying to investigate practice-based issues, and because it allows you to focus directly on your ongoing, everyday activities, you will have strong motivation to see it through in order to find some solutions. As you read through the sections in this chapter, you will probably recognise many of the steps and procedures involved in AR as things that you do anyway as part of your teaching. This just gives you a good framework on which to hang them together in a more formal and complete way to ensure that you and your students (and possibly your colleagues or other teachers) get maximum benefit from your efforts. And although it takes time to look at your activities in a more formal and detailed way, in the words of Michael Wallace (1998: 1) 'there is ample evidence that this approach can provide all sorts of interesting and helpful professional insights'.

This chapter begins with the very explicit aim of reducing the traditional fracture between those who practise and those who research practice in language teaching. As such, it holds a very important place in this volume, as a discussion which is not always found in books about practice. The legitimacy of qualified teachers to be researchers faces diminishing opposition, but many novice teachers and their tutors have not always considered action research to be a worthy contender for a place on teacher education programmes at certain levels. In recent times, however, we are moving towards a realisation that this should be a core component of a teacher's identity and, as such, it should be encouraged from the very beginning (van Looy and Goegebeur 2007, Wallace 1998) and right throughout one's career. All of these issues are introduced in Section 9.2, before a more procedural account of action research is presented as an appropriate methodology for investigating classroom contexts in Section 9.3. Specific issues, problems and questions which are suitable for this type of research are then discussed in some detail in the third core section.

9.2   BEING TEACHER AND RESEARCHER

9.2.1   CONCEPTS, FINDINGS AND TEXTS

Teacher research, or practitioner research (these terms are often used synonymously), has been given several labels and definitions over the years, some of which will be explored in this and the next section. A large-scale study reported by Borg (2013) is based on 15 years of research and 1,730 participating teachers and managers from contexts in Africa, Asia, Australia and New Zealand, Europe, the Middle East, and North and South America. Using a range of data-gathering techniques, Borg explores, among other things, how the participants conceive research and what they perceive to be its important characteristics. He concludes that:

> Language teachers' conceptions of research are predominantly associated with what has been called a 'standard' view of scientific research (Robson, 2002: 19) – i.e. one associated with statistics, objectivity and hypothesis testing. Similar views were expressed by managers in the questionnaires, though the interviews with these managers highlighted a broader range of conceptions of research. Thus they did refer to activities that were formally academic but gave more prominence to reflective, analytical, and evaluative activities whose focus was on professional

development, improving classroom practice and enhancing student learning. (Borg 2013: 69)

Without wanting to go into the details of distinctions between what has traditionally been termed 'scientific' research and 'non-scientific' research (see Brown 2014: ch. 1), it is sufficient to say at this point that a broad view of what can be counted as legitimate teacher research is advocated here. The important distinction, in my opinion, is rather that between what is merely 'reflection' as discussed in Chapter 8 and what can reasonably be defined as 'research'. You can explore this distinction for yourself in the tasks at the end of this section and also in the contents of Section 9.3. Taking this broad view also allows teacher research to be more inclusive, and many of the activities in which you engage on a regular basis as part of your practice can, in some cases with some modification, become part of the world of research. It is then perfectly feasible that on one or many occasions in your professional career, you will engage in doing some research. And this can occur despite some of the barriers that are often cited as preventing such engagement. Borg (2013: 18; see also Burns 2010: 6) summarises these perceived obstacles, from previous accounts in the literature, as follows:

- Non-collaborative school cultures
- Limitations in teachers' awareness, beliefs, skills, and knowledge
- Limited resources (including time)
- Lack of teacher motivation
- Economic matters
- Unsupportive leadership
- Political issues.

As with all things, if you are interested and motivated in professional development through research activities, you will find a way to do it, even on a small scale. So, then, the question arises: 'why should I do AR?' For a teacher who is committed to developing in this way 'there is growing evidence that language teachers from all over the world would get immense satisfaction from doing AR, especially when they can work collaboratively with other colleagues to explore common issues' (Burns 2010: 7). More specifically, the benefits cited include teaching and research skills development, faster professional development, more effective materials development, innovation, and the generation of useful theory (Denny 2005: 8, cited in Burns 2010: 7).

Having briefly discussed teachers' conceptions of research, and the barriers and rationale for engaging, we will now move towards exploring the nature of AR and how it fits within professional development activities. On the basis of our discussions of RP in Chapter 8, and as a useful point of departure, it is worthwhile drawing on Wallace's representation of professional development strategies in Figure 9.1 and thinking about where research is situated within this framework and what that means (Wallace 1998: 14).

The strategies identified on this framework fork to the right where some of the activities, such as attending conferences, lead to professional reflection and potentially changes in practice. We saw in Chapter 8 how these can be useful but

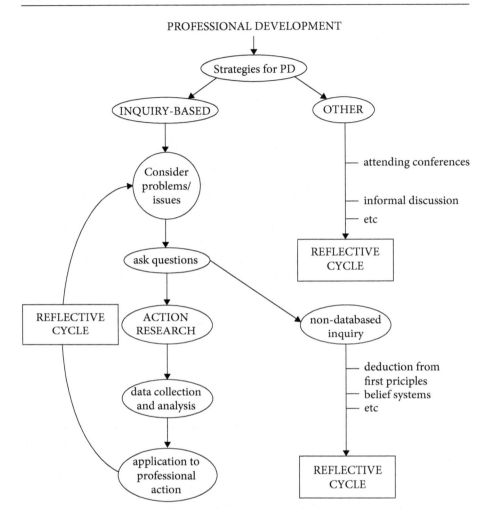

Figure 9.1   Professional development strategies (Wallace 1998: 14)

some commentators, including Wallace (1998: 13–14), consider that certain types of informal reflection can be 'more therapeutic than productive. Contemplating problems does not necessarily lead to solving them . . . There is therefore a case for also having available as a source for our reflection certain systematic approaches and techniques which will help us to make sense of our experiences, and perhaps through such *structured reflection* come to a solution' (italics in original). Therefore on the left of the fork we see a different, more structured and formal type of reflective cycle around the process of AR. This is the focus of our discussions in the remainder of this chapter.

Table 9.1 Professional development strategies

Strategy	Pros	Cons	My preferences/ possibilities	My desired outcomes
Action research				
Conferences				
Collaborative discussions				
Reading professional publications				
Professional organisations				
Peer observations				
Other				

TASK 9.1   PROFESSIONAL DEVELOPMENT STRATEGIES

Discuss each of the strategies in Table 9.1 and fill in the various columns. Feel free to add other strategies that you think might be useful for you or others.

TASK 9.2   YOUR PERCEPTIONS OF RESEARCH

A. Think about how you perceive research. Read the following scenarios from Borg (2013: 53). For each one, discuss in pairs/groups whether you would categorise it as research or not, and explain why.

1. A teacher noticed that an activity she used in class did not work well. She thought about this after the lesson and made some notes in her diary. She tried something different in her next lesson. This time the activity was more successful.

2. A teacher read about a new approach to teaching writing and decided to try it out in his class over a period of two weeks. He video recorded some of his lessons and collected samples of learners' written work. He analysed this information, then presented the results to his colleagues at a staff meeting.

3. A university lecturer gave a questionnaire about the use of computers in language teaching to 500 teachers. Statistics were used to analyse the questionnaires. The lecturer wrote an article about the work in an academic journal.

4. Midway through a course, a teacher gave a class of 30 students a feedback form. The next day, 5 students handed in their completed forms. The teacher read these and used the information to decide what to do in the second part of the course.

5. A teacher trainer asked his trainees to write an essay about ways of motivating teenage learners of English. After reading the assignments, the

trainer decided to write an article on the trainees' ideas about motivation. He submitted his article to a professional journal.

B.   On the basis of the discussions you had when completing (A), place the following in order of most to least important as features of good research:

- The results are presented or published.
- There are a large number of participants.
- Surveys are used.
- The research is objective.
- Variables are controlled.
- The results are analysed statistically.
- The results apply to many teaching contexts.
- An experiment is used.
- Ideas for teachers' use are generated.
- The research is based on existing literature.
- The research is ethical.
- The research is replicable.
- The research has practical value.
- The research makes a new contribution to knowledge.

TASK 9.3   DEFINITIONS OF RESEARCH

On the basis of your discussions around the previous two tasks, spend some time exploring definitions online, survey your 'friends' on social media, and write a definition of (1) teacher research and (2) action research that best reflect your perceptions and beliefs about each of these concepts.

9.3   THE ACTION RESEARCH APPROACH

9.3.1   CONCEPTS, FINDINGS AND TEXTS

Many types of research are valuable for language teachers but the one that fits most easily in a book on practice is AR, and that will be the focus of our attention from here. Historically, according to Wallace (1987), the first stage in the development of AR was between the 1920s and 1950s in the United States (for example, Corey 1953). During this period there was a growing interest in the application of more scientific methods to the study of social and educational contexts. As such, when it originally began to develop, AR was seen to be a method for applying theories produced by the disciplines in question to their practices in order to test their effectiveness. Due to its close affinity with positivism (a system that believes that every rationally justifiable assertion can be scientifically verified or is capable of logical or mathematical proof), it was rejected as inappropriate and unsuitable in the 1950s by social scientists. A renewed interest in AR for educational purposes came in the

United Kingdom in the 1970s. According to Zwozdiak-Myers (2012: 50), this came in response to an increased concern that traditional educational research did not meet the needs of teachers and schools, and a belief that professionalism could be enhanced if teachers adopted a researcher role. AR was proposed as a method for teachers to test policies and curriculum proposals in order to establish how they work in practice, so that the results could in turn inform more effective policy and changes. This type of AR advocated more interpretative and qualitative methodologies which placed teachers and students, their beliefs, experiences, thoughts and interpretations. at the centre (see Brown 2014: ch. 5). As such, it has become a process for improving personal practice, though some commentators would argue that it is a collaborative activity with a focus on changing systems and contexts in a more general sense (see, for example, Carr and Kemmis 1986, McNiff 2013). This latter perspective adopts a socio-political stance to the study of education and is often referred to as critical praxis (Hollingsworth and Sockett 1994). Edge (2001: 5) provides a useful list of the potential orientations of AR, along with examples, as follows:

- means oriented: we know that we are trying to teach people to write English on the course. How can we improve the ways in which we do so?
- ends oriented: we know that these students want to become librarians. How sure are we about the importance of teaching them to write?
- theory oriented: as we investigate our teaching of writing, how can we articulate our increased understanding of what is happening here? How can we connect with other written records in order to theorise our practice and perhaps, contribute to the theory that informs us?
- institution oriented: to what extent is my writing course, through its goals, its topics, and my practice, contributing to an integrated educational programme through which the institution mediates between its students and its social context?
- society oriented: to what extent is my writing course, through its goals, its topics, and my practice, promoting values that I believe in (e.g. contributing to a healthy dialogic relationship among students, teachers, institution and society at large)?
- teacher oriented: where is my own personal and professional development in this? What is the contribution to collegiality and, thereby, the kind of society I want to live in?

Whatever the orientation, in this chapter I use the term with reference to local practice and change, and having conducted a number of AR projects in the past myself, I am inclined to agree with Nunan (1992b: 18):

> While collaboration is highly desirable, I do not believe that it should be seen as a defining characteristic of action research. Many teachers who are interested in exploring processes of teaching and learning in their own context are either unable, for practical reasons, or unwilling, for personal reasons, to do

collaborative research. The work that such people carry out should not necessarily be excluded as action research.

There is also the added argument that the investigation of some types of problems is more suitable for individual than group attention. However, where collaboration (in the sense of dialogue with others) is possible, it can be beneficial. We can therefore identify four key features of AR:

- It focuses on a social situation (often the classroom, in the case of teacher AR).
- It can involve collaboration and dialogue with others.
- It involves the systematic collection of data, making it different from intuitive reflection.
- It is exploratory in nature.

If you are more familiar with scientific methods used for research you will notice some differences. AR does not aim to confirm a hypothesis in the way scientific research does. It is more qualitative and reflective, though it does make use of guiding hypotheses. It does not establish formal control and experimental groups, nor does it rely on pre- or post-testing techniques. It does not use quantitative inferential and statistical analysis and does not pretend to be generalisable. And, as it is localised, it does not lead to general results that will apply to other contexts (though others may gain insights from your results). To quote Burns (2010: 2):

> The central idea of the *action* part of AR is to intervene in a deliberate way in the problematic situation in order to bring about changes and, even better, improvements in practice. Importantly, the improvements that happen in AR are ones based on information (or to use the research term, *data*) that an action researcher collects systematically . . . So, the changes made in the teaching situation arise from solid information rather than our hunches or assumptions about the way we think things are.

Having discussed the characteristics, orientations and definitions of AR, let us now turn to the process involved in conducting research within this approach. The four-stage, cyclical model of AR is probably the best known and most widely used. Each cycle involves the following stages:

1. Develop a *plan*.
2. *Act* to implement the plan.
3. *Observe* the effects of the action.
4. *Reflect*.

Figure 9.2 represents the often-cited Kemmis and McTaggart (1988) model of AR and illustrates how the cycles can continue until satisfactory outcomes/solutions are found.

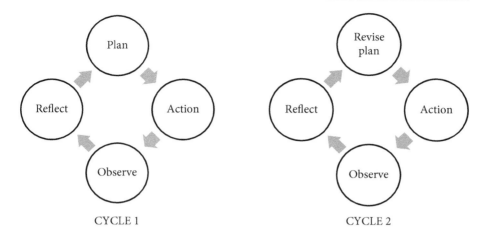

Figure 9.2   Cyclical action research model (based on Kemmis and McTaggart1988)

McKernan (1996) offers a slightly elaborated model to illustrate the stages involved in AR, using somewhat different terminology, adding the stage of needs assessment and distinguishing between developing and implementing the plan. And there are many other variations. The model that you choose to follow will depend on your particular needs and preferences at a particular point in time around a specific problem you have identified. In order to find a solution or improve practices using AR approaches, it is highly likely that your research will involve human participants, for example, learners and colleagues.

It is important to remember that ethical issues arise whenever you study people's activities through data-collection techniques such as interviews, observations, recordings, note-taking etc., any of which may interfere with their privacy or comfort. It is your responsibility to protect the well-being of the participants involved in your research and not to put them at risk in any way (physically or emotionally). This is even more acute when dealing with what are often defined as vulnerable groups such as minors. If you do not have a code of ethical practice in research available in your institution then you should follow the principles and guidelines published by professional organisations such as BAAL (British Association of Applied Linguistics) or BERA (British Educational Research Association) (see also Burns 2010: 33–7).

TASK 9.4   DEFINING ACTION RESEARCH

Read the following definitions of AR and, in discussion, say which you prefer and why:

The study of a social situation with the view to improving the quality of the action in it. (Elliot 1991: 69)

Small scale intervention in the functioning of the real world and a close
examination of the effects of such intervention. (van Lier 1996: 32)

Action research is defined as any systematic inquiry conducted by teachers,
administrators, counselors, or others with a vested interest in the teaching and
learning process or environment for the purpose of gathering information about
how their particular schools operate, how they teach, and how their students
learn. (Mertler 2011: 4)

TASK 9.5   PARTICIPATORY ACTION RESEARCH

'Participatory action research' (PAR) (Auerbach 1994) is another term you may come
across in your reading. Explore Dr Jason J. Campbell's talks on PAR on YouTube.
What are the differences, if any, between PAR and AR?

TASK 9.6   EXPLORING ACTION RESEARCH RESOURCES

Explore the following web resources and evaluate their usefulness for teachers
wanting to do AR:

Jean McNiff's webpage: http://www.jeanmcniff.com
Sage's student study site for Mertler (2011): http://www.sagepub.com/mertler3study/
default.htm
www.actionresearch.net

9.4   THE BEGINNING, MIDDLE AND END OF ACTION RESEARCH

9.4.1   CONCEPTS, FINDINGS AND TEXTS

In this final core section of Chapter 9, I would like you to work your way through
the four stages of the AR cycle so that you begin to understand and appreciate what
is involved at each stage. As you do this, try to use real issues that you have in your
own teaching situations as the vehicle to move you through the process. As it is one
of only a few complete volumes currently dedicated to AR in language teaching (see
also Edge 2001, Wallace 1998), I often refer to Anne Burns' book throughout this
section (Burns 2010).

Stage 1: Planning the research
Using the phrase 'identifying research questions', which is often found in more conventional research methods books, makes it sound as if you have to invest a big effort
into going out and finding research questions, when in fact they should easily surface
and find their way to you as the part of the first stage of AR. All you need to do is to
be open to considering where they might come from, judging them as worthy AR
projects and labelling them as such so that you can begin on the procedural stages
of the journey. The key consideration to remember is that you are looking for an

improvement in some aspect of problematic practice, or a solution to some sort of practice-based problem. The general area of focus could emerge from a number of different sources: cooperative development discussions (see Chapter 8), observations of teaching (your own or others'), reflective diaries or blogs that you keep about your teaching, informal discussions with your learners or colleagues, a published article that you read, etc. Fischer (2001) discusses four general points of reference from which an AR focus may emerge: your teaching; your learners; the curriculum; your philosophies, values and beliefs about teaching. The last of these, which we have discussed as teacher cognition in some detail in earlier chapters, can have the potential to influence our AR in unintended ways. This is why we need to consider carefully the issue of research validity. 'Validity in research raises important questions, such as: *How can you ensure the methods used for collecting data are trustworthy? How can you be sure that your conclusions are solidly based on the data you have collected?*' (Burns 2010: 25).

Once you have identified a general area for your AR, you probably need to refine it further so that it becomes a question that is suitable for the process. Burns (2010: 30) offers the following advice for shaping appropriate research questions:

> First, avoid questions you can do little about. For example, choosing a question that has to do with changing the whole of the required syllabus in your school or district will not take you far . . . Second, tailor your questions to fit within the time limit you have available. Trying to track students' progress across a year, for example, might take you beyond the bounds of the time and resources you have available. Also, focus on one issue to see where it takes you rather than trying to look at multiple aspects, [which] is likely to lead to 'AR burn-out' and give you mixed and unclear outcomes. Finally, choose areas of direct relevance and interest to you, your immediate teaching context, or your school.

Having refined the research question appropriately it is time to prepare further by identifying appropriate resources and materials. There are two areas that will be of value:

- reading the relevant published research literature
- identifying appropriate people and equipment.

Most of the teachers I have worked with have found that a very useful starting place is reading previous research publications that relate to the focus for their AR. Consulting books, journals and online artefacts can help to guide your research, give ideas about focus or design, identify problems that may arise, save time and effort (by not making the same mistakes or reinventing the wheel), and give other accounts against which to compare your results (thereby strengthening validity). Many publishers (for example, Routledge, CUP, Wiley-Blackwell) now have a range of handbooks/guides/readers around topics of interest to language teachers. These books give very comprehensive overviews of specific research areas, and are an accessible way for new researchers to help identify the type of research that is being done and who the major researchers in the field are. Another useful resource that I and my students often consult is the TIRF

(The International Research Foundation for English Language Education) website, which provides reference lists of publications around numerous topics. You will find these by going to the homepage and clicking on 'access to resources' and then on 'reference lists', where they are presented through links on an alphabetical listing by topic. Other online resources such as the ERIC (Educational Resources Information Centre) database (see Burns 2010: 41–2 for instructions on how to use ERIC), Google Scholar, JStore, researchers' profile websites and their institutional repositories are also valuable and worth exploring.

As the final part of the planning phase, you need to consider the people you may need to involve in your research. Of course there are the participants, but you may also wish to involve others such as colleagues, managers, administrators, parents, librarians or technicians. AR is usually collaborative in some way, so consider the roles that others will play and how they can be included in ethical ways, with their full knowledge and consent. Their level of involvement will depend on your aims, your context and your own preferences. In addition to 'human resources' you also need to consider the materials and equipment required for your data collection and analysis (software and hardware). Audio- and/or video-recordings are often collected as data in AR, and their intrusive and disruptive influence is very much diminished in a world where mobile media abound and are habitually used by most people. Burns (2010: 47) provides some useful hints for recording:

- Test the equipment in advance
- Make sure you have spare power sources and storage (memory, disks etc.)
- Ask participants to minimise background noise that might affect the quality of the recording (movement, whispering, touching equipment etc.)
- Have the microphone as close as possible to the speaker, or at an equal distance from all speakers if recording more than one person
- Record in a place that is as quiet as possible
- Use a cloth under the microphone to reduce surface noise
- Remember to turn your equipment on and check intermittently that it is still recording.

Stage 2: Putting the plan into action
The next stage of AR involves collecting data or evidence (with the appropriate ethical approvals). The techniques used can be categorised according to two different but related paradigms. Firstly, there is the distinction between quantitative techniques (those which produce data that can be numerically or statistically analysed) and qualitative ones (those which gain insight and allow for description rather than statistics; see Holliday 2007: chs 4 and 5 for a discussion on legitimate qualitative data sources). Secondly, there are observation-based methods (what you see, for example notes, classroom recordings, photographs) and non-observation-based ones (what you need to know, for example, interviews, focus groups, surveys). Any, many or all of these may be suitable to collect the data which will help you link your AR question, action and reflection. In fact, much research now involves using mixed methods to

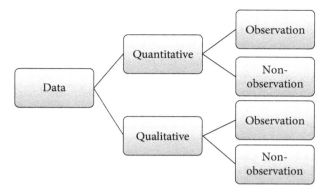

Figure 9.3   Action research data-collection techniques

gain multiple perspectives and insights (Brown 2014). Figure 9.3 provides a simple visual representation.

The three most common data-collection techniques that I and teachers that I know have used over the years are observations, interviews and questionnaires (see also D. E. Murray 2010). I will give each one brief attention here.

Observations of classroom practices and resulting transcriptions are given some attention in Burns (2010: 57–72) and Wallace (1998: ch. 6). Observations within an AR cycle should generally be quite formal, focused (on the AR question), objective, reflective and evaluated using the documented evidence (notes, recordings etc.). They can take the form of self- or peer observations and may be done by individuals or groups, as you decide within the context of your research. There are a number of questions/issues to be considered in advance of observation (see also Chapter 4):

- What setting, participants, activities, events, behaviours and interactions do you want to observe?
- Where, when and how often will you observe?
- How will you observe (for example, observation sheets/templates, notes, recordings and transcriptions, using what sorts of technologies)?

Interviews can take place with individuals or with groups of participants. As well as saving on interview time (though not necessarily time spent scheduling and co-ordinating), the advantage of group interviews is that the responses can be more detailed and insightful as a result of participants prompting and developing ideas together. On the other hand, the major disadvantage is that 'the results cannot be generalized, the emerging group culture may interfere with individual expression . . . the group may be dominated by one person and "groupthink" is a possible outcome' (Fontana and Frey 2000: 652). You will need to make an informed decision about which group configuration suits your purposes, as well as the most appropriate interview format. Interviews can take three formats for the purposes of AR:

- Structured: these usually follow a predetermined schedule and consist of closed questions which direct the participants in one of a number of ways. These interviews are usually inflexible and while they may provide easily analysable data, the major disadvantage is that they may not provide the insights you need to address your action point.
- Semi-structured: these consist of a number of key questions which can be used to collect data in the way a structured interview does, but with flexibility when these questions are also used as prompts for further exploration and discussion.
- Unstructured: these are the most flexible and allow a completely open style, usually to gather complementary evidence. Their success can rely heavily on the skills of the interviewer to move the discussion in the appropriate directions to uncover the information needed in relation to the research question.

Questionnaires are a useful tool when you wish to get information or opinion from a number of participants that is large enough to makes it unfeasible to interview them all. Questionnaires are useful for eliciting information about demographics, habits and perceptions/opinions/beliefs (Dörnyei 2003: 8–9), and can consist of a number of different types of items:

- closed items such as scales, yes/no questions and multiple-choice items
- open items, which can be completely free or partially guided.

Questionnaires, in order to be valid and reliable, need to be very well designed and piloted before wider distribution. They need to be clear, concise and not biased in a way that will lead the participant in a particular direction or way of thinking. This can be difficult to achieve, even for an experienced researcher, so if you decide not to use a pre-existing and trialled questionnaire, and to design one of your own, I would strongly suggest that you read more extensively about questionnaire design (for example, Burns 2010: 81–9, Christison and Bassano 1995).

Stage 3: Observing the results
This stage of AR is all about making sense of the evidence you have collected in a way that focuses on finding a way forward with your research question or practice-based problem. Burns (1999: 157–60) proposes a useful framework for the analysis, which I adapt here for present purposes:

1. Assemble your data: collect your data plus any reflections you have made along the way, and go through it to start identifying key patterns or trends that may address your question
2. Code the data: tag (label specific categories, for example, questions) or transcribe the data in a way which categorises patterns or functions and makes them easy to retrieve for later analysis. There are a number of useful coding systems which you can adopt/adapt (for example, Walsh 2011), as well as tagging software such as NVivo (see Bazeley and Jackson 2013 for full details on how to use this software in qualitative research). The coding should only be as complex and detailed as

you require for the purposes of your research. In other words, try not to spend time coding details such as overlaps and interruptions in classroom language if this is not relevant to your research focus.

3. Compare the data: cross-reference the various datasets that you have collected and begin to chart the results on table, charts etc. or extract appropriate quotations. This comparison should be as concise as possible.

4. Build meanings and interpretations: think deeply and critically about the results in a way that goes beyond the detailed description and focuses on the overall broad question. This will involve posing many questions and developing explanations about what the research means, and is often best done in the context of previous research findings which can help direct relative interpretations.

5. Report outcomes: think about how you will tell your whole research story and share it orally or in writing with others, either locally or more openly through a publication.

Stage 4: Reflecting and planning for further action research
Based on the findings in Stage 3, the final stage of the process requires focused and critical reflection around a number of key elements (your practice, the research process, your feelings and philosophies), and is thereby a type of evaluation of success. Sharing your research with others either formally or informally can deepen your reflections even further through the contributions, questions and feedback you get from them. You will then be in a position to make an informed decision about whether this is the end of this particular AR project, or whether it needs to continue into another cycle in order to make a fully informed decision about whether and how to change and improve your practice.

TASK 9.7   ACTION RESEARCH QUESTIONS

As a precursor to the tasks in this section I strongly recommend that you watch Anne Burns speaking about AR principles and processes, on her own webpage or on YouTube as part of the TESOL talks series at http://www.youtube.com/watch?v=U4kLZLhxWzk.

A. Read the following, discuss whether you think they are good AR questions and explain why or why not.
   1. What is CALL?
   2. Does using social media help improve my learners' writing skills?
   3. What kind of pronunciation practice activities will help my intermediate-level learners improve their pronunciation?
   4. How do Polish learners of English perceive current EAL (English as an additional language) supports available in Irish secondary schools, and what gaps do they identify?
   5. Why are most Dutch nationals such good speakers of English?

B. Write a rough draft of a research question for your own AR.
C. Refine and narrow it by asking the following ten questions:

1. Is the question small and focused?
2. Is the question ethical?
3. Does the question lead to data collection and analysis?
4. Is the question clear and concise?
5. Is the question related to current research on practice in TESOL?
6. Is there any bias in the question?
7. Is the question open-ended (for example using *what, why, how* question words)?
8. Is the question related to my own localised practice?
9. Is there a logical link between the question, the data and the type of conclusion you are looking for?
10. Is the question going to ultimately lead to a change/improvement in practice?

D.   Now rewrite your question, bearing these factors in mind. This is usefully done with a partner, whose input may be valuable.

TASK 9.8   ACTION RESEARCH AND DEEP REFLECTION

A.   Think about and, with a partner, formulate between six and ten key questions that could help to direct deep reflection as part of Stage 4 of the process.
B.   Either in person or virtually, using information and communications technology, interview someone who has conducted a piece of AR, using your questions. Discuss with a partner whether they elicit deep and meaningful reflection that could help inform further planning.

TASK 9.9   LEARNING FROM PUBLISHED ACTION RESEARCH PROJECTS

Find an account of an AR project in teaching from a quality online source (confer with your tutor if you are unsure), either as a published piece or as an oral presentation. Which elements of the study might be useful for you to adopt in conducting a study around the question you formulated in Task 9.7? Which elements will not be useful and why?

9.5   FURTHER READING ONE

Mann, S. (1999) 'Opening the insider's eye: starting action research', *Language Teacher*, 23: 12, 11–13.
This article was written to encourage teachers to become researchers in an effort to bridge the gap between those who formulate theory and those involved in practice. Mann suggests that AR allows for more of a teachers' perspective on what happens in their own classrooms. This position stems partially from the notion of 'participant inquiry': the idea that those on the inside are best placed to understand the complexities around what is involved in a teacher's job. Such recognition began to gain a lot

of credence in the 1990s through the work of people such as Allwright and Bailey (1991). The author suggests that AR is a mechanism which best allows the profession to describe teaching from the inside, which is important as a formal process because:

> Teachers can best document significant interventions and modifications in practice but they may not realise or be able to describe this complexity until they have begun a process of reflection or reading or both. A great number of teacher actions are unconscious or routinised. Indeed it would not be possible to do all the things that a teacher does in the classroom if all the actions were conscious . . . Action research is a way to engage with classroom teaching and bring more of it to a conscious level, a way to uncover what has become invisible . . . If action research has two simple ingredients then, they are:
>
> – Opening teachers' eyes to what has become familiar
> – Developing a sustained focus on one aspect of teaching. (p. 11)

Mann goes on to describe the starting steps involved in action research, which is the total scope of this article. The first starting step is identifying an idea for research, first in general terms and then with more of a focus for investigation. He advises that teachers might think about beginning with something small they would like to explore and that can be managed while working as a teacher. The second starting step is narrowing the focus, which involves taking a big (potentially daunting) issue and transforming it into something small enough to manage. He suggests two techniques to help with this process: focusing circles (Edge 1992) and mind maps (Buzan and Buzan 1996).

- Focusing circles – this is a technique from Edge (1992: 37–8) which enables you to narrow your focus by drawing a small circle at the centre (inside) of a larger one. The issue, topic or problem is written in the small circle, and the larger one is divided into four segments. In each of these segments an aspect of the topic is written. One of these four segments then becomes the centre of the next circle and so on.
- Mind maps – most teachers have, at some time, used mind maps or spider webs. Probably the most comprehensive guide to the use of mind mapping is provided by Buzan and Buzan (1996). Here the issue is written at the centre of a piece of paper, and related factors branch out from the centre.

From using both of these techniques with students he worked with, Mann suggests that each of these involves different ways of thinking. In focusing circles, it was found that the thinking was selective and involved choices and justifications. In mind maps, the focus was more on making connections. The former was found to be more useful in AR to define and narrow the research area/question. Taking into account similar advice from other authors on the topic, Mann suggests that it is very important to get the research focus right as it may determine the success of the project, and that part of getting it right includes not making it too broad, avoiding questions that cannot be answered, limiting the duration and addressing issues that relate directly to your teaching context.

Some potentially useful questions are proposed by the author, based on Wallace (1998: 21):

- Purpose – Why are you engaging in this research?
- Topic – What area are you going to investigate?
- Focus – What is the precise question you are going to ask yourself within that area?
- Product – What is the likely outcome of the research, as you intend it?
- Mode – How are you going to conduct the research?
- Timing – How long have you got to do the research? Is there a deadline for its completion?
- Resources – What are the resources, both human and material, that you can call upon to help you complete the research?
- Fine tuning – As you proceed with your research, do you suppose you will have to rethink your original question?

The final starting step in Mann's framework involves talking through the more focused research idea with colleagues. This allows for articulation, questioning and feedback, and fits well with the notion of 'dialogic understanding' (Bakhtin 1981). Mann supports the value of individual undertakings helped by others, in contrast to some of the more collaborative approaches to AR. He refers to early versions of what became Edge's (1992) model of cooperative understanding (as discussed in more detail in Chapter 8 of this volume), where colleagues can act as a sounding board to bounce ideas off, rather than offering advice and direction.

At the end of the article there is an account of some of the potential problems that can sometimes arise with AR. However, Mann is quite positive and suggests that by following some of the advice given by Nunan (1993) and Burns (1999) these can be overcome. This advice includes having assistance from those trained in AR methodology; securing release time from teaching to conduct the research; and setting up focus teams. Finally, given that this article was written in 1999, when access to the Internet was just beginning to grow, the conclusion makes mention of the increased opportunities it might afford for AR teachers to overcome situations where they find themselves working in isolation.

FURTHER READING ONE TASK

1. Think of two general areas in which you might like to conduct some AR. Take one through a focusing circles process and the other through a mind maps process.
2. Which process did you find more useful, enjoyable or difficult? Say why.
3. What potential problems might you face in conducting the research project you identified for yourself in earlier tasks, and how could you overcome them?

9.6 FURTHER READING TWO

Allwright, D. (2003) 'Exploratory practice: Rethinking practitioner research in language teaching', *Language Teaching Research*, 7: 2, 113–41.
See also Dick Allwright's seminar on exploratory practice with research students at Warwick, June 2009, at http://www2.warwick.ac.uk/fac/soc/al/intranet/masters/elt_sm-copy/conference09/dick_allwright/research_student_seminar.
This article is the introduction to a special issue of *Language Teaching Research* devoted to the theme of exploratory practice (EP), which is a form of practitioner research different from AR. The article also outlines the underlying principles and the nature of EP. Allwright begins by outlining some of the things he believes we have got wrong in relation to practitioner research, and then outlines the resultant rethinking which led to EP, which bases itself on some new proposals:

- First, we should, above our concern for instructional efficiency, prioritise the quality of life in the language classroom.
- Secondly, instead of trying to develop ever 'improved' teaching techniques, we should try to develop our understandings of the quality of language classroom life.
- Thirdly, we should expect working helpfully for understanding to be a fundamentally social matter, not an asocial one. Simple causal relationships are most unlikely to apply, but all practitioners, learners as well as teachers, can expect to gain, 'to develop', from this mutual process of working for understanding. (p. 114)

The author describes the origins of EP from two perspectives. Firstly, in his own earlier academic work and writings, he alludes to the fact that he had unintentionally made classroom research practically impossible by the demands it could place on teachers. Therefore in 1991 (Allwright and Bailey 1991), he published some statements of global principle for a revised type of teacher research:

a) First, and foremost, I proposed that research should aim at the development of situational understanding. This principle has retained all its importance over the years, [and] contrasted with the stated aim of Action Research, for example, to produce practical solutions to isolated problems . . .
b) I also proposed that in relating to language teachers, 'academic' researchers like myself could best act as research consultants, not, as was usual, research directors. So we would advise, if asked, on the conduct of investigations, but not control the research agenda . . .
c) I simultaneously proposed that learners be fully involved as contributors to what was necessarily a social investigative enterprise, with their own research agendas, and with their own interest in understanding language classroom life. For examples, see especially Perpignan, 2001, and Slimani-Rolls [2003].
d) Finally, I advocated working with 'puzzles', rather than 'problems'. This was partly to avoid the negative connotations of 'problem', given that many

teachers around the world feared that admitting to classroom 'problems' might endanger their contracts, and partly to involve areas of classroom life that were not obviously 'problematic'. (pp. 116–17)

Secondly, EP had very practical origins for the author, in his work in Rio de Janeiro over two months teaching a course on classroom research to a group of local practitioners. During this period, he realised that some of his proposals were misguided and impractical, given the reality of the teachers' lives, professional and personal. The author reports that these experiences consolidated his thinking around the practicality of what he had proposed in the principles above. More specifically, he talks about focusing on 'quality of life' rather than 'quality of work' in the classroom, and asserts that EP must make a contribution to the former before it can hope to contribute to the latter. Understanding is key to this process, and Allwright discusses the notion of 'understanding' and the difficulty associated with articulating it through language, which in effect is restrictive for this purpose. In other words, any account of understanding is only a limited depiction of the understanding itself. Nonetheless he places value on the articulation of 'situated understandings' as part of EP local thinking.

Using some of the *local* experiences and thinking from Rio, along with more general principles articulated *globally* in his 1991 book, led to the development of some principles and practices that can be described as EP. With many caveats and with much resistance, he offers the following 'principled description' of what exploratory practice involves (pp. 127–31):

1. Practitioners (preferably teachers and learners together) working to understand:
   (a) what they want to understand, following their own agendas;
   (b) not necessarily in order to bring about change;
   (c) not primarily by changing;
   (d) but by using normal pedagogic practices as investigative tools, so that working for understanding is part of the teaching and learning, not extra to it;
   (e) in a way that does not lead to 'burn-out', but that is indefinitely sustainable;
2. in order to contribute to:
   (f) teaching and learning themselves;
   (g) professional development, both individual and collective.

The associated set of general principles is presented as follows:

- Principle 1: put 'quality of life' first
- Principle 2: work primarily to understand language classroom life
- Principle 3: involve everybody
- Principle 4: work to bring people together
- Principle 5: work also for mutual development
- Principle 6: integrate the work for understanding into classroom practice (let the need to integrate guide the conduct of the work for understanding)
- Principle 7: make the work a continuous experience (avoid time-limited funding).

Towards the end of the article, Allwright discusses the importance of EP as a collegial activity, particularly in relation to Principles 3, 4 and 5. Collegiality can happen in a number of different ways within different groups: teachers and learners; teachers within the same school; teachers and colleagues in training and in development; teachers' associations; and, with some difficulty within hierarchical structures, managers, principals etc. Finally, the author re-emphasises the importance of the cyclical relationship between global and local, and briefly presents some examples of the kind of work that has been undertaken using the EP framework, including voluntary work with teacher groups, as consultancies, within academic and practitioner research, and research about EP.

FURTHER READING TWO TASK

1. Discuss what you perceive to be the main differences between EP and AR (think about purposes, principles, process and outcomes). Do you have a preference for one over the other? Why? Are they compatible or mutually exclusive?
2. Take the research 'puzzle' you identified for Mann's article above and move it through the EP process. What does it look like? What are the practical pros and cons of using EP?

9.7   SUMMARY

This chapter began with discussion of the importance and place of research in the professional lives of teachers from their initial education programme right through to the end of their careers. In a very general sense, teacher research engagement can happen in a number of ways, and I believe that this can be different for each individual and context. In tertiary education, the links between teaching and research have been emphasised for a number of years. This is to be expected as there is the potential for a more natural and easy alignment between the activities and expectations at that level. In this arena, teaching and research can have many dimensions: research activity, evidence-based teaching, a research-based curriculum, a culture of inquiry, communities of scholars, research-aligned teaching and teaching enhanced research (Brew 2006). These dimensions are worth considering for all teachers, who at the very least can keep abreast of relevant current research and allow this to inform their teaching content and pedagogy. This is becoming ever easier through the availability of online materials and courses (for example MOOCs), and more manageable through the creation of personal learning networks (PLNs) (Hanson-Smith 2016; see Chapter 10 for further discussion).

A brief discussion of Wallace's 1998 framework outlining distinctions between inquiry-based and non-inquiry-based options for professional development in Section 9.2 led to a more refined and detailed consideration of direct teacher engagement in conducting research in Section 9.3. The nature of AR as a suitable framework is outlined along with a description of a typical AR cycle. The more detailed steps and processes involved are presented in Section 9.4 with a discussion around the four stages of planning, putting the plan into action, observing the results, and reflecting and planning for further AR. My underlying and fundamental conviction in writing this chapter is that all teachers can be involved in research in some way as a professional development activity. The entrance point and movement along the cline from simply reading research findings to conducting your own research can be at your own discretion and will inevitably vary according to your professional and personal circumstances over the course of your career.

9.8   ADDITIONAL READINGS

Allwright, D. (2005) 'Developing principles for practitioner research: The case of exploratory practice', *Modern Language Journal*, 89, 353–66.

Bailey, K. (2001) 'Action research, teacher research, and classroom research in language teaching', in Celce-Murcia, M. (ed.), *Teaching English as a Second or Foreign language* (3rd edn), Boston: Heinle and Heinle, 489–98.

Crookes, G. (1993) 'Action research for second language teachers: Going beyond teacher research', *Applied Linguistics*, 14: 2, 130–44.

Edge, J. (ed.) (2001) *Action Research: Case Studies in TESOL Practice*, Alexandria: TESOL.

Gray, D. E. (2014) *Doing Research in the Real World*, London: Sage (ch. 13 and accompanying online resources).

McNiff, J. (2013) *Action Research: Principles and Practice*, Abingdon: Routledge.

Mertler, C. (2011) *Action Research: Improving Schools and Empowering Educators*, London: Sage.

10

CONCLUSION

This book has brought you through the various iterative stages of the many components of your TP that you need to consider. At the outset, I asked you to begin to develop your teacher identity, and in the final two chapters, we have returned to the notion of the teacher in a constant state of explorative learning. I have considered what I hold to be the pillars of practice in each of the core chapters and trust that I have involved you in the discussions of each in an accessible yet critical way. I hope that you now appreciate, in a more holistic way, the merits of engaging in the practice component of your TESOL programme, or indeed as an early-career teacher. I reinforce one of my very early assertions that although we know a lot about teaching, there is still a lot we do not know. Therefore, you are at the beginning of a journey and not at the end, having read this book and worked through the various tasks. Like your students, you are a self-directed and independent learner, now ready to take responsibility for your ongoing development as a teacher.

Even when you are working in a scaffolded environment with a teacher educator, a tutor or a cooperating teacher, you need to begin to have an independent voice and ownership over your own development. This can be difficult and may seem paradoxical in a context where you (and others) consider yourself a novice. There are disadvantages to doing too much TP and being 'over-supervised'. It does not allow you to take risks, try new things and develop independently. In previous research with novice teachers I found a tendency towards wanting to be supervised more (Farr 2011: ch. 8). In this research, teachers and tutors agree that TP feedback has some impact on future performance, but there is uncertainty about whether increased amounts of feedback continue to have positive impact. It may be that there is a point of maximum effect. I also found that most teachers would prefer to have between 30 per cent and 80 per cent of their practice supervised, but that tutors believe that teachers should be more independent and typically suggest between 10 per cent and 60 per cent supervision (Farr 2011: 166). Analysing typical discourse in feedback discussions also shows that the discourse is dominated by the tutor and is primarily directive. This is despite the espoused beliefs of both teachers and tutors that this should be more cooperative, with teachers taking responsibility for the content and direction of the discussion. After all, you are primary in terms of the experience and learning opportunity. There is huge value in the teacher's own perspective in the pursuit of good teaching, which is far from being a scientific discipline and is highly contextually dependent and variable.

In more general terms, there are also many other learning opportunities that you can engage with to improve your practice, either during or following a formal teacher education programme. Hanson-Smith (2016) suggests self-help options for teachers through personal learning environments (PLEs) using social media and video resource sites, and in the phenomenon of MOOCs. Learning through a MOOC is a relatively recent innovation, which has gained a lot of momentum and attracted a lot of debate in higher education circles. It involves taking a free online programme of study for a short duration, usually through one of the major platforms such as FutureLearn (UK-based) or Coursera (US-based). They can be extremely useful if you need flexibility around your job and/or if you have a specific niche need that has not been met through other educational programmes you have followed (or are likely to in the future). I have followed some MOOCs myself and have recommended them to my student teachers as complementary resources to their programme content. Hanson-Smith (2016) outlines some of the advantages in relation to the field of educational technology, which include the following: they can adapt quickly to technological changes and new content inclusion; they are relatively short and can fit with work schedules; they are generally free; materials are generally downloadable; they often run on mobile device interfaces; and they are suitable for self-motivated learners, which teachers usually are.

Finally, I would like to conclude by thinking about the shifting, evolving nature of teaching and learning and related research as an impetus to continue to learn and keep abreast of practice-relevant developments. At the time of completing this volume I scanned through the table of contents of the articles in the latest editions of three practice-oriented language teaching journals: *ELT Journal* (general teaching), *ReCALL* (technology focus) and *Classroom Discourse* (language in teaching). I present my findings below and task you with using this as a baseline to see how the field of English language teaching develops in coming years.

ELT Journal
Aki Siegel
    Editor's choice: What should we talk about? The authenticity of textbook topics
Christopher J. Hall
    Moving beyond accuracy: From tests of English to tests of 'Englishing'
Nicola Galloway and Heath Rose
    Using listening journals to raise awareness of Global Englishes in ELT
Raquel Serrano, Elsa Tragant, and ÀngelsLlanes
    Summer English courses abroad versus 'at home'
W. L. Quint Oga-Baldwin andYoshiyuki Nakata
    Optimizing new language use by employing young learners' own language
Ming Huei Lin, Ji-Jhen Li, Po Yi Hung, and Hui-Wen Huang
    Blogging a journal: Changing students' writing skills and perceptions

ReCALL
Lina Lee and Alfred Markey
    A study of learners' perceptions of online intercultural exchange through Web 2.0 technologies

Hora (Fatemeh) Hedayati and S. Susan Marandi
  Iranian EFL teachers' perceptions of the difficulties of implementing CALL
EulineCutrimSchmid and Volker Hegelheimer
  Collaborative research projects in the technology-enhanced language classroom:
  Pre-service and in-service teachers exchange knowledge about technology
DoganYuksel and BanuInan
  The effects of communication mode on negotiation of meaning and its noticing
Lily Lim
  Engaging student interpreters in vocabulary building: Web search with computer workbench

Classroom Discourse
JuupStelma
  Developing intentionality and L2 classroom task-engagement
Cécile Petitjean
  Social representations of turn-taking in classrooms: From compulsory to post-compulsory
  schooling in French-speaking Switzerland
Li Wei
  Translanguaging knowledge and identity in complementary classrooms for multilingual
  minority ethnic children
DoganYuksel
  Teachers' treatment of different types of student questions
Julia Hüttner
  Agreeing to disagree: 'Doing disagreement' in assessed oral L2 interactions

1 EXAMPLES OF PUBLISHED MATERIALS

Title	Publisher	Website
General English coursebooks		
Advance Your English	CUP	http://www.cambridge.org/us/cambridgeenglish/catalog/adult-courses/advance-your-english
Clockwise	OUP	https://elt.oup.com/catalogue/items/global/adult_courses/clockwise/?cc=global&selLanguage=en
Cutting Edge	Longman	http://www.pearsonlongman.com/newcuttingedge
Face2Face	CUP	http://www.cambridge.org/us/cambridgeenglish/catalog/adult-courses/face2face
Inside Out	Macmillan	http://www.macmillanenglish.com/courses/inside-out
Language in Use	CUP	http://www.cambridge.org/gb/cambridgeenglish/catalog/adult-courses/language-use
Landmark	OUP	https://elt.oup.com/catalogue/items/global/adult_courses/landmark/?cc=global&selLanguage=en
Natural English	OUP	https://elt.oup.com/student/naturalenglish/?cc=global&selLanguage=en
New English File	OUP	https://elt.oup.com/student/englishfile/?cc=global&selLanguage=en
New Headway	OUP	https://elt.oup.com/student/headway/?cc=global&selLanguage=en
Total English	Longman	http://www.pearsonlongman.com/newtotalenglish
Specific skills coursebooks		
Cambridge English Skills	CUP	http://www.cambridge.org/us/search?iFeelLucky=false&currentTheme=Learning&query=cambridge+english+skills
Effective Reading	Macmillan	http://www.macmillanenglish.com/courses/effective-reading
Oxford Online Skills Program	OUP	https://elt.oup.com/catalogue/items/global/adult_courses/oxford_online_skills_program/?cc=hu&selLanguage=hu&mode=hub
Speakout	Longman	http://www.pearsonlongman.com/speakout
Systems coursebooks		
Advanced Grammar in Use	CUP	http://www.cambridge.org/us/cambridgeenglish/catalog/grammar-vocabulary-and-pronunciation/advanced-grammar-use-2nd-edition

Title	Publisher	Website
Systems coursebooks		
English Grammar in Use	CUP	http://www.cambridge.org/us/cambridgeenglish/catalog/grammar-vocabulary-and-pronunciation/english-grammar-use-4th-edition
English Vocabulary in Use	CUP	http://www.cambridge.org/us/search?site=CE&iFeelLucky=false&query=VOCABULARY+IN+USE
Language Practice	Macmillan	http://www.macmillanenglish.com/category/skills-grammar-and-vocabulary
Macmillan English Grammar in Context	Macmillan	http://www.macmillanenglish.com/courses/macmillan-english-grammar-in-context
Practical English Grammar	OUP	https://elt.oup.com/catalogue/items/global/grammar_vocabulary/a_practical_english_grammar/?cc=global&selLanguage=en
Exam resources		
IELTS Foundation	Macmillan	http://www.macmillanenglish.com/courses/ielts-foundation
IELTS Masterclass	OUP	https://elt.oup.com/catalogue/items/global/exams_testing/ielts_masterclass/?cc=global&selLanguage=en&mode=hub
New Proficiency Gold	Longman	http://www.pearsonelt.com/products/New%20Proficiency%20Gold%20Course%20Book/9780582507272
Objective First	CUP	http://www.cambridge.org/ie/elt/catalogue/subject/project/item7397280/Objective-First/?site_locale=en_IE&currentSubjectID=382392
EAP resources		
Academic Connections	Longman	http://www.pearsonelt.com/courses/Academic%20Connections/679
Academic Encounters	CUP	http://www.cambridge.org/ie/elt/catalogue/subject/project/item7066695/Academic-Encounters-2nd-Edition/?site_locale=en_IE&currentSubjectID=382373
Headway Academic Skills	OUP	https://elt.oup.com/catalogue/items/global/adult_courses/headway_academic_skills_ielts_study_skills_edition/?cc=global&selLanguage=en&mode=hub
Skillful	Macmillan	http://www.macmillanenglish.com/courses/skillful

Title	Publisher	Website
ESP resources		
Global	Macmillan	http://www.macmillanenglish.com/courses/global
International Express	OUP	https://elt.oup.com/catalogue/items/global/ business_esp/international_express/intermediate/97 80194597869?cc=global&selLanguage=en&mode= hub
International Legal English	CUP	http://www.cambridge.org/ie/elt/catalogue/subject/ project/item6453005/ International-Legal-English/?site_locale=en_ IE&currentSubjectID=2561588
Market Leader	Longman	http://www.pearsonelt.com/products/Market%20 Leader%203rd%20Edition%20Advanced%20 Coursebook%20&%20DVD-Rom%20 Pack/9781408237038
Resources for young learners		
Best Buddies	Macmillan	http://www.macmillanenglish.com/courses/ best-buddies
English Adventure	Longman	http://www.pearsonelt.com/products/English%20 Adventure%20Level%201%20Pupils%20Book%20 plus%20Picture%20Cards/9780582791688
English Time	OUP	https://elt.oup.com/catalogue/items/global/young_ learners/english_time_second_edition/?cc=global& selLanguage=en&mode=hub
Family and Friends	OUP	https://elt.oup.com/catalogue/items/global/ young_learners/family_and_friends_second_editio n/?cc=global&selLanguage=en&mode=hub
Fun for Starters, Movers and Flyers	CUP	http://www.cambridge.org/ie/elt/catalogue/subject/ project/item2698388/ Fun-for-Starters,-Movers-and-Flyers/?site_ locale=en_IE&currentSubjectID=382388

2   EXAMPLES OF ONLINE MATERIALS

Title	Website
Online sites for teachers	
BBC English	http://www.bbc.co.uk/worldservice/learningenglish
Camsoft	http://www.camsoftpartners.co.uk/websites.htm
Dave's ESL Café	http://www.eslcafe.com
Developing Teachers	http://www.developingteachers.com
English Club	http://www.englishclub.com
English-To-Go	http://www.english-to-go.com/index.cfm
English Zone	http://www.english-zone.com
ESL Flow	http://www.eslflow.com
ESL Gold	http://www.eslgold.com
ITESL	http://iteslj.org/ESL3a.html
OneStopEnglish	http://www.onestopenglish.com
Pearson ELT Grammar	http://www.pearsonelt.com/grammar
Speech in Action	http://www.speechinaction.org
Teaching English	http://www.teachingenglish.org.uk
World English	http://www.world-english.org
CALL packages	
Babbel	http://www.babbel.com/learn-english-online
Longman English Interactive	http://www.longmanenglishinteractive.com/home.html
Living Language	http://www.livinglanguage.com/products/english/online-course
Planet English	http://www.planetenglish.com
Rocket Languages	http://www.rocketlanguages.com/english/premium/general.php
Rosetta Stone	http://www.rosettastone.ie/lp/tukbrand14/?cid=se-br-gg-ie-2014&rd=0
TellMeMore	http://www.tellmemore-online.com/en/learn_english_uk_online.htm
TenseBuster	http://www.clarityenglish.com/program/tensebuster.php
Transparent Language	http://www.transparent.com/learn-english
Understanding and Using English Grammar Interactive	http://www.pearsonlongman.com/ae/multimedia/programs/uuegi.htm
WordSmart	http://www.wordsmart.com

Title	Website
Language practice apps	
English Irregular Verbs	iTunes; Google Play (free)
Headway Phrase A Day	iTunes; Google Play
PB Phonics	iTunes (free)
Pronunciation Checker	Google Play (free)
Quizlet	iTunes; Google Play (free)
The Language Wheel	iTunes (free)
Sounds	iTunes; Google Play (free)
Word Reference	iTunes; Google Play (free)

3   EXAMPLES OF CORPUS-INFORMED MATERIALS

Title	Publisher	Website
Corpus-based reference books		
Cambridge Grammar of English	CUP	http://www.cambridge.org/us/cambridgeenglish/catalog/grammar-vocabulary-and-pronunciation/cambridge-grammar-english
Longman Grammar of Spoken and Written English	Longman	http://www.longmanhomeusa.com/catalog/products/product-details/?pid=F-0EH-5&sid=Grammar+Practice
Corpus-informed coursebooks		
English Unlimited	CUP	http://www.cambridge.org/us/cambridgeenglish/catalog/adult-courses/english-unlimited
Top Notch	Longman	http://www.pearsonelt.com/topnotch/
Touchstone	CUP	http://www.cambridge.org/us/cambridgeenglish/catalog/adult-courses/touchstone
Corpus-informed skills books		
English Vocabulary in Use Advanced	CUP	http://www.cambridge.org/us/cambridgeenglish/catalog/grammar-vocabulary-and-pronunciation/english-vocabulary-use-advanced
English Grammar Today: An A–Z of Spoken and Written Grammar	CUP	http://www.cambridge.org/us/cambridgeenglish/catalog/grammar-vocabulary-and-pronunciation/english-grammar-today/english-grammar-today-z-spoken-and-written-grammar-cd-rom
English Grammar Today Workbook	CUP	http://www.cambridge.org/us/cambridgeenglish/catalog/grammar-vocabulary-and-pronunciation/english-grammar-today/english-grammar-today-workbook
The Inside Series	OUP	https://elt.oup.com/catalogue/items/global/skills/inside_series/?cc=global&selLanguage=en&mode=hub
Real Grammar: A Corpus-Based Approach to English	Longman	http://www.pearson.com.au/products/A-C-Biber-Conrad/Real-Grammar-A-Corpus-Based-Approach-to-English/9780135155875?R=9780135155875

4   EXAMPLES OF ONLINE CORPORA AND CONCORDANCERS

Title	Website
Backbone	http://webapps.ael.uni-tuebingen.de/backbone-search/faces/initialize.jsp
BASE	http://www2.warwick.ac.uk/fac/soc/al/research/collect/base
BNC	http://www.natcorp.ox.ac.uk
Corpus BYU	http://corpus.byu.edu
ICLE	https://www.uclouvain.be/en-cecl-icle.html
Lextutor	http://www.lextutor.ca
MICASE	http://quod.lib.umich.edu/m/micase
MICUSP	http://micusp.elicorpora.info
Oxford Text Archive	http://ota.ahds.ac.uk
PolyU Language Bank	http://langbank.engl.polyu.edu.hk/indexl.html
PolyU Learner English Corpus	http://langbank.engl.polyu.edu.hk/indexl.html
Sacodeyl	http://sacodeyl.inf.um.es/sacodeyl-search2
Santa Barbara Corpus	http://www.linguistics.ucsb.edu/research/santa-barbara-corpus
Sketch Engine	http://ca.sketchengine.co.uk/open
Webcorp	http://www.webcorp.org.uk/live

5A   REVIEW OF KEY TERMS AND CONCEPTS

Read the terms and concepts listed in the table below and define them in your own words. Then check your answers with the glossary provided in Appendix 5B.

Concept/Term	Your understanding of the meaning
1. Teaching approach	
2. Teaching methodology	
3. Scaffolding	
4. Speech modification	
5. Face needs of learners	
6. Face-threatening actions	
7. Language proficiency level	
8. Critical language pedagogy	
9. Affective dimensions of learning	
10. Error	
11. Elicitation	
12. Teacher talk	
13. Language variety	
14. Language register	
15. Language style	
16. Colloquial language use	
17. Target language use	
18. Intercultural competence	

5B   GLOSSARY

Concept/Term	Meaning
1. Teaching approach	The theory and principles underlying a particular set of teaching practices
2. Teaching methodology	The practices and procedures used in teaching and the beliefs which underlie them
3. Scaffolding	The support provided to learners to enable them to perform tasks which may be beyond their capacity
4. Speech modification	A type of communication strategy in which a speaker typically simplifies speech to make it more accessible
5. Face needs of learners	The positive image or impression of oneself that one shows or intends to show to others
6. Face-threatening actions	A speech act that threatens the face of a person being addressed
7. Language proficiency level	The degree of skill with which a person can use a language
8. Critical language pedagogy	An approach to teaching that seeks to examine critically the conditions underlying teaching and the social and cultural purposes of its use
9. Affective dimensions of learning	The emotional factors that may influence language learning and language use
10. Error	A fault made by speakers during the production of sounds, words or grammar
11. Elicitation	A questioning technique or procedure used to draw information/opinions/answers from a learner
12. Teacher talk	The variety of language used by a teacher when in the process of teaching learners
13. Language variety	The language spoken within a speech community
14. Language register	The type of language used by a professional group of people
15. Language style	The way an individual uses language, which often ranges from more colloquial to formal speech
16. Colloquial language use	An informal type of speech used amongst people who know each other well
17. Target language use	The use of the language which is being formally taught to learners
18. Intercultural competence	Developing understandings and expertise in relation to other cultures

Source: adapted from Richards and Schmidt (2003)

6   TEACHER DRESS AND BEHAVIOUR

Teacher details: (age/culture/ institution)	Attitudes towards dress	Attitudes towards behaviour
Teacher 1		
Teacher 2		
Teacher 3		

7   TEACHER STRATEGIES

Teacher 1 strategies	Teacher 2 strategies
I realised I needed to spend more time preparing the language part of the lesson as it involved more than I thought. I also got the students more involved in working out the answers in pairs and I listened and wrote up the correct answers on the board. It worked better and I could relax and chat to them more. The whole atmosphere changed and now I don't dread teaching them and have got to know some of them quite well.	I decided to dress a bit more formally and wear shoes with a heel to give me some height. It actually made me feel more in command. Then when I needed to give an instruction, I went to the front and stood in the middle so the students could all see me, and I raised my arm up high to signal to stop talking. This was an idea my supervisor said to try and they did stop talking after a minute or two. I feel more confident now.

8   PEDAGOGIC OPTIONS/RESPONSES TO DIFFERENT TYPES OF DISCIPLINE PROBLEMS

- Encourage students to work with different partners
- Change interactional pairs frequently
- Nominate effectively to make sure other students get opportunities to speak
- Give extra homework
- Seek the advice of a more experienced teacher
- Speak to the student in question in a firm but fair way, and explain how you would like them to change their behaviour
- Refer the matter to the director of the school or your line manager
- Contact the parents (if a child/teenager)
- Decide on a code of behaviour with the class at the start of the course
- Check to see if there is a school policy and follow it
- Keep a diary of incidents
- Remind the whole class regularly about the importance of good discipline if learning goals are to be achieved
- Give students opportunities to comment on/raise issues (i.e. surveys)
- Allow the students to work alone
- Minimise opportunities for cheating – prevention is better than punishment

REFERENCES

Abbitt, J. T. (2011) 'Measuring technological pedagogical content knowledge in preservice teacher education: A review of current methods and instruments', *Journal of Research on Technology in Education*, 43: 4, 281–300.

Akbari, R. (2007) 'Reflections on reflection: A critical appraisal of reflective practices in L2 teacher education', *System*, 35: 2, 192–207.

Allwright, R. (1980) 'Turns, topics, and tasks: Patterns of participation in language learning and teaching', in Larsen-Freeman, D. (ed.), *Discourse Analysis in SLA*, Rowley, MA: Newbury House, 165–87.

Allwright, D. (2003) 'Exploratory practice: Rethinking practitioner research in language teaching', *Language Teaching Research*, 7: 2, 113–41.

Allwright, D. (2005) 'Developing principles for practitioner research: The case of exploratory practice', *Modern Language Journal*, 89, 353–66.

Allwright, D. and Bailey, K. M. (1991) *Focus on the Language Classroom: An Introduction to Classroom Research for Language Teachers*, Cambridge: Cambridge University Press.

Anderson, L. W., Krathwohl, D. R., Airasian, P. W., Cruikshank, K. A., Mayer, R. E., Pintrich, P. R., Raths, J. and Wittrock, M. C. (2001) *A Taxonomy for Learning, Teaching, and Assessing: A Revision of Bloom's Taxonomy of Educational Objectives*, New York: Longman.

Argyris, C. and Schön, D. A. (1974) *Theory in Practice: Increasing Professional Effectiveness*, San Francisco: Jossey-Bass.

Arnold, J. (1999) *Affect in Language Learning*, Cambridge: Cambridge University Press.

Auerbach, E. (1994) 'Participatory action research', *TESOL Quarterly*, 28: 4, 673–703.

Bailey, K. (2001) 'Action research, teacher research, and classroom research in language teaching', in Celce-Murcia, M. (ed.), *Teaching English as a Second or Foreign Language* (3rd edn), Boston: Heinle and Heinle, 489–98.

Baker, F. (2010) 'Using corpora in language testing', in O'Keeffe, A. and McCarthy, M. (eds), *The Routledge Handbook of Corpus Linguistics*, London: Routledge, 633–45.

Bakhtin, M. M. (1981) *The Dialogic Imagination: Four Essays by M. M. Bakhtin*, ed. Holquist, M., trans. Emerson, C. and Holquist, M., Austin: University of Texas Press.

Banbrook, L. and Skehan, P. (1989) 'Classrooms and display questions', in Brumfit, C. and Mitchell, R. (eds), *Research in the Language Classroom*, London: Modern English Publications and the British Council, 141–52.

Barduhn, S. (2002) 'Why develop? It's easier not to', in Edge, J. (ed.), *Continuing Professional Development: Some of Our Perspectives*, Whitstable: IATEFL, 10–13.

Bazeley, P. and Jackson, K. (2013) *Qualitative Data Analysis with NVIVO* (2nd edn), London: Sage.

Belenky, M. F., Clinchy, B., Goldberger, N. R. and Tarule, J. M. (1986) *Women's Ways of Knowing*, New York: Basic Books.

Bell, D. (2007) 'Do teachers think that methods are dead?', *ELT Journal*, 61: 2, 135–46.

Benson, P. (2001) *Teaching and Researching Autonomy in Language Learning*, Harlow: Pearson Education.

Benson, P. (2013) *Teaching and Researching Autonomy in Language Learning* (2nd edn), Abingdon and New York: Routledge.

Benson, P. and Voller, P. (eds) (2013) *Autonomy and Independence in Language Learning*, Abingdon and New York: Routledge.

Biber, D., Conrad, S. and Reppen, R. (1998) *Corpus Linguistics: Investigating Language Structure and Use*, Cambridge: Cambridge University Press.

Biber, D., Johansson, S., Leech, G., Conrad, S. and Finegan, E. (1999) *Longman Grammar of Spoken and Written English*, London and New York: Longman.

Bishop, J. L. and Verleger, M. A. (2013) 'The flipped classroom: A survey of the research', paper presented at the 120th ASSE Annual Conference and Exposition, Atlanta, 23–6 June. Available at: http://www.studiesuccesho.nl/wp-content/uploads/2014/04/flipped-classroom-artikel.pdf.

Blake, R. J. (2008) *Brave New Digital Classroom: Technology and Foreign Language Learning*, Washington: Georgetown University Press.

Bloom, B. S., Engelhart, M. D., Furst, E. J., Hill, W. H. and Krathwohl, D. R. (1956) *Taxonomy of Educational Objectives: The Classification of Educational Goals. Handbook I: Cognitive Domain*, New York: David McKay.

Borg, M. (2004) 'The apprenticeship of observation', *ELT Journal*, 58: 3, 274–6.

Borg, S. (2009) 'English language teachers' conceptions of research', *Applied Linguistics*, 30: 3, 358–88.

Borg, S. (2013) *Teacher Research in Language Teaching: A Critical Analysis*, Cambridge: Cambridge University Press.

Boud, D., Keogh, R. and Walker, D. (1985) *Reflection: Turning Experience into Learning*, London: Kogan Page.

Braun, S. (2005) 'From pedagogically relevant corpora to authentic language learning contents', *ReCALL*, 17: 1, 47–64.

Brew, A. (2006) *Research and Teaching: Beyond the Divide*, New York: Palgrave Macmillan.

Brezina, V. and Gablasova, D. (2013) 'Is there a core general vocabulary? Introducing the New General Service List', *Applied Linguistics*, 36: 1, 1–22.

Britzman, D. P. (2000) 'Teacher education in the confusion of our times', *Journal of Teacher Education*, 51, 200–5.

Brown, H. D. (1994) *Principles of Language Learning and Teaching*, White Plains: Pearson Longman.

Brown, H. D. (2001) *Teaching by Principles: An Interactive Approach to Language Pedagogy*, Englewood Cliffs: Prentice Hall.

Brown, J. D. (2014) *Mixed Methods Research for TESOL*, Edinburgh: Edinburgh University Press.

Brown, P. and Levinson, S. (1987) *Politeness: Some Universals in Language Usage*, Cambridge: Cambridge University Press.

Bruner, J. (1985) 'Vygotsky: A historical and conceptual perspective', in Wertsch, J. V. (ed.), *Culture, Communication and Cognition: Vygotskian Perspectives*, New York: Cambridge University Press, 21–34.

Bruner, J. (1986) *Actual Minds, Possible Worlds*, Cambridge, MA: Harvard University Press.

Burns, A. (1999) *Collaborative Action Research for English Language Teachers*, Cambridge: Cambridge University Press.

Burns, A. (2010) *Doing Action Research in English Language Teaching: A Guide for Practitioners*, New York: Routledge.

Butler, Y. G. (2004) 'What level of proficiency do elementary school teachers need to attain to teach EFL? Case studies from Korea, Taiwan, and Japan', *TESOL Quarterly*, 38: 2, 245–78.

Buzan, T. and Buzan, B. (1996) *The Mind Map Book: How to Use Radiant Thinking to Maximise Your Brain's Untapped Potential*, London: Plume.

Bygate, M. (2000) 'Introduction to the special issue: Tasks in language pedagogy', *Language Teaching Research*, 4: 3, 185–92.

Byram, M. (1997) *Teaching and Assessing Inter-Cultural Communicative Competence*, Clevedon: Multilingual Matters.

Cameron, L. (2001) *Teaching Language to Young Learners*, Cambridge: Cambridge University Press.

Candlin, C. N. and Breen, M. (1980), 'Evaluating and designing language teaching materials', *Practical Papers in English Language Education*, 2, Lancaster: Institute for English Language Education, University of Lancaster.

Carr, W. and Kemmis, S. (1986) *Becoming Critical: Education, Knowledge and Action Research*, London: Falmer Press.

Carrier, M. (1997) 'ELT online: The rise of the Internet', *ELT Journal*, 51: 3, 279–309.

Carter, R. and McCarthy, M. (2006) *Cambridge Grammar of English: A Comprehensive Guide to Spoken and Written Grammar and Usage*, Cambridge: Cambridge University Press.

Carter, R. and Nunan, D. (eds) (2001) *The Cambridge Guide to Teaching English to Speakers of Other Languages*, New York: Cambridge University Press.

Cazden, C. B. (1986) 'Classroom discourse', in Wittrock, M. C. (ed.), *Handbook of Research on Teaching*, New York: Macmillan, 432–43.

Chamberlin, C. R. (2000) 'Nonverbal behaviors and initial impressions of trustworthiness in teacher–supervisor relationships', *Communication Education*, 49: 4, 352–64.

Chambers, A. (2005) 'Integrating corpus consultation into language studies', *Language Learning & Technology*, 19: 2, 111–25.

Chambers, A. (2007) 'Popularising corpus consultation by language learners and teachers', in Hidalgo, E., Quereda, L. and Santana, J. (eds), *Corpora in the Foreign Language Classroom*, Amsterdam: Rodopi, 3–16.

Chambers, A. (2010) 'What is data-driven learning?', in O'Keeffe, A. and McCarthy, M. (eds), *The Routledge Handbook of Corpus Linguistics*, London: Routledge, 345–58.

Chambers, A., Farr, F. and O'Riordan, S. (2011) 'Language teachers with corpora in mind: From starting steps to walking tall', *Language Learning*, 39: 1, 85–104.

Chapelle, C. and Jamieson, J. (2008) *Tips for Teaching with CALL: Practical Approaches to Computer-Assisted Language Learning*, New York: Longman.

Chaudron, C. L. (1988) *Second Language Classroom: Research on Teaching and Learning*, New York: Cambridge University Press.

Cheng, M. M. H., Tang, S. Y. F. and Cheng, A. Y. N. (2012) 'Practicalising theoretical knowledge in student teachers' professional learning in initial teacher education', *Teaching and Teacher Education*, 28: 6, 781–90.

Chinnery, G. M. (2006) 'Emerging technologies: Going to the MALL – mobile assisted language learning', *Language Learning & Technology*, 10: 1, 9–16.

Chomsky, N. (1986) *Knowledge of Language: Its Nature, Origin and Use*, Westport: Praeger.

Christison, M. A. and Bassano, S. (1995) 'Action research: Techniques for collecting data through surveys and interviews', *CATESOL Journal*, 8, 89–103.

Clarke, A. (1995) 'Professional development in practicum settings: Reflective practice under scrutiny', *Teaching and Teacher Education*, 11: 13, 243–61.

Coffield, F., Moseley, D., Hall, E. and Ecclestone, K. (2004) *Learning Styles and Pedagogy in*

Post-16 Learning: A Systematic and Critical Review. http://sxills.nl/lerenlerennu/bronnen/
Learning%20styles%20by%20Coffield%20e.a..pdf

Copeland, W. D. (1980) 'Affective dispositions of teachers in training toward examples of supervisory behavior', *Journal of Educational Research*, 74: 1, 37–42.

Copland, F. (2010) 'Causes of tension in post-observation feedback in pre-service teacher training: An alternative view', *Teaching and Teacher Education*, 26: 3, 466–72.

Copland, F., Garton, S. and Burns, A. (2013) 'Challenges in teaching English to young learners: Global perspectives and local realities', *TESOL Quarterly*, 28: 4, 738–62.

Corey, S. (1953) *Action Research to Improve School Practice*, New York: Teachers College, Columbia University.

Coxhead, A. (2000) 'A new academic word list', *TESOL Quarterly*, 34: 2, 213–38.

Coxhead, A. (2010) 'What can corpora tell us about English for academic purposes?', in O'Keeffe, A. and McCarthy, M. (eds), *The Routledge Handbook of Corpus Linguistics*, London: Routledge, 458–70.

Crawford, R. (2013) *The ICT Teacher's Handbook* (2nd edn), New York and Abingdon: Routledge.

Creese, A. (2008) 'Linguistic ethnography', in Creese, A., Martin, P. and Hornberger, N. (eds), *Encyclopedia of Language and Education. Vol. 9.* New York: Springer, 229–41.

Crookes, G. (1993) 'Action research for second language teachers: Going beyond teacher research', *Applied Linguistics*, 14: 2, 130–44.

Crookes, G. (2003) *A Practicum in TESOL: Professional Development through Practice*, New York: Cambridge University Press.

Cullen, R. (2002) 'Supportive teacher talk: The importance of the F-move', *English Language Teaching Journal*, 56: 2, 117–27.

Cunningsworth, A. (1995) *Choosing Your Coursebook*, Oxford: Heinemann.

Cutrim-Schmid, E. (2016) 'Interactive whiteboards and language learning', in Farr, F. and Murray, L. (eds), *The Routledge Handbook of Language Learning and Technology*, New York: Routledge.

Cutting, J. (2015) *Language in Context in TESOL*, Edinburgh: Edinburgh University Press.

Davies, S. and Parkinson, B. (1994) 'Peer observation and post-observation discussion', *Edinburgh Working Papers in Applied Linguistics*, 5, 30–49.

DeGrazia, J. L., Falconer, J. L., Nicodemus, G. and Medlin, W. (2012) 'Incorporating screencasts into chemical engineering courses', *Proceedings of the ASEE Annual Conference & Exposition, 2012*, www.asee.org/search?utf8=%E2%9C%93&search=zappe+flipping&commit=Search

Derewianka, B. (2003) 'Developing electronic materials for language teaching', in Tomlinson, B. (ed.), *Developing Materials for Language Teaching*, London: Continuum, 199–220.

Dewey, J. (1933) *How We Think*, Chicago: Henry Regnery.

Dobbs, J. (2001) *Using the Whiteboard*, Cambridge: Cambridge University Press.

Dörnyei, Z. (2001) *Motivation Strategies in the Language Classroom*, Cambridge: Cambridge University Press.

Dörnyei, Z. (2003) *Questionnaires in Second Language Research: Construction, Administration and Processing*, Mahwah: Lawrence Erlbaum.

Dörnyei, Z. and Murphey, T. (2003) *Group Dynamics in the Language Classroom*, Cambridge: Cambridge University Press.

Dörnyei, Z. and Ushioda, E. (2011) *Teaching and Researching Motivation* (2nd edn), London: Pearson Education.

Doyle, W. (1984) *Effective Classroom Practices for Secondary Schools*. Austin: Research and Development Centre for Teacher Education.

Dunn, R., Dunn, K. and Price, G. E. (1975) *The Learning Style Inventory*, Lawrence: Price Systems.

Dunn, R., Dunn, K. and Price, G. E. (1978) *Teaching Students through Their Individual Learning Styles*, Reston: Reston Publishing.

Edge, J. (1984) 'Feedback with face', *English Language Teaching Journal*, 38: 3, 204–6.

Edge, J. (1992) 'Co-operative development', *English Language Teaching Journal*, 46: 1, 62–70.

Edge, J. (1993) *Essentials of English Language Teaching*, London: Longman.

Edge, J. (ed.) (2001) *Action Research: Case Studies in TESOL Practice*, Alexandria: TESOL.

Edge, J. (2002) *Continuing Cooperative Development: A Discourse Framework for Individuals as Colleagues*, Ann Arbor: University of Michigan Press.

Edge, J. (2011) *The Reflexive Teacher Educator in TESOL*, New York and London: Routledge.

Edge, J. and Richards, K. (1998) 'Why *best practice* is not good enough', *TESOL Quarterly*, 32: 3, 569–76.

Ehrman, M. and Oxford, R. (1990) 'Adult language learning styles and strategies in an intensive training setting', *Modern Language Journal*, 74: 3, 311–26.

Elliot, J. (1991) *Action Research for Educational Change*, Milton Keynes: Open University Press.

Ellis, R. (1997) 'The empirical evaluation of language teaching materials', *ELT Journal*, 51: 1, 36–42.

Fanselow, J. F. (1990) '"Let's see": Contrasting conversations about teaching', in Richards, J. C. and Nunan, D. (eds), *Second Language Teacher Education*, Cambridge: Cambridge University Press, 182–97.

Farr, F. (2005) 'Reflecting on reflections: The spoken word as a professional development tool in language teacher education', in Hughes, R. (ed.), *Spoken English, Applied Linguistics and TESOL: Challenges for Theory and Practice*, Basingstoke: Palgrave Macmillan, 182–215.

Farr, F. (2008) 'Evaluating the use of corpus-based instruction in a language teacher education context: Perspectives from the users', *Language Awareness*, 17: 1, 25–43.

Farr, F. (2011) *The Discourse of Teaching Practice Feedback: An Investigation of Spoken and Written Modes*, New York: Routledge.

Farr, F. and Murray, L. (eds) (2016) *The Routledge Handbook of Language Learning and Technology*, New York: Routledge.

Farr, F. and O'Keeffe, A. (eds) (2004) *The Limerick Corpus of Irish English (L-CIE)*, Limerick: University of Limerick.

Farr, F. and Riordan, E. (2012) 'Students' engagement in reflective tasks: An investigation of interactive and non-interactive discourse corpora', *Classroom Discourse*, 3: 2, 126–43.

Farr, F. and Riordan, E. (2015) 'Tracing the reflective practices of student teachers in online modes', *ReCALL*, 27: 1, 104–23.

Farr, F., Chambers, A. and O'Riordan, S. (2010) 'Corpora for materials development in language teacher education: Underlying principles and useful data', in Mishan, F. and Chambers, A. (eds), *Perspectives on Language Learning Materials Development*, Berlin: Peter Lang, 33–62.

Farrell, T. S. C. (2007) *Reflective Language Teaching: From Research to Practice*, London: Continuum.

Farrell, T. S. C. (2012) 'Reflecting on reflective practice: (Re)visiting Dewey and Schön', *TESOL Journal*, 3: 1, 7–16.

Farrell, T. S. C. (2015) *Promoting Teacher Reflection in Second Language Education: A Framework for TESOL Professionals*, New York: Routledge.

Feenberg, A. (2002) *Transforming Technology: A Critical Theory Revisited*, Oxford: Oxford University Press.

Fendler, L. (2003) 'Teacher reflection in a hall of mirrors: Historical influences and political reverberations', *Educational Researcher*, 32, 16–25.

Fischer, J. C. (2001) 'Action research: Rationale and planning', in Burnaford, G., Fischer, J. and Hobson, D. (eds), *Teachers Doing Research: The Power of Action through Inquiry* (2nd edn), Hillsdale: Lawrence Erlbaum, 29–48.

Flowerdew, L. (2012) *Corpora and Language Education*, London: Palgrave Macmillan.

Fontana, A. and Frey, J. (2000) 'The interview: From structured questions to negotiated text', in Denzin, N. and Lincoln, Y. (eds), *The Sage Handbook of Qualitative Research* (2nd edn), London: Sage, 645–72.

Freeman, D. (1982) 'Observing teachers: Three approaches to in-service training and development', *TESOL Quarterly*, 16: 1, 21–8.

Freeman, D. (1991) '"To make the tacit explicit": Teacher education, emerging discourse, and conceptions of teaching', *Teaching and Teacher Education*, 7: 5/6, 439–54.

Freeman, D. (2004) 'Language, sociocultural theory, and L2 teacher education: Examining the technology of subject matter and the architecture of instruction', in Hawkins, M. R., *Language Learning and Teacher Education: A Sociocultural Approach*, New York: Multilingual Matters, 169–97.

Gaies, S. and Bowers, R. (1990) 'Clinical supervision of language teaching: The supervisor as trainer and educator', in Richards, J. C. and Nunan, D. (eds), *Second Language Teacher Education*, Cambridge: Cambridge University Press, 167–81.

Gardner, R. C. and Lambert, W. E. (1972) *Attitudes and Motivation in Second-Language Learning*, Rowley: Newbury House.

Garrett, P. and Shortall, T. (2002) 'Learners' evaluations of teacher-fronted and student-centered activities', *Language Teaching Research*, 6, 125–7.

Garrison, J. W. and Rud, A. G. (1995) *The Educational Conversation: Closing the Gap*, Albany: SUNY Press.

Gatbonton, E. (2008) 'Looking beyond teachers' classroom behavior: Novice and experienced ESL teachers pedagogic knowledge', *Language Teaching Research*, 12: 2, 161–82.

Gebhard, J. G. (1990) 'Models of supervision: Choices', in Richards, J. C. and Nunan, D. (eds), *Second Language Teacher Education*, Cambridge: Cambridge University Press, 156–66.

Gillen, J. (2014) *Digital Literacies*, Abingdon: Routledge.

Gilmore, A. (2009) 'Using online corpora to develop students' writing skills', *ELT Journal*, 63: 4, 363–72.

Gilquin, G. and Granger, S. (2010) 'How can data-driven learning be used in language teaching?', in O'Keeffe, A. and McCarthy, M. (eds), *The Routledge Handbook of Corpus Linguistics*, London: Routledge, 359–70.

Golombek, P. R. (1998) 'A study of language teachers' personal practical knowledge', *TESOL Quarterly*, 32: 3, 447–64.

Gore, J. and Zeichner, K. (1991) 'Action research and reflective teaching in preservice teacher education: A case study from the United States', *Teaching and Teacher Education*, 7: 2, 119–36.

Gower, R., Phillips, D. and Walters, S. (2005) *Teaching Practice: A Handbook for Teachers in Training*, Oxford: Macmillan.

Graddol, D. (2006) *English Next: Why Global English May Mean the End of 'English as a Foreign Language'*, Plymouth: English Company.

Granger, S. (2013) 'The passive in learner English: Corpus insights and implications for pedagogical grammar', in Ishikawa, S. (ed.), *Papers from LCSAW2013. Vol. 1*, Kobe: Kobe University, 5–16.

Gray, D. E. (2014) *Doing Research in the Real World*, London: Sage.

Gray, J. (2002) 'The global coursebook in English language teaching', in Block, D. and Cameron, D. (eds), *Globalisation and Language Teaching*, London: Routledge, 151–67.

Griffiths, V. (2000) 'The reflective dimension in teacher education', *International Journal of Educational Research*, 33: 5, 539–55.

Halliday, J. (1998) 'Techncisim, reflective practice and authenticity in teacher education', *Teaching and Teacher Education*, 14, 597–605.

Hanks, P. (2009) 'The impact of corpora on dictionaries', in Baker, P. (ed.), *Contemporary Corpus Linguistics*, London: Continuum, 214–36.

Hanson-Smith, E. (2016) 'Teacher education and technology', in Farr, F. and Murray, L. (eds), *The Routledge Handbook of Language Learning and Technology*, New York: Routledge.

Harley, B., Allen, P., Cummins, J. and Swain, M. (eds) (1990) *The Development of Second Language Proficiency*, New York: Cambridge University Press.

Harmer, J. (2007) *How to Teach English*, Harlow: Pearson.

Hawkins, M. R. (2004) 'Social apprenticeships through mediated learning in language teacher education', in Hawkins, M. R. (ed.) *Language Learning and Teacher Education. A Sociocultural Approach*, New York: Multilingual Matters, 89–110.

Healey, D., Hanson-Smith, E., Hubbard, P., Ioannou-Georgiou, S., Kessler, G. and Ware, P. (2011) *TESOL Technology Standards Framework*, Alexandria: TESOL Inc.

Helm, F. and Guth, S. (2016) 'Telecollaboration and language learning', in Farr, F. and Murray, L. (eds), *The Routledge Handbook of Language Learning and Technology*, New York: Routledge.

Holec, H. (1981) *Autonomy in Foreign Language Learning*, Oxford: Pergamon.

Holliday, A. (1994) *Appropriate Methodology and Social Context*, Cambridge: Cambridge University Press.

Holliday, A. (2005) *The Struggle to Teach English as an International Language*, Oxford: Oxford University Press.

Holliday, A. (2007) *Doing and Writing Qualitative Research* (2nd edn), London: Sage.

Hollingsworth, S. and Sockett, H. (1994) 'Positioning teacher research in educational reform: An introduction', in Hollingsworth, S. and Sockett, H. (eds), *Teacher Research and Educational Reform*, Chicago: University of Chicago Press, 1–20.

Hoover, N. L., O'Shea, L. J. and Carroll, R. G. (1988) 'The supervisor–intern relationship and effective interpersonal communication skills', *Journal of Teacher Education*, 39: 2, 17–21.

Horwitz, E., Horwitz, M. and Cope, J. (1986) 'Foreign language learning classroom anxiety', *Modern Language Journal*, 70: 1, 125–32.

Housner, L. D. and Griffey, D. C. (1985) 'Teacher cognition: Differences in planning and interactive decision making between experienced and inexperienced teachers', *Research Quarterly for Exercise and Sport*, 56: 1, 45–53.

Howard, A. and Donaghue, H. (eds) (2014) *Teacher Evaluation in Second Language Education*, London: Bloomsbury.

Hughes, A. and Hadfield, J. (2005) *How to Teach Young Learners*, London: Pearson.

Hughes, R. (2010) 'What a corpus tells us about grammar teaching materials', in O'Keeffe, A. and McCarthy, M. (eds), *The Routledge Handbook of Corpus Linguistics*, London: Routledge, 401–41.

Hunston, S. (1995) 'Grammar in teacher education: The role of a corpus', *Language Awareness*, 4: 1, 15–31.

Hunter, M. (1984) 'Knowing, teaching, and supervising', in Hosford, P. L. (ed.), *Using What We Know About Teaching*, Alexandria: Association for Supervision and Curriculum Development, 169–92.

Hyland, K. (2006) *English for Academic Purposes: An Advanced Resourcebook*, London and New York: Routledge.

Islam, C. and Mares, C. (2003) 'Adapting classroom materials', in Tomlinson, B. (ed.), *Developing Materials for Language Teaching*, London: Continuum, 86–100.

Jay, J. K. and Johnson, K. L. (2002) 'Capturing complexity: A typology of reflective practice for teacher education', *Teaching and Teacher Education*, 18, 73–85.

Jenkins, J. (2007) *English as a Lingua Franca: Attitudes and Identity*, Oxford: Oxford University Press.

Jensen, E. (1998) *Superteaching* (3rd edn), San Diego: Brain Store.

Jianping Xu (2009) 'A survey study of autonomous learning by Chinese non-English major post-graduates', *English Language Teaching*, 4: 2, 25–32.

Johns, T. (1991) 'Should you be persuaded: Two samples of data-driven learning materials', *English Language Research Journal*, 4, 1–16.

Kadir-Hussein, A. and Che-Haron, S. (2012) 'Autonomy in language learning', *Journal of Education and Practice*, 3: 8, 103–11.

Kayi-Adar, H. (2013) '"No, Rolanda, completely wrong! " Positioning, classroom participation and ESL learning', *Classroom Discourse*, 4: 2, 130–50.

Kemmis, S. and McTaggart, R. (1988) *The Action Research Planner* (3rd edn), Geelong: Deakin University Press.

Kennedy, M. (1990) *Policy Issues in Teacher Education*, Michigan: National Centre for Research on Teacher Learning.

Kern, R. and Malinowski, D. (2016) 'Limitations and boundaries in language learning and technology', in Farr, F. and Murray, L. (eds), *The Routledge Handbook of Language Learning and Technology*, New York: Routledge.

Klimt, B. and Yang, Y. (2004) 'The Enron corpus: A new dataset for email classification research', presented at the European Conference on Machine Learning, Italy.

Knight, D. (2011) 'The future of multimodal corpora', *RBLA, Belo Horizonte*, 11: 2, 391–415.

Koerner, M., O'Connell-Rust, F. and Baumgartner, F. (2002) 'Exploring roles in student teaching placements', *Teacher Education Quarterly*, 29: 2, 35–58.

Kolb, D. (1984) *Experiential Learning: Experience as the Sources of Learning and Development*, Englewood Cliffs: Prentice Hall.

Korthagen, F. (2004) 'In search of the essence of a good teacher: Towards a more holistic approach in teacher education', *Teaching and Teacher Education*, 20: 1, 77–97.

Korthagen, F. and Vasalos, A. (2005) 'Levels in reflection: Core reflection as a means to enhance professional growth', *Teachers and Teaching: Theory and Practice*, 11: 1, 47–71.

Kramsch, C. (1995) 'Embracing conflict versus achieving consensus in foreign language education', *ADFL Bulletin*, 26: 3, 6–12.

Kramsch, C. (1998) *Language and Culture*, Oxford: Oxford University Press.

Krashen, S. D. (1985) *The Input Hypothesis: Issues and Implications*, London: Longman.

Krashen, S. D. and Terrell, T. D. (1983) *The Natural Approach: Language Acquisition in the Classroom*, Englewood Cliffs: Prentice Hall.

Kumaradivelu, B. (1999) 'Critical classroom discourse analysis', *TESOL Quarterly*, 33: 3, 453–84.

Kumaradivelu, B. (2006) 'TESOL methods: Changing tracks, challenging trends', *TESOL Quarterly*, 40: 1, 59–81.

Lakoff, G. (1973) 'Hedges: A study in meaning criteria and the logic of fuzzy concepts', *Journal of Philosophical Logic*, 2: 4, 458–508.

Lave, J. and Wenger, E. (1991) *Situated Learning: Legitimate Peripheral Participation*, Cambridge: Cambridge University Press.

Lee, D. Y. W. (2010) 'What corpora are available?', in O'Keeffe, A. and McCarthy, M. (eds), *The Routledge Handbook of Corpus Linguistics*, London: Routledge, 107–21.

Leech, G. (1997) 'Teaching and language corpora: A convergence', in Wichmann, A., Fligelstone, S., McEnery, T. and Knowles, G. (eds), *Teaching and Language Corpora*, London: Longman, 1–23.

Levy, M. (2009) 'Technologies in use for second language learning', *Modern Language Journal*, 93: 1, 769–82.

Lindstromberg, S. (2004) *Language Activities for Teenagers*, Cambridge: Cambridge University Press.

Little, D. (1995) 'Learning as dialogue: The dependence of learner autonomy on teacher autonomy', *System*, 23: 2, 175–81.

Littlejohn, A. (2013) 'Self-access work and curriculum ideologies', in Benson, P. and Voller, P. (eds), *Autonomy and Independence in Language Learning*, Abingdon and New York: Routledge, 181–91.

Littlewood, W. (2007) 'Communicative and task based language teaching in East Asian classrooms', *Language Teaching*, 40: 3, 243–49.

Long, M. and Sato, C. (1983) 'Classroom foreigner talk discourse: Forms and functions of teacher questions', in Seliger, H. and Long, M. H. (eds), *Classroom Oriented Research in Second Language Acquisition*, Rowley: Newbury House, 268–85.

Lortie, D. C. (1975) *School-Teacher: A Sociological Study*, Chicago and London: University of Chicago Press.

Macaro, E. (2003) *Teaching and Learning a Second Language: A Guide to Recent Research and its Applications*, London and New York: Continuum.

Mann, S. (1999) 'Opening the insider's eye: Starting action research', *Language Teacher*, 23: 12, 11–13.

Mann, S. and Walsh, S. (2013) 'RP or "RIP": A critical perspective on reflective practice', *Applied Linguistics Review*, 4: 2, 291–315.

Mann, S. G. (2003) 'An evaluation of tutor-led feedback in the context of initial teacher training in EFL', in Gollin, J., Ferguson, G. and Trappes-Lomax, H. (eds), *IALS Conference Proceedings*, Edinburgh: IALS [CD].

Mares, C. (2003) 'Writing a coursebook', in Tomlinson, B. (ed.) *Developing Materials for Language Teaching*, London: Continuum, 130–40.

Master, P. (1983) 'The etiquette of observation', *TESOL Quarterly*, 17: 3, 497–501.

McCarten, J. (2007) *Teaching Vocabulary: Lessons from the Corpus, Lessons for the Classroom*, Cambridge: Cambridge University Press.

McCarten, J. (2010) 'Corpus-informed course book design', in O'Keeffe, A. and McCarthy, M. (eds), *The Routledge Handbook of Corpus Linguistics*, London: Routledge, 413–27.

McCarten, J. and McCarthy, M. J. (2010) 'Bridging the gap between corpus and course book: The case of conversation strategies', in Mishan, F. and Chambers, A. (eds), *Perspectives on Language Learning Materials Development*, Oxford: Peter Lang, 11–32.

McCarthy, M. J. (2006) *Explorations in Corpus Linguistics*, Cambridge: Cambridge University Press.

McCarthy, M. J. (2002) 'Good listenership made plain: British and American non-minimal response tokens in everyday conversation', in Reppen, R., Fitzmaurice, S. M. and Biber, D. (eds), *Using Corpora to Explore Linguistic Variation*, Amsterdam: John Benjamins, 49–72.

McCarthy, M. J. (2003) 'Talking back: "Small" interactional response tokens in everyday conversation', *Research on Language and Social Interaction*, 36, 33–63.

McDonagh, J. and Shaw, C. (1993) *Materials and Methods in ELT: A Teacher's Guide*, London: Blackwell.

McEnery, T. and Kifle, N. A. (2002) 'Epistemic modality in argumentative essays of second-language writers', in Flowerdew, J. (ed.), *Academic Discourse*, Harlow: Longman, 182–95.

McEnery, T. and Xiao, R. (2010) 'What corpora can offer in language teaching and learning', in Hinkel, E. (ed.), *Handbook of Research in Second Language Teaching and Learning. Vol. 2*, London: Routledge, 364–80.

McKernan, J. (1996) *Curriculum Action Research: A Handbook of Methods and Resources for the Reflective Practitioner*, London: Kogan Page.

McNiff, J. (2013) *Action Research: Principles and Practice*, Abingdon: Routledge.

Medgyes, P. (1994) *The Non-Native Teacher*, Houndmills: Macmillan.

Mertler, C. (2011) *Action Research: Improving Schools and Empowering Educators*, London: Sage.

Meunier, F. (2002) 'The pedagogic value of native and learner corpora in EFL grammar teaching', in Granger, S., Hung, J. and Petch-Tyson, S. (eds), *Computer Learner Corpora, Second Language Acquisition and Foreign Language Teaching*, Amsterdam: John Benjamins, 119–41.

Mishan, F. (2004) 'Authenticating corpora for language learning: A problem and its resolution', *ELT Journal*, 58: 3, 219–27.

Mishan, F. (2005) *Designing Authenticity into Language Learning Materials*, Bristol: Intellect.

Mishan, F. (2013) 'Modes of delivery', in Tomlinson, B. (ed.), *Applied Linguistics and Materials Development*, London: Bloomsbury, 287–302.

Mishan, F. and Chambers, A. (eds) (2010) *Perspectives on Language Learning Materials Development*, Oxford: Peter Lang.

Mishan, F. and Timmis, I. (2015) *Materials Development for TESOL*, Edinburgh: Edinburgh University Press.

Mishra, P. and Koehler, M. J. (2006) 'Technological pedagogical content knowledge: A framework for teacher knowledge', *Teachers College Record*, 108: 6, 1017–54.

Mitchell, A. (1997) 'Teacher identity: A key to increased collaboration', *Action in Teacher Education*, 19: 3, 1–14.

Moskowitz, G. (1971) 'Interaction analysis: A new modern language for supervisors', *Foreign Language Annals*, 5, 211–21.

Moskowitz, G. (1978) *Caring and Sharing in the Foreign Language Class: A Sourcebook on Humanistic Techniques*, Rowley: Newbury House.

Mukundan, J. and Nimehchisalem, V. (2008) 'Educational software and English teaching courseware: Promising panaceas?', *Journal of NELTA*, 13: 1–2, 71–9.

Murray, D. E. (2010) 'Learning by doing: The role of data collection in action research', in Park, G., Widodo, H. P. and Cirocki, A. (eds), *Observation of Teaching: Bridging Theory and Practice through Research on Teaching*, Munich: LINCOM EUROPA, 49–61.

Murray, D. E. and Christison, M. (2011) *What English Language Teachers Need to Know. Vol. II*, New York and Abingdon: Routledge.

Murray, N. (2010) 'Pragmatics, awareness- raising, and the cooperative principle', *English Language Teaching Journal*, 64: 3, 293–301.

Nesselhauf, N. (2004) 'Learner corpora and their potential for language teaching', in Sinclair, J. (ed.), *How to Use Corpora in Language Teaching*, Amsterdam: John Benjamins, 125–52.

Nesselhauf, N. (2005) *Collocations in a Learner Corpus*, Amsterdam: John Benjamins.

Nguyen, L. V. (2008) 'Technology-enhanced EFL syllabus design and materials development', *English Language Teaching*, 1: 2, 135–42.

Nunan, D. (1988) *Syllabus Design*, Oxford: Oxford University Press.

Nunan, D. (1989) 'The teacher as researcher', in Brumfit, C. and Mitchell, R. (eds), *Research in the Language Classroom*, London: Modern English Publications and the British Council, 16–32.

Nunan, D. (1992a) *Language Learning and Teaching*, Cambridge: Cambridge University Press.

Nunan, D. (1992b) *Research Methods in Language Learning*, Cambridge: Cambridge University Press.

Nunan, D. (1993) 'Action research in language education', in Edge, J. and Richards, K. (eds), *Teachers Develop Teachers Research: Papers on Classroom Research and Teacher Development*, Oxford: Heinemann, 39–50.

Nunan, D. (2013) 'Designing and adapting materials to encourage learner autonomy', in Benson, P. and Voller, P. (eds), *Autonomy and Independence in Language Learning*, Abingdon and New York: Routledge, 192–203.

Nunan, D. and Lamb, C. (1996) *The Self-Directed Teacher*, Cambridge: Cambridge University Press.

O'Keeffe, A. and Farr, F. (2003) 'Using language corpora in language teacher education: Pedagogic, linguistic and cultural insights', *TESOL Quarterly*, 37: 3, 389–418.

O'Keeffe, A., McCarthy, M. and Carter, R. (2007) *From Corpus to Classroom: Language Use and Language Teaching*, Cambridge: Cambridge University Press.

O'Keeffe, A., Clancy, B. and Adolphs, S. (2011) *Introducing Pragmatics in Use*, London: Routledge.

O'Neill, R. (1991) 'The plausible myth of learner-centredness: Or the importance of doing ordinary things well', *English Language Teaching Journal*, 45: 4, 293–304.

Orland-Barak, L. (2002) 'The impact of the assessment of practice teaching on beginning teaching: Learning to ask different questions', *Teacher Education Quarterly*, 29: 2, 99–122.

O'Sullivan, I. and Chambers, A. (2006) 'Learners' writing skills in French: Corpus consultation and learner evaluation', *Journal of Second Language Writing*, 15, 49–68.

Oxford, R. (1990) *Language Learning Strategies: What Every Teacher Should Know*, Boston: Heinle and Heinle.

Oxford, R. (ed.) (1996) *Language Learning Strategies Around the World: Cross-Cultural Perspectives*, Hawaii: University of Hawai'i Press.

Oxford, R. (1997) 'Cooperative learning, collaborative learning, and interaction: Three communicative strands in the language classroom', *Modern Language Journal*, 81: 4, 443–56.

Oxford, R. (2001) 'Language learning strategies', in Carter, R. and Nunan, D. (eds), *Teaching English to Speakers of Other Languages*, New York: Cambridge University Press, 166–72.

Park, G., Widodo, H. P. and Cirocki, A. (eds) (2010) *Observation of Teaching: Bridging Theory and Practice through Research on Teaching*, Munich: LINCOM.

Peacock, M. (1997) 'The effect of authentic materials on the motivation of EFL learners', *ELT Journal*, 51: 2, 144–56.

Pennington, M. C. (1990) 'A professional development focus for the language teaching practicum', in Richards, J. and Nunan, D. (eds), *Second Language Teacher Education*, Cambridge: Cambridge University Press, 132–52.

Pennycook, A. (1989) 'The concept of method, interested knowledge, and the politics of language teaching', *TESOL Quarterly*, 23, 589–618.

Perpignan, H. (2001) *Teacher-Written Feedback to Language Learners: Promoting a Dialogue for Understanding*, unpublished thesis (PhD), Lancaster University.

Peters, K. H. and March, J. K. (1999) *Collaborative Observation*, Thousand Oaks: Corwin Press.

Phillips, D. (1997) 'Teacher training: Observation and feedback', in McGrath, I. (ed.), *Learning to Train: Perspectives on the Development of Language Teacher Trainers*, Hemel Hampstead: Prentice Hall, 82–8.

Phillips, D. T. and Quilligan, M. (2014) 'Teaching an introductory course in soil mechanics using problem-based learning', presented at the ICEER International Conference on Engineering Education and Research, McMaster University, Canada, 24–6 August.

Placek, J. (1983) 'Conceptions of success in teaching: Busy, happy, and good?', in Templin, T. and Oslin, J. (eds), *Teaching in Physical Education*, Champaign: Juman Kinetics, 5–56.

Prodromou, L. (1992) 'What culture? Which culture?', *English Language Teaching Journal*, 46: 1, 39–59.

Prodromou, L. (2003) 'In search of the successful user of English', *Modern English Teacher*, 12: 2, 5–14.

Prodromou, L. (2008) *English as a Lingua Franca: A Corpus-based Analysis*, London: Continuum.

Prodromou, L. and Mishan, F. (2008) 'Materials used in Western Europe', in Tomlinson, B. (ed.), *English Language Teaching Materials: A Critical Review*, London: Continuum, 193–212.

Rampton, B. (2007) 'Neo-Hymesian linguistic ethnography in the UK', *Journal of Sociolinguistics*, 11: 5, 1–19.

Rees-Miller, J. (1994) 'Comments on Janie Rees-Miller's "A critical appraisal of learner training: Theoretical bases and teaching implications": The author responds', *TESOL Quarterly*, 28: 4, 776–81.

Reid, J. M. (1987) 'The learning style preferences of ESL students', *TESOL Quarterly*, 21: 1, 87–111.

Reppen, R. (2010) *Using Corpora in the Language Classroom*, Cambridge: Cambridge University Press.

Revell, J. and Norman, S. (1997) *In Your Hands: NLP in ELT*, London: Saffire.

Richards, J. C. (2002) *Methodology in Language Teaching: An Anthology of Current Practice*, Cambridge and New York: Cambridge University Press.

Richards, J. C. and Lockhart, C. (1996) *Reflective Teaching in Second Language Classrooms*, New York: Cambridge University Press.

Richards, J. C. and Rodgers, T. S. (1986) *Approaches and Methods in Language Teaching*, Cambridge: Cambridge University Press.

Richards, J. C. and Schmidt, F. (2003) *Longman Dictionary of Language Teaching and Applied Linguistics*, London: Longman.

Riordan, E. (2012) 'Online reflections: The implementation of blogs in language teacher education', in Farr, F. and Moriarty, M. (eds), *Learning and Teaching: Irish Research Perspectives*, Berlin: Peter Lang, 195–224.

Riordan, E. and Murray, L. (2010) 'A corpus-based analysis of online synchronous and asynchronous modes of communication within language teacher education', *Classroom Discourse*, 1: 2, 181–98.

Riordan, E. and Murray, L. (2012) 'Sharing and collaborating between an online community of novice teachers: CMC in language teacher education', *Journal of E-Learning and Knowledge Society*, 8: 3, 91–103.

Robson, C. (2002) *Real World Research* (2nd edn), Oxford: Blackwell.

Rodgers, C. R. and Raider-Roth, M. B. (2006) 'Presence in teaching', *Teachers and Teaching: Theory and Practice*, 12: 3, 265–87.

Römer, U. (2004) 'Comparing real and ideal language learner input: The use of an EFL textbook corpus in corpus linguistics and language teaching', in Aston, G., Bernardini, S. and Stewart, D. (eds), *Corpora and Language Learners*, Amsterdam: John Benjamins, 185–99.

Römer, U. (2011) 'Corpus research applications in second language teaching', *Annual Review of Applied Linguistics*, 31, 205–25.

Rossouw, D. (2009) 'Educators as action researchers: Some key considerations', *South African Journal of Education*, 29, 1–16.

Rubdy, R. (2003) 'Selection of materials', in Tomlinson, B. (ed.), *Developing Materials for Language Teaching*, London: Continuum, 37–57.

Rukthong, A. (2008) *Readiness for Autonomous Language Learning: Thai University Learners' Beliefs about EFL Learning and Use of Learning Strategies*, unpublished thesis (Master's), Mahidol University, Bangkok.

Sappington, J., Kinsey, K. and Munsayac, K. (2002) 'Two studies of reading compliance among college students', *Teaching of Psychology*, 29: 4, 272–4.

Schellekens, P. (2007) *The Oxford ESOL Handbook*, Oxford: Oxford University Press.

Schmidt, R. (1993) 'Awareness and second language acquisition', *Annual Review of Applied Linguistics*, 13, 206–26.

Schön, D. (1987) *Educating the Reflective Practitioner: Toward a New Design for Teaching and Learning in the Professions*, San Francisco: Jossey-Bass.

Schön, D. A. (1983) *The Reflective Practitioner: How Professionals Think in Action*, New York: Basic Books.

Schön, D. A. (1991) 'Introduction', in Schön, D. A. (ed.), *The Reflective Turn: Case Studies In and On Educational Practice*, Aldershot: Arena, 1–11.

Scollon, R. and Scollon, S. B. K. (1981) *Narrative, Literacy and Face in Interethnic Communication*, Norwood: Ablex.

Scrivener, J. (2011) *Learning Teaching: The Essential Guide to English Language Teaching* (3rd edn), London: Macmillan.

Selinker, L. (1971) 'Interlanguage', *International Review of Applied Linguistics in Language Teaching*, 10: 1–4, 209–32.

Shamin, F. (1996) 'In or out of the action zone: Location as a feature of interaction in large ESL classes in Pakistan', in Bailey, K. M. and Nunan, D. (eds), *Voices from the Language Classroom*, Cambridge: Cambridge University Press, 123–44.

Sharma, P. and Westbrook, K. (2016) 'Online and blended language learning', in Farr, F. and Murray, L. (eds), *The Routledge Handbook of Language Learning and Technology*, New York: Routledge.

Shimahara, N. K. (1998) 'The Japanese model of professional development: Teaching as craft', *Teaching and Teacher Education*, 14: 5, 451–62.

Shomoossi, N. and Ketabi, S. (2007) 'A critical look at the concept of authenticity', *Electronic Journal of Foreign Language Teaching*, 4: 1, 149–55.

Shulman, L. (1986) 'Those who understand: Knowledge growth in teaching', *Educational Researcher*, 15: 2, 4–14.

Shulman, L. (1987) 'Knowledge and teaching: Foundations of the new reform', *Harvard Educational Review*, 57, 1–22.

Sinclair, J. M. (1997) 'Corpus evidence in language description', in Wichmann, A., Fligelstone, S., McEnery, T. and G. Knowles (eds), *Teaching and Language Corpora*, London: Longman, 27–39.

Sinclair, J. M. and Coulthard, R. M. (1975) *Towards an Analysis of Discourse: The English Used by Teachers and Pupils*, Oxford: Oxford University Press.

Sinclair, J. M. and Renouf, A. (1988) 'A lexical syllabus for language learning', in Carter, R. and McCarthy, M. (eds), *Vocabulary in Language Teaching*, London: Longman, 140–58.

Singleton, J. (1989) 'Japanese folkcraft pottery apprenticeship: Cultural patterns of an educational institution', in Coy, M. W. (ed.), *Apprenticeship: From Theory to Practice and Back Again*, New York: SUNY Press, 13–30.

Skehan, P. (2002) 'Theorising and updating aptitude', in Robinson, P. (ed.), *Individual Differences and Instructed Language Learning*, Amsterdam: John Benjamins, 69–93.

Skehan, P. (2014) *Individual Differences in Second Language Learning*, Abingdon: Routledge.

Slimani-Rolls, A. (2003) 'Exploring a world of paradoxes: An investigation of group work', *Language Teaching Research*, 7: 2, 221–39.

Spiro, J. (2013) *Changing Methodologies in TESOL*, Edinburgh: Edinburgh University Press.

Spratt, M., Humphreys, G. and Chan, V. (2002) 'Autonomy and motivation: Which comes first?', *Language Teaching Research*, 6: 3, 245–66.

Stockwell, G. (2016) 'Mobile language learning', in Farr, F. and Murray, L. (eds), *The Routledge Handbook of Language Learning and Technology*, New York: Routledge.

Swain, M. (1985) 'Communicative competence: Some roles of comprehensible input and comprehensible output in its development', in Gass, S. and Varonis, E. (eds), *Input in Second Language Acquisition*, Rowley: Newbury House, 235–53.

ThangSiew Ming (2009) 'Investigating autonomy of Malaysian ESL learners: A comparison between public and private universities', *Southeast Asian Journal of English Language Studies*, 15, 98–124.

Thornbury, S. (2000) 'A dogma for EFL', *IATEFL Issues*, 153, 2.

Thornbury, S. (2011) 'Language teaching methodology', in Simpson, J. (ed.), *The Routledge Handbook of Applied Linguistics*, Abingdon: Routledge, 185–99.

Tilstone, C. (1998) *Observing Learning and Teaching*, Abingdon: David Fulton.

Tomlinson, B. (1998) 'Introduction', in Tomlinson, B. (ed.), *Materials Development in Language Teaching*, Cambridge: Cambridge University Press, 1–24.

Tomlinson, B. (2001) 'Materials development', in Carter, R. and Nunan, D. (eds), *The Cambridge Guide to Teaching English to Speakers of Other Languages*, Cambridge: Cambridge University Press, 66–71.

Tomlinson, B. (2003a) 'Humanizing the coursebook', in Tomlinson, B. (ed.), *Developing Materials for Language Teaching*, London: Continuum, 162–73.

Tomlinson, B. (2003b) 'Introduction', in Tomlinson, B. (ed.), *Developing Materials for Language Teaching*, London: Continuum, 1–11.

Tomlinson, B. (2003c) 'Materials evaluation', in Tomlinson, B. (ed.), *Developing Materials for Language Teaching*, London: Continuum, 15–36.

Tomlinson, B. (ed.) (2008a) *English Language Learning Materials: A Critical Review*, London: Continuum.

Tomlinson, B. (2008b) 'Language acquisition and language learning materials', in Tomlinson, B. (ed.), *English Language Learning Materials: A Critical Review*, London: Continuum, 3–14.

Tomlinson, B. (2012) 'Materials development for language learning and teaching', *Language Teaching*, 45: 2, 143–79.

Tomlinson, B. (2013a) 'Classroom research of language classes', in Tomlinson, B. (ed.), *Applied Linguistics and Materials Development*, London: Bloomsbury, 43–60.

Tomlinson, B. (2013b) 'Second language acquisition and materials development', in Tomlinson, B. (ed.), *Applied Linguistics and Materials Development*, London: Bloomsbury, 11–30.

Toto, R. and Nguyen, H. (2009) 'Flipping the work design in an industrial engineering course', *39th Frontiers in Education Conference*, 1–4.

Tsui, A. B. M. (1985) 'Analysing input and interaction in the second language classroom', *RELC Journal*, 16: 1, 8–32.

Tsui, A. B. M. (1995) *Introducing Classroom Interaction*, London: Penguin.

Tsui, A. B. M. (1996) 'Reticence and anxiety in second language learning', in Bailey, K. M. and Nunan, D. (eds), *Voices from the Language Classroom*, Cambridge: Cambridge University Press, 145–67.

Tusting, K. and Maybin, J. (2007) 'Linguistic ethnography and interdisciplinarity: Opening the discussion', *Journal of Sociolinguistics*, 11: 5, 575–83.

Ur, P. (1991) *A Course in Language Teaching*, Cambridge: Cambridge University Press.

Ushioda, E. and Dörnyei, Z. (2012) 'Motivation', in Gass, S. and Mackey, A. (eds), *The Routledge Handbook of Second Language Acquisition*, New York: Routledge, 396–409.

van Lier, L. (1996) *Interaction in the Language Curriculum*, London: Longman.

van Looy, L. and Goegebeur, W. (2007) 'Teachers and teacher trainees as classroom researchers: Beyond Utopia?', *Educational Action Research*, 15: 1, 107–26.

van Manen, M. (1977) 'Linking ways of knowing to ways of being practical', *Curriculum Inquiry*, 6: 3, 205–88.

Vásquez, C. (2011) 'TESOL teacher identity and the need for "small story" research', *TESOL Quarterly*, 45: 3, 535–45.

Vásquez, C. and Reppen, R. (2007) 'Transforming practice: Changing patterns of participation in post-observation meetings', *Language Awareness*, 16: 3, 153–72.

Vásquez, C. and Urzúa, A. (2009) 'Reported speech and reported mental states in mentoring meetings: Exploring novice teacher identities', *Research on Language and Social Interaction*, 42: 1, 1–19.

Vygotsky, L. S. (1978) *Mind in Society: The Development of Higher Psychological Processes*, Cambridge, MA: Harvard University Press.

Waite, D. (1993) 'Teachers in conference: A qualitative study of teacher–supervisor face-to-face interactions', *American Educational Research Journal*, 30: 4, 675–702.

Wajnryb, R. (1992a) *Classroom Observation Tasks: A Resource Book for Language Teachers and Trainers*, Cambridge: Cambridge University Press.

Wajnryb, R. (1992b) 'The lightbulb has to want to change: Supervision as a collaborative process', *TESOL in Context*, 21: 1, 6–8.

Wallace, M. (1987) 'A historical review of action research: Some implications for the education of teachers in their management role', *Journal of Education for Teaching*, 13: 2, 97–115.

Wallace, M. (1998) *Action Research for Language Teachers*, Cambridge: Cambridge University Press.

Walsh, S. (2001) *Characterising Teacher Talk in the Second Language Classroom: A Process Model of Reflective Practice.*, unpublished thesis (PhD), Queen's University, Belfast.

Walsh, S. (2002) 'Construction or obstruction: Teacher talk and learner involvement in the EFL classroom', *Language Teaching Research*, 6: 1, 3–23.

Walsh, S. (2003) 'Developing interactional awareness in the second language classroom', *Language Awareness*, 12: 2, 124–42.

Walsh, S. (2006) *Investigating Classroom Discourse*, London and New York: Routledge.

Walsh, S. (2010) 'What features of spoken and written corpora can be exploited in creating language teaching materials and syllabuses?', in O'Keeffe, A. and McCarthy, M. (eds), *The Routledge Handbook of Corpus Linguistics*, London: Routledge, 333–44.

Walsh, S. (2011) *Exploring Classroom Discourse: Language in Action*, London and New York: Routledge.

Walsh, S. (2013) *Classroom Discourse and Teacher Development*, Edinburgh: Edinburgh University Press.

Walter, E. (2010) 'Using corpora to write dictionaries', in O'Keeffe, A. and McCarthy, M. (eds), *The Routledge Handbook of Corpus Linguistics*, London: Routledge, 428–43.

Wang, S. and Vásquez, C. (2012) 'Web 2.0 and second language learning: What does the research tell us?', *CALICO Journal*, 29: 3, 412–30.

West, M. (1953) *A General Service List of English Words*, London: Longman.

White, J. and Lightbown, P. M. (1984) 'Asking and answering in ESL classes', *Canadian Modern Language Review*, 40, 228–44.

Wolf, K. and Dietz, M. (1998) 'Teaching portfolios: Purposes and possibilities', *Teacher Education Quarterly*, Winter, 9–23.

Woodward, T. (1997) 'Trainer training: A question matrix', in McGrath, I. (ed.), *Learning to Train: Perspectives on the Development of Language Teacher Trainers*, Hemel Hempstead: Prentice Hall, 3–10.

Wragg, E. C. (2012) *An Introduction to Classroom Observation* (classic edn), Abingdon: Routledge.

Yaping, Z. (2005) 'An investigation into learner autonomy in college English teaching', *CELEA Journal*, 28: 2, 95–100.

Young, A. and Fry, J. D. (2008) 'Metacognitive awareness and academic achievement in college students', *Journal of the Scholarship of Teaching and Learning*, 8: 2, 1–10.

Zaare, M. (2013) 'An investigation into the effect of classroom observation on teaching methodology', *Procedia: Social and Behavioral Sciences*, 70, 605–14.

Zappe, S., Lieicht, R., Messner, J., Litzinger, T. and Lee, H. W. (2009) '"Flipping" the classroom to explore active learning in a large undergraduate course', *Proceedings, American Society for Engineering Education Annual Conference & Exposition, 2009*, www.asee.org/search?utf8=%E2%9C%93&search=zappe+flipping&commit=Search

Zeichner, K. and Liston, D. (1996) *Reflective Teaching: An Introduction*, Mahwah: Lawrence Erlbaum.

Zwozdiak-Myers, P. (2012) *The Teacher's Reflective Practice Handbook*, Abingdon and New York: Routledge.

INDEX